Feet and Wheels to Chimborazo

A unique climbing and cycling
adventure to the summit of Ecuador

MARK HORRELL

"I visited the enchanted springs of the Amazon, and I wanted to climb the watchtower of the world. I searched for the footsteps of La Condamine and Humboldt. Boldly I followed them; nothing could stand in my way."

Simón Bolívar, My Delirium on Chimborazo

Feet and Wheels to Chimborazo

CONTENTS

CONTENTS

PROLOGUE

Beside the entrance to the restaurant was a 2m statue of a man in a Victorian greatcoat and knee-high boots, sitting on a rock. His right hand was clasping an open book on his right knee, and his left hand was clenched into a fist. He looked ahead with a determined expression as if a passage from the book had given him pause for thought.

Or was he sneering? The statue had been spray-painted with cheap silver paint, the sort you might find in the bargain bin at your local supermarket. Perhaps that's what he was annoyed about. I'd be pretty annoyed if someone had thrown a tin of that stuff over me too – and I'm not even a distinguished Victorian gentleman.

I recognised him immediately. It was Edward Whymper, an English wood engraver who had travelled to Ecuador in 1880 and made the first ascent of most of the country's highest peaks. You may wonder why anyone would recognise an old wood engraver, but I had read a lot about this one. He was a pioneering mountaineer and explorer, and kind of a hero to me.

But right at that moment, I didn't like him one bit – especially with that pompous expression on his face.

We were on a lonely stretch of desert road in the

highlands of Ecuador, and Edita and I had pedalled hard to get there. My stomach was doing things to my insides that are better not to describe, but which you may well have experienced if you've ever eaten a hot curry rather too quickly. The climb had taken a lot out of me. I was reaching the limits of my endurance.

Whymper was guarding the restaurant, the only one we had seen since leaving Guaranda that morning, many kilometres and 1,500 vertical metres below us. I needed food, and the bathroom would have been useful too. But the restaurant was closed.

I don't know what constituted a profanity in Whymper's day, but my mind wandered.

'Damnation, you quim-scraping rapscallion. Spawn of a blood-curdling dingle-dangler.'

Neither phrase felt quite forceful enough, or expressed the passion running through me at that moment, so I used a simpler, more modern phrase involving fornication. That should leave no doubt.

Thanks to Whymper and an enormous pizza I'd eaten in Guaranda, I'd had nothing but a few snacks all morning. My stomach had been on hunger strike for two days. The pizza had oozed cheese like a genetically modified cow. It contained three types of meat and every known Andean vegetable, including the more unusually shaped ones. It was our first meal in days that hadn't been chicken soup and rice.

I loved that pizza. Thinking back, it was everything a hungry cyclist could wish for – so good that my stomach wanted me to eat it all over again. But when it was presented to me for a second time on the floor of our hotel shower, it no longer seemed quite so appealing.

I was still suffering from food poisoning this morning, but we needed to continue with our cycle ride. We had climbed up through the Andes to the foothills of

Chimborazo at an altitude of 4,100m. Chimborazo is a giant, ice-clad volcano, and the focus of our journey. It had captivated explorers for centuries. Whymper had been the first person to reach its summit. My legs should have been tingling with anticipation to get back on the bike, but extreme physical exercise, altitude sickness, food poisoning, and a profound dislike of cycling made for a heady cocktail.

I couldn't wait (to get it over with and put my feet up, preferably somewhere as far away from a set of pedals as I could get).

We left Whymper behind us and continued our journey. The scenery was monotonous. Chimborazo had been our constant companion since Guaranda, beckoning us higher, a dome of snow like a Christmas pudding drizzled in rum sauce. It winked at us, but now it had disappeared into cloud somewhere on our left. Deprived of its gaze, I could see only miles and miles of rolling desert stretching before me – red sandy hillsides peppered with fist-sized rocks.

The road forged a way through. Long, straight stretches disappeared over a brow or behind a bank, and there were no landmarks to keep me engaged. Edita zoomed far ahead of me. 'Zoomed' is maybe the wrong word; she zoomed only in the way that a tortoise zooms to a snail. I expect she was hurting too, but she was stronger than me now and I was holding her back. Vicuñas munched on chuquiragua bushes by the side of the road. Golden-maned and giraffe-necked, they are a symbol of the Andes. Dozens of them scrambled down a bank; they looked a bit like tiny camels.

Camels.

If only I could ride a camel to Chimborazo, like Lawrence of Arabia charging through the desert. They aren't the prettiest animals and I knew they could be smelly, but surely a camel had to be more comfortable than this confounded bike? You don't have to pedal a camel, and you can nestle between the humps.

My stomach rumbled in time to the judders, like an old bull elephant being tickled in its sleep. Physically I was a wreck. Long hours of straddling a bike meant that had I been a horse, they couldn't even have put me to stud. Every rotation of the pedals was a struggle; at each kilometre marker I stopped and slumped over the handlebars. I probably had altitude sickness too. Soon I would have nothing more to give.

As the long straight sections followed one another and the scenery remained the same, only the green kilometre markers by the side of the road relieved the tedium. These were counting down the distance to our destination. I counted 11, 10, 9, but with each one I became weaker and slower.

Draping myself over the handlebars gave only temporary respite. I needed to lie down in the sand and sleep for a good half hour. Perhaps that would give me fresh energy. Or maybe I could wait for Pablo, our driver, and sleep in the support vehicle.

The support vehicle… I could even take it to Riobamba! But then our challenge would be over. I would have failed.

I stopped the bike, got off and strode out to the flattest area of sand that I could find. Edita stopped ahead of me and I knew she was watching, but I was too tired to care. Without waiting to lower myself gently, I crashed down on my back and closed my eyes.

A short while later I was still lying on my back, dreaming of salad. I wasn't excited about salad, but I hoped it would wash away the memory of pizza.

I felt a shadow cast over me, and I heard Edita's voice.

'I need to go now. It's getting cold.'

I didn't know that she had turned around and come back to me. I didn't know how long she had been waiting as I slept. Or how long I'd been asleep.

'You go then. I think I'll lie here just a little longer.'

I looked around from my position lying by the roadside. Still the road stretched before us, its surface as rough as a cheese grater. If I still had a tether then I must have reached its end several miles back.

The wind whistled and my brain hummed, but otherwise all was silent.

What was I doing here?

I don't even like cycling. Why was I here, exhausted beyond belief, and lying in the desert, miles from anywhere? What had brought me to this point?

I was happy walking and climbing mountains. These things gave me an interesting life. Why introduce a bike into it?

It's a long story, but I will start at the beginning – a time before I met Edita, and Ecuador was just a place on the map.

What am I doing here?

PART ONE

THE AVENUE OF THE VOLCANOES

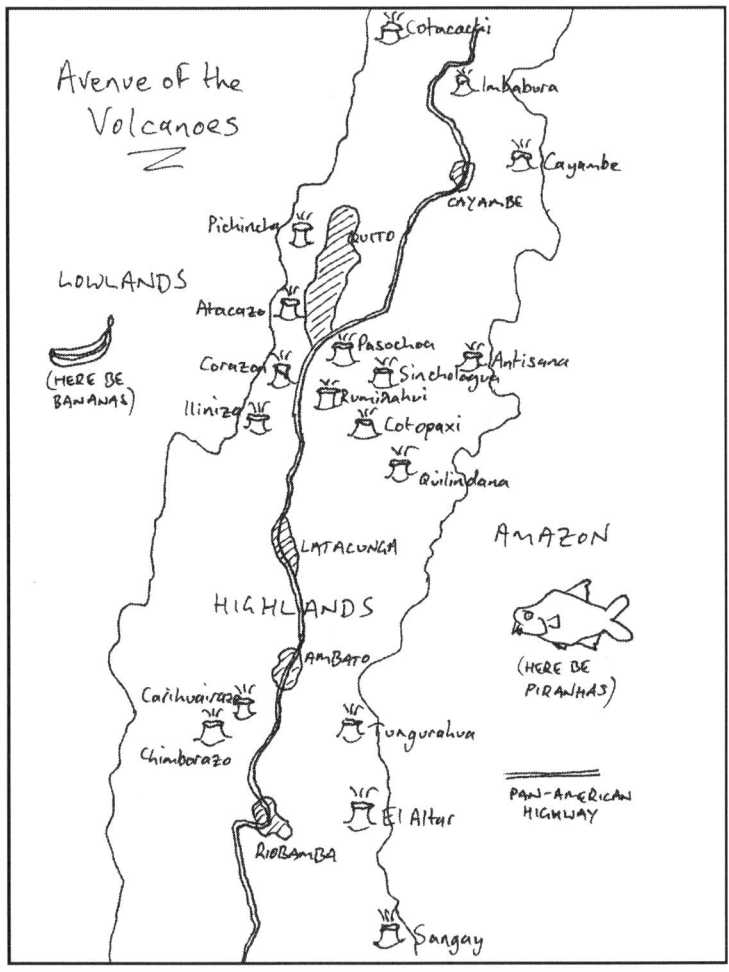

Avenue of the Volcanoes

Cotacachi
Imbabura
Cayambe
CAYAMBE
Pichincha
QUITO
LOWLANDS
Atacazo
(HERE BE BANANAS)
Pasochoa
Corazon
Antisana
Sincholagua
Iliniza
Rumiñahui
Cotopaxi
Quilindana
AMAZON
LATACUNGA
HIGHLANDS
AMBATO
(HERE BE PIRANHAS)
Carihuairazo
Chimborazo
Tungurahua
PAN-AMERICAN HIGHWAY
El Altar
RIOBAMBA
Sangay

1 THE CENTRE OF THE EARTH

It was Thierry who first invited me to Ecuador. I met him on a group trekking holiday in Ethiopia. He and I shared a tent for two weeks on that trip, but on our first night, we shared a hotel room.

This produced an incident I will never forget. I took an afternoon nap, to be woken by a creaking sound coming from the next bed. I looked up and saw Thierry sitting at the end of the bed, his hand gyrating vigorously up and down on a cylindrical object between his legs.

'Jesus Christ, what are you doing?' I said.

He turned my way, and I recoiled instinctively. He was holding a 7in cylinder in his hand. It had a large black handle and a tube that dangled in his water bottle.

'It is my water purification system,' he said.

I laughed in relief. 'Thank god. Why don't you use chlorine tablets, like any normal person?'

He looked hurt.

'It is good. It works well.'

'I'm sorry,' I replied. 'I didn't mean it like that. I thought you were doing something else. You scared the shit out of me.'

Despite my rude awakening that first afternoon, we got on well. We were two of the quicker members of the group, so we often walked together and found ourselves waiting for the others to catch up. We kept in touch and met regularly in London. I lived a reclusive lifestyle and didn't go out much, but Thierry would contact me every few months to invite me to a restaurant. He was something of a restaurant connoisseur with an interest in fine wine and dining. Although he'd lived in London for many years, he still spoke English with a comically French accent.

In true Gallic tradition, he cycled everywhere and never used public transport. He was unspeakably fit and went for a swim in his local lido every morning before going to work. On one occasion I remember turning up for dinner over an hour late. I excused myself by describing the horror journey I'd had across London: constant travel disruption, a train stopping in a tunnel, and separate buses crawling through traffic.

'Why didn't you just take a Boris Bike?' Thierry said. 'You would have been here in just a few minutes.'

A cycle hire service introduced by the controversial Mayor of London, Boris Johnson, had been given the affectionate nickname 'Boris Bikes'. It was still in its infancy; I had never taken one, and I didn't know anyone else who had.

'You're right, Thierry. I would have been here very quickly. Why didn't I take a Boris Bike? It didn't even occur to me.'

It was years before I eventually straddled a Boris (to coin a phrase). This was because I prefer to walk than cycle.

Thierry and I sometimes joined the same expeditions for our Christmas holidays. In Mexico, we climbed a number of volcanoes, including the country's highest peak, Pico de Orizaba (5,611m). This was the closest thing to an active volcano I had climbed, and certainly the most impressive crater I had ever looked down into. Despite being a straightforward plod up a snow cone, this was an enjoyable climb. For much of it, all we could see above us was a cone of snow and ice, gradually reducing in size as we ascended. The slope was steep, but the ice was hard and crusty, with no fresh snow to wade through. This made the terrain easy underfoot.

After about three hours of ascent, the slope ended abruptly when we reached the crater rim. Suddenly we found ourselves standing at the top of a sheer cliff looking down into a deep and surprisingly compact crater. Beyond it, through a blanket of cotton-wool clouds, we caught glimpses of the green Mexican plateau far beneath. It was an amazing scene, rather like those pictures of the earth taken from a space station in orbit. I felt like I was floating in outer space, looking down onto the surface of the earth.

The summit was a small, flat area of gravel marked by a cross. It was not only the highest point in Mexico, but the third-highest in North America. The feeling of height was amplified by Orizaba's isolation. That part of Mexico is characterised by a broad high-altitude plateau populated with isolated volcanoes. Only Popocatépetl and Iztaccíhuatl on the far western horizon, the second and third-highest mountains in Mexico, remotely rivalled our position. The crater seemed immense. It dropped away sharply below us, leaving no sense of its depth. For all we knew it could have drilled down into the centre of the earth.

It left a deep impression on me, and started my love affair with volcanoes.

By then I already knew that Ecuador was the country best known for climbable volcanoes. I was making a transition from trekker to mountaineer in 2004 when I climbed Mera

Peak in Nepal. I was a keen hill walker, and I started learning some alpine skills to enable me to climb higher, glaciated mountains.

These skills included learning to walk with an ice axe and crampons, and climb while roped together with other people. The ice axe was used more like a walking stick on the sort of easy mountains I liked to climb. You may be thinking that it's somewhat generous to describe walking along with an axe swinging in your hand as a 'skill', but it was also important to learn how to use the axe to arrest a fall on a steep snow slope – something you don't have much time to learn when it actually happens.

Crampons are metal spikes attached to the sole of a boot to facilitate walking across snow and ice. The skill is to avoid catching the points of one crampon in the straps of the other and falling spread-eagled on the ground with your face in snow. This happened frequently to fellow students on the first ever mountaineering course I attended in the French Alps. The trick was to walk with your legs wide apart, as though you had a large object dangling between your legs (easier for some people than others). The worst part of falling was not horrific injury, but a bollocking from the guide, whose principal motivational technique was to make less competent clients feel like prize-winning bellends.

Finally, the main purpose of the rope is to prevent anyone falling into a crevasse. These cracks in the ice are often hidden beneath fresh snow, and not easily spotted. Many are deep enough to give you plenty of time to wish you'd been kinder to your parents before landing at the bottom. But, luckily, most are narrow enough so that if any climber on a rope falls into one, the other attached climbers can hold them in place until they are able to climb out again. I preferred to walk second on the rope behind the guide, so that when I did fall in, I could pre-empt his stern words by blaming him for widening the crevasse as he landed in soft snow on the other side.

People who have been in crevasses for any length of time will tell you that it's one of the most unpleasant things they have ever experienced; some of these people have even used the toilets in Kathmandu Airport.

But if you think I'm exaggerating, and you have one of those freezers the size of a human, with a lid that opens upwards like a coffin, here's a little simulation you can do. Go and lie in it; ask one of your friends to close it behind you and sit on it, then spend the next few minutes wondering when (and if) they are going to let you out again. That's what spending time in a crevasse is like, except you won't find a packet of garden peas down there to nibble on.

My tent mate Huw and I were at a similar stage in our climbing careers, and we'd chosen to climb Mera Peak because it was a good beginner's mountain. It rises to an impressive 6,476m, and its standard route is primarily a gentle snow slope with a steeper section just below the summit. We spent much of our downtime discussing other trips and other mountains. We were both trekkers at heart, and not interested in climbing anything super technical, but mountains that were essentially treks up snow and ice were on our radar.

'You should consider Cotopaxi in Ecuador,' Huw said. 'It's exactly two metres higher than Kilimanjaro, but its summit is covered in ice. It's quite a bit more technical. Steeper than Mera Peak, a few more crevasses, but overall it's not too bad.'

'I've heard of Cotopaxi,' I replied. 'Isn't it an active volcano?'

This was before I'd been to Mexico, and watching *The Lord of the Rings* had coloured my mental image of active volcanoes. When I was a small child, I had visited Rotorua in

New Zealand, where I had seen geysers spouting sulphur-infused water vapour that smelled like rotten eggs. I was certain every crater contained red bubbling lava, and must be unspeakably hot. I was pretty sure that 'active' also meant there must be regular eruptions that shot boulders 50m in the air like a mediaeval catapult. This was an additional hazard that I was keen to avoid, particularly if I were to be roped to someone who wasn't as good as me at getting out of the way.

Huw had confronted the same issues when deciding whether to climb Cotopaxi, and he convinced me that my idea of what climbing an active volcano must be like was, in point of fact, stupid.

Huw's description of the scenery in that part of Ecuador piqued my interest, but he had some regrets about his own climb. They had been slow in ascending. By the time he reached the summit the sky had clouded over, and there were no views. He didn't even mention the crater.

I filed Cotopaxi away in my memory. My next encounter with it came during an event organised by a tour company offering trips to Ecuador. A craggy old mountain guide presented a slide show about an expedition to Ecuador's volcanoes.

Ecuador is one of the smaller countries in South America – slightly larger than the United Kingdom, but with a greater range of scenery. It's divided into three distinct geographical regions. The western coastal side, touching the Pacific Ocean, is flat and agricultural, with many fruit plantations. The eastern side of the country is rainforest. Its rivers drain into the Amazon and eventually travel over 3,000km into the Atlantic Ocean. Of more interest to me was the third region. The coast and the Amazon are divided by the Andes mountain range, which cuts through Ecuador from north to south in a central belt. When the German scientist Alexander von Humboldt travelled through Ecuador in 1802, he observed two parallel chains, and he dubbed the corridor between them the *Avenue of the Volcanoes*.

In reality the part of the Andes that passes through Ecuador is a highland plateau, populated by isolated volcanoes. As the craggy mountain guide clicked through the slides, it occurred to me that here was a very civilised place to go high-altitude mountaineering. Quito sits on Humboldt's corridor at 2,850m, and is the second-highest capital city in the world after La Paz in Bolivia. If you start your holiday by flying in to Quito airport then your body starts acclimatising as soon as you get off the plane.

As for the climbing, most of the volcanoes that rise above 4,000m to 5,000m can be climbed as day hikes. The guide described an expedition of about two weeks' duration that involved climbing four or five peaks. These increased in difficulty as the trip went on, beginning with easy walks to get accustomed to the altitude, with the big glacier peaks at the end.

The early part of the trip looked more like an exotic wine tour than a mountaineering expedition. He showed us photos of people walking up gentle grassy hills. These were interspersed with shots of luxury *haciendas* with rustic adobe walls and thatched roofs, pleasant dining rooms, and climbers tucking in to juicy steaks and red wine. These were the comfortable lodges they stayed in between day hikes.

Things got more interesting when they started climbing the bigger peaks. The warm-up to Cotopaxi was a mountain called Cayambe, which looked like an interesting peak in its own right. It was another large, glaciated volcano, almost as high as Cotopaxi. They climbed at night. Dawn broke during their ascent to reveal a blanket of cloud far below. Isolated peaks broke through the blanket, their summits distinctly triangular. I had always imagined the Andes as a chain of mountains linked by long ridges, but this landscape was very different. One photo showed the black triangle of Cayambe's own shadow projected onto the clouds, a phenomenon that is unimpressive on more complex mountains where the shadows lack any distinctive shape, but I have since observed many times when climbing volcanoes.

The shadow of Cayambe's summit cast across the land below as climbers make their way up

Cayambe's summit was a snowy plateau. The view was a sea of clouds that stretched beyond every horizon. Two mountains penetrated through in the far distance like ships on the waves, one a trapezium and the other a triangle. Both were snow capped.

'That's Antisana and Cotopaxi,' the mountain guide said. 'They're about fifty miles away. When you see them like that, you really want to climb them all.'

I knew what he meant. I wanted to climb them all too,

but the question was – when?

Before I had time to think about it, there was the rest of the slide show to watch.

'We just had one more volcano to do: Cotopaxi. It was a struggle, though. We'd eaten one of these the night before.'

He moved on to the next slide, which featured something that looked suspiciously like a rat that had been pickled in formaldehyde sitting on a plate. Its head was intact and staring skywards, and its tiny paws were held in the air, as though it had just finished jumping to the right in the process of performing the Time Warp. If it was about to be eaten, then it looked like it was intending to introduce itself to its diner beforehand, rather like the animal that wants to be eaten in Douglas Adams' *The Restaurant at the End of the Universe*.

The vegetarians in the room let out a collective 'uuurrrgggh'.

'It's a guinea pig,' he continued. 'I wouldn't recommend them, they're a bit gristly, and ours made a few of the team sick.'

Guinea pigs are a common delicacy in the Andes of Ecuador, Peru and Bolivia, and eating one is a rite of passage for every tourist who isn't vegetarian. The main issue is the way they are cooked and presented. They are usually roasted whole over a spit, head and limbs still attached. They retain this shape when they are shoved on a plate in front of you. There's no getting away from the fact that you're eating a rodent. If a cow's head were to be presented in a similar fashion, complete with horns, ears, dilated nostrils, and lips frozen in the act of saying 'moo', eating a steak would probably seem less palatable.

Whatever the side effects of the guinea pig, they did manage to reach the summit, but Cotopaxi was as Huw had described it: trapezoidal Antisana was visible during the ascent, but then the mists rolled in, and the summit photos revealed little more than thick cloud.

'I know these shots look like they could have been taken in Scotland,' our presenter quipped, 'but I promise you that's the summit of Cotopaxi. That's one of the things with Ecuador. When it's great, it's really great, but sometimes you've got to be lucky with the weather.'

There was no mention of Cotopaxi's crater, or that they'd been climbing an active volcano. It was a snow peak, and the landscape was not remotely like the Mordor of *The Lord of the Rings*. There was nothing to fear from climbing volcanoes after all – and I wanted to give it a try one day. The highlands of Ecuador looked a stunningly beautiful place to explore, and the accommodation looked comfortable too, if not the food. I knew I had to go there.

I was more familiar with Ecuador by the time Thierry suggested a visit. I knew that while Ecuador had many volcanoes over 4,000m in altitude, there were four that stood head and shoulders above the others. These were the four big glaciated volcanoes: Antisana (5,753m), Cayambe (5,790m), Cotopaxi (5,897m) and Chimborazo (6,310m). Cotopaxi was the best known among tourists because it was the most visible on a clear day from Quito, and also because it had been well marketed as a tourist attraction. It was a mountain that any reasonably active person – or so we were given to believe – could tackle and have a good chance of reaching the summit. Its volcanic activity had given it a certain notoriety. There was a major eruption in 1877, and another in 1904. It was still active, and another eruption was likely in the not-too-distant future.

But Cotopaxi wasn't the highest mountain in Ecuador,

and for most of its history it hadn't been the most famous either. That accolade went to Chimborazo. Chimborazo was well known in the 18th century, before the Himalayas had been thoroughly explored and before anyone even knew that Everest existed. It was believed to be the highest mountain in the world, and for this reason it was of more interest to explorers than Cotopaxi.

But the first people to travel to Ecuador and climb some of its volcanoes were not mountaineers, but scientists; and their purpose was to resolve a furious scientific debate about the earth's shape.

When he sailed across the Atlantic and reached the Americas in 1492, Christopher Columbus proved that the earth was neither flat nor (as the writer Terry Pratchett believed) perched on the back of a giant floating turtle. But by the early 18th century, some people were pretty sure it wasn't a perfect sphere either. This was clear not only from observations by astronomers but also from sailors who were reliant on the sky for navigation.

Scientists were agreed that it was a spheroid (or oval-shaped to you and me), but on which axis was it squashed? On one side of the debate were the Cartesians, advocates of the French philosopher René Descartes, who believed the earth was prolate, or longer at the poles. On the other side were the Newtonians, followers of the British mathematician Isaac Newton, who believed the earth was oblate, or bulging around the equator.

In 1735 a French astronomer, Louis Godin, led an expedition to the equator to try and resolve the question. Its aim was simple: to measure the length of a degree of latitude at the equator. French scientists already knew what the length was at 45ºN in France. If a degree of latitude was longer at the equator, then the Cartesians would be correct and the earth would be prolate. But if a degree of latitude turned out to be shorter at the equator, then the scientists would have to accept that an Englishman, Isaac Newton, was right and the earth was oblate.

I know what you're thinking. These were French scientists; they still remembered the Hundred Years' War. They were never going to let Newton win the argument; the expedition would be a stitch-up. But as Thierry has shown, not all Frenchmen despise the English; and anyway, scientists are not that petty. They're more interested in discovering the truth than putting one over on their adversaries across the channel. Godin was himself a supporter of Newton's theory, as was the French writer Voltaire (though he was famously a bit of a rebel).

Although Godin was nominally leader of what is now known as the French Geodesic Mission, the expedition is better known for the contributions of its two main scientists Pierre Bouguer (English translation 'Peter Bugger') and Charles-Marie de La Condamine.

Measuring the length of a degree of latitude isn't as simple as it sounds. You can't just roll out a very long tape measure and read off the length. This isn't only because they don't make tape measures that long, but because the land was far from flat. The scientists therefore had to do that Pythagoras thing that some of you may remember from school. You know: the square on the hippopotamus is equal to the sum of the squares on the two adjacent sides.

There were no hippopotamuses in Ecuador, but by measuring the sides and angles of a series of triangles, all the way from their baseline in Quito to the town of Cuenca, 300km to the south, they could calculate the overall distance. This was quite a fun, outdoorsy type of job, because it involved climbing mountains in order to make the observations. They then had to make some astronomical observations to calculate the number of degrees of latitude in the distance they had measured. Needless to say, it's easier these days. You can just use Google Earth.

They started by measuring the length of a baseline, from which all their other calculations would be based. They chose a place called Yaruqui, a village 15km east of Quito, where there is a long, flat plain that is now the location of Quito's international airport. Above Yaruqui is a fairly innocuous hillside called Pambamarca, which is an eroded volcano rising to an altitude of 4,062m. This was to be the apex of the first triangle. The apex of the second triangle would be formed by Pichincha, a rather more alarming volcano that shoots up to 4,794m above Quito. I say 'shoots up' because one of its summits, Guagua Pichincha, is one of Ecuador's most active volcanoes. It last erupted in 1999, spewing a 20km mushroom cloud into the air that showered Quito, a city of 2.6 million people, in volcanic ash.

The scientists wouldn't have been able to see their base stations in the Yaruqui plain from Guagua Pichincha, the highest of Pichincha's summits, but they could from Rucu Pichincha (4,698m), the second summit. Because the mountain is relatively accessible from a highly populated area, they didn't make its first ascent, but theirs is one of the earliest recorded accounts. Bouguer, La Condamine and a Spanish naval officer, Antonio de Ulloa, climbed Rucu Pichincha in August 1737, and ended up staying on top for 23 days. Constant cloud prevented them from making observations.

Over the next few months, the scientists worked their way south. At the mountain stations they sometimes had to wait a month or more to get enough clear weather to complete their readings. It's now known that Ecuador's dense cloud cover is a combination of trade winds from the northern and southern hemispheres meeting at the equator, and moist tropical air rising from the Amazon rainforest.

It took them over two years to reach Cuenca. Bouguer then travelled to Esmeraldas on the Pacific coast to measure the height of Pichincha from sea level. This was to ensure the altitudes of all the other mountains were correct. He went in June 1740 but – you won't believe this – Pichincha was in cloud the whole time he was there, apart from a three-minute period on 18 July, during which he 'did not have time to examine the different points'[1] (which, I believe, is a Gallic euphemism for going to the bathroom at a key moment). Finally, in August, a break in the weather enabled him to measure the altitude of Iliniza, a twin-summited extinct volcano west of Cotopaxi.

With their work apparently at an end more than five years after they left France, Bouguer noticed that one of their instruments had been giving faulty results. They had to face the inevitable and do many of the measurements all over again, contending with more wind and snow on foggy mountainsides.

It was at this moment that La Condamine received an old French newspaper in the mail, dated from 18 months earlier and reporting that the French Geodesic Mission had left Ecuador and was on its way back to France. How they must have laughed when they read this.

By the time they finally completed all their work for a second time, in January 1743, most of the team had been in Ecuador for nearly seven years. They had lost one man to malaria, another had been murdered during a bullfight in Cuenca, the team's two Spanish naval captains had nipped to the coast for a few months to fight a quick war with the British, they'd witnessed a huge eruption of the volcano Sangay, and lived through a major earthquake in Quito that flattened houses 80km away.

Despite this, although they didn't know it at the time, the overall aim of the expedition turned out to be a ripping success. Bouguer calculated that the length of a degree of latitude at the equator was 110,598m. This is just 22m more than the actual distance, which wasn't established until 1924. That's pretty amazing. As any Englishman could have told them, 22m is roughly the length of a cricket pitch.

They had also explored Ecuador's Central Highlands thoroughly and were some of the first explorers to climb its mountains. And in case you're wondering, they discovered that the world is oblate. Newton was right – it bulges at the equator as a result of spinning on its axis.

This would turn out to be of major significance for another of Ecuador's mountains, Chimborazo – but more on that later.

2 ANTISANA

There was a gentle tap at the door and I sat up in bed. I looked at my watch; it was five o'clock in the morning and light outside. I had been expecting Thierry to arrive at midnight. Actually, I had been expecting him for the last two days, but it was December, and heavy snow back in Europe had been grounding flights. Thierry had made it as far as Amsterdam, but more snow on the runway meant that his onward flight was cancelled, and the only replacement went via Lima in Peru.

I opened the door of our hotel room. Thierry was grinning from ear to ear.

'That was crazy,' he said as I invited him in.

'Your flight from Lima was delayed too?' I asked.

'It departed on time, but I fell asleep on the flight, and when I woke up we were landing in Bogotá.'

'Bogotá in Colombia? You got on the wrong flight, you idiot.'

'I got on the right flight, but when it reached Quito there was too much cloud to land, so it continued to Colombia.'

I tried to keep a straight face, but it was too much.

'So already I 'ave been in Lima, in Bogotá and in Quito, and it is not yet 5.30. Now I am going to get some sleep.'

I roared with laughter.

It was already my third day in Quito and I was liking it here, as I expected I would. We were hoping to climb Antisana, which was supposed to be a more technical mountain than Cotopaxi, but I didn't quite know what this meant. When we first met in Ethiopia five years earlier, we were both trekkers who were eager to climb something more difficult. Since then our climbing had taken us in different directions. While I had been concentrating more on altitude, Thierry had been doing guided rock climbs of increasing difficulty. His technical climbing skills were more advanced than mine, but I expected Ecuador's volcanoes to be more to my liking, at a high altitude with a certain amount of glacier travel.

I didn't expect Antisana to be especially difficult, and we were due to start with a series of easy hikes as a warm-up, but first we had a more immediate problem.

That morning we were intending to climb Rucu Pichincha, the volcano above Quito where Bouguer, La Condamine and Ulloa spent 23 days in 1737. The climb took them several hours, and for Ulloa it took two days. On his first attempt he was overcome by altitude sickness, a condition that was little understood in the 1730s. It's a consequence of the reduced air pressure and lower oxygen levels at high altitude. Minor symptoms include headaches and appetite loss, but in more serious cases fluid builds up in the lungs or the brain, and can lead to death if not dealt with quickly.

Fortunately, there is a simple cure for altitude sickness; victims recover completely by descending to a lower altitude. There also a simple method to prevent it happening in the first place: the longer you spend at altitude, the more your body adapts, a process known as acclimatisation. By sleeping at a moderate altitude for several nights, you can increase your chances of going to high altitude safely, in much the same way that you can increase your chances of enduring a Beyoncé concert by listening to a two-hour podcast of banshees wailing.

Anyway, Ulloa collapsed on Rucu Pichincha and lost consciousness. The porters carried him down to their camp, where he slept overnight. By the morning he had recovered enough to make a second attempt. The team erected a hut on the narrow summit, but the structure was so small they could barely creep inside. They would have known little about spending time at altitude. They had expected to suffer from tropical heat at the equator, but at 2,850m above sea level, Quito had a more temperate climate. On the summit of Rucu Pichincha, 2,000m higher, it was another matter. They suffered intensely from cold, and their summit thermometer regularly dipped below freezing.

Most of the time violent winds and extreme cold confined them to their hut. Hail and snow battered them. They lived in fear of the wind tearing their hut off the summit and hurling them down to the *páramo* grasslands hundreds of metres below. Snow piled up on the roof, and they had to rush outside with shovels to clear it away before the roof collapsed. Sometimes they found drifts of snow piled against the door, barricading them in. Their hands and feet swelled in the cold, and their lips chapped so badly they bled when they spoke.

Conditions were better for their porters, who had moved in to a cave lower down, among the grasslands beneath Rucu Pichincha's rocky summit walls. The porters were able to keep warm by burning chuquiragua, a local bush similar to juniper. Chuquiragua is native to the highlands of Ecuador and Peru, and has a bright orange flower known as the 'Flower of the Andes'. It grows abundantly at higher altitudes, even on desert slopes where other plants can't survive.

The porters climbed up from time to time to resupply the intrepid scientists in their summit box, and check they were OK. Sometimes they found them barricaded in by the snow. They dug the poor men out, presumably after hearing a gentle *rat a tat tat* on the door and anguished cries of 'help'.

The snow, wind and cold were unpleasant, but it was the cloud that turned the scientists' job into an impossible task. It kept drifting across the summit, and most of the time Bouguer, La Condamine and Ulloa found themselves shrouded in a thick fog that made observation impossible. From time to time the clouds lowered and warm sunshine bathed the summit. The scientists would rush outside, eager to take some readings, only to find a sea of clouds below them, obscuring the survey stations at either end of the baseline down on the Yaruqui plain.

By September they had been more than three weeks on the summit and had little to show for it in terms of scientific data, though they'd spent some merry hours playing I Spy inside their box. Here's a previously unpublished transcript from one of the expedition journals.

'I spy with my little eye, something beginning with "F",' La Condamine said.

'Fog!' Bouguer and Ulloa cried in unison.

'No,' La Condamine replied with a mischievous glint in his eye. 'Fuck all! Hahaha…'

Eventually they had to descend from the summit before madness set in, and they established another observation station lower down.

Times had moved on; we knew a little more about altitude than they did. We knew that we were unlikely to collapse on the way up like Ulloa had done, as long as we took things slowly and drank plenty of water. It seemed likely that Ulloa, the Spanish naval officer who was only 21 years old, may have been racing. I had noticed over the years that it's the youngsters who tend to get sick at high altitude, because they always want to prove themselves by being quicker than everybody else. The key to acclimatisation is to take things slowly.

We were an experienced bunch, and most of us had acclimatised for two nights at 2,850m in Quito. But for Thierry it was different. He had only just arrived and was tired from his flights. To climb so high before he'd given himself time to acclimatise could be dangerous for him. He said he would come with us, but he would see how he was feeling, and the summit might be too much.

Pichincha has two main summits, 4,698m Rucu Pichincha, the older and lower summit which is now extinct (*rucu* means 'old' in the native Quechua language), and 4,794m Guagua Pichincha, the higher summit, whose volcanic activity has caused it to be raised from the earth more recently. The word *guagua* means 'baby' in Quechua, which interestingly is the same word that babies use in English. There is also a third summit, Padre Encantado ('bewitched priest' in Spanish) lying roughly in between the two. Legend has it that a rock pillar on this summit is the petrified remains of a Franciscan friar who went up it to pray when he and two companions became lost in thick fog.

Between them these summits form a single massif rising directly to the west of Quito. Guagua Pichincha is believed to have been active for around 2,000 years, and Spanish conquistadors had recorded its eruptions as early as the 16th century. The largest was in 1660, when a huge eruption belched ash and pumice 25km into the air. It caused an ash cloud to blot out the sun for four days and plunge Quito into darkness. Lava flows swept down the sides of the volcano, but thankfully the mountain's topography – with Rucu Pichincha rising between Guagua Pichincha and Quito – meant that Ecuador's capital was protected.

The eruption on 5 October 1999 wasn't as devastating, but it still produced an 8km ash column that darkened the sky with a huge grey cloud. Two or three millimetres of ash were deposited over northern Quito, and the cloud caused the international airport, which was then located in the middle of the city, to be closed. There was another eruption similar in size two days later.

There aren't many places in the world where it's possible to get to a very high altitude as easily as Quito. A city at 2,850m with a 4,798m mountain right above it is already off to a good start. Many of Ecuador's volcanoes have four-wheel drive tracks snaking up to their higher reaches. Pichincha has a cable car, the *teleférico,* which opened in 2005. This takes visitors from the outskirts of the city all the way to Cruz Loma, a shoulder of the mountain at 4,100m. It's now possible to reach the páramo grasslands straight from Quito. This high-altitude ecosystem is a feature of the Andes of Peru, Ecuador, Colombia and Venezuela. Characterised by tall, dense grasses called *paja* by the locals, the páramo is an area of alpine tundra above the tree line, containing a number of unusual plant species.

The páramo is famous for wet and windy weather. These conditions wouldn't be wildly unfamiliar to our small party of six. Although I already knew Thierry, I had only just met the others. We were led by Felipe, an Ecuadorian mountain guide, who had climbed all of Ecuador's highest mountains multiple times and was a paramedic. The other members were a Scottish husband and wife called Angus and Ruth, who were keen climbers, and a young barrister called Tony.

Angus had many tales of derring-do that conjured images of a ruthless adventurer, oozing testosterone as he battled onwards, letting nothing stand in the way of achieving his ambition. But other stories hinted at his softer side. In one, he and his climbing friends were trekking back to Lukla after climbing Ama Dablam, a hard technical peak in the Himalayas. A young woman they were trekking with offered him her T-shirt in exchange for a hand-printed Ama Dablam T-shirt he'd had made especially before he left Scotland. Instead of accepting her offer or bargaining for a little bit more, Angus politely asked her to put the T-shirt back on again.

Tony had been ill for the last two days after picking up an illness in the Amazon jungle.

'Sorry for being antisocial,' he said at breakfast. 'I've been domiciled in my room for a couple of days.'

Tony was tall, good-looking, and his jokes were funnier than mine. There isn't a lot more I need to say about him at this stage, though his tendency to use legal terminology was a little jarring. Quite clearly I was going to detest him.

I may have been expecting crappy weather, but it was a fine day as we drove up to the teleférico, and we were in for a treat. Quito is an unusual city; shaped like an airport runway, it's hemmed in by Pichincha to the west and a long ridge to the east that forms a barrier between the city and the Yaruqui plain 500m below. East to west the city is no more than 6km at its widest point, but it sprawls for over 50km from north to south.

It took just 15 minutes in the cable car to rise nearly 1,000m from the fringes of Quito to a shoulder of hillside high above. As we swung above the ridge opposite that forms Quito's eastern boundary, it was as though the curtains had been raised over a stage and the scenery of volcanoes appeared dramatically before us. Volcano after volcano stretched across the horizon, each isolated and distinct. Felipe named them all as the cable car glided slowly up the hill.

'These smaller peaks to the right are Sincholagua, Pasochoa, Rumiñahui and Corazón, and the one with two summits is Iliniza. We will be climbing Rumiñahui and Iliniza Norte in a few days.'

'Wow, such an amazing view,' Ruth said.

'But with just one caveat – it's a bit cloudy,' Tony said.

'To the left of these, and just behind them, you can see Cayambe, Antisana and Cotopaxi,' Felipe continued.

The three giant volcanoes towered over everything. They were each about 60km away and would be unmistakeable on a clear day, but a streak of clouds along the horizon merged with their snowcaps and hid them slightly. I came to understand that this was common, and we were lucky to have them as clear as we did. Even so, we saw enough to get some idea of their profiles. While Cayambe and Cotopaxi were both clearly conical and the classic volcano shape, Antisana's topography was a little more complex, with multiple summits breaking through the clouds.

The theatre of volcanoes beyond Quito distracted us from the climate zones passing in sequence immediately below the car. In the space of a few minutes we had passed above pine forest and across farmland, and now we were dangling just a few metres above the bleak moorland of the páramo.

It took just a quarter of an hour to reach the higher cable car station at Cruz Loma, where radio masts stood sentinel on a grassy promontory overlooking Quito. The city sprawled far beneath us, but we turned our attention to the view west. Within 15 minutes we had emerged into a different world. Tall grasses swished around our knees in the breeze, and we looked across a treeless plateau of yellow and brown to a line of three distinct peaks. Furthest from us, a moon-like dome peeped above a grassy ridge.

'That's Guagua Pichincha at the back,' Felipe said, 'then you can see Padre Encantado in the middle. We're going up the closest one, Rucu Pichincha.'

Padre Encantado stood directly between the two

Pichinchas, and was a prominent bulge in the rolling hills, but the nearest of the three peaks drew our gaze. The jagged rocks of Rucu Pichincha rose above the grassland like the scaly back of a sleeping dragon.

'It reminds me of Stac Pollaidh,' Angus said, alluding to a compact but famous peak in the Scottish Highlands.

We were 4,000m higher, but in some ways he was right. The two peaks are similar in scale and form, rising in isolation above the surrounding moors.

The route to the base of the mountain lay along an eroded pathway up a gentle ridge. It took us about an hour to reach it as the clouds gradually settled over its top. The mountain can be tackled directly by scrambling up its back and continuing to the summit, but we skirted to the right beneath it. After circling around the base on a dusty trail edged with chuquiragua and red-fingered lycopodium, we started up a dusty scree slope that was so badly eroded that it had almost become sand. Felipe was leading us up, but his guide's instinct suddenly made him turn around and look back.

Thierry was a long way behind us and moving very slowly. We waited for him to catch up, and when he reached us he was wheezing like Darth Vader.

'Are you OK, Thierry?' Felipe said.

'I don't know. I think I am struggling.'

'You are not acclimatised. You only arrived this morning, and we are over 4,000m. I don't think you should climb any higher.'

Thierry looked up the scree slope and the rocky face above it. The clouds had been descending imperceptibly as we climbed and now they had engulfed the summit. Only Felipe knew how much further we had to climb. Thierry looked back down the way we had come. We could still see most of the route back to Cruz Loma and it seemed a good time for Thierry to turn around before the trail became more difficult.

'I think I will go back now,' he said. 'I don't want to rush my acclimatisation. I will wait for you back at the cable car.'

Felipe didn't say anything more. We watched Thierry descend as we stopped for a drink, then we continued onwards, zigzagging up slopes that were thick with sand and tiring to ascend.

At last we climbed above the sand and reached a rocky ridge. It was here that things started to get more serious. The ridge narrowed to an eroded crumble of black volcanic rock. We followed Felipe as he scrambled left across a slanting rock face. We had no rope between us, and it reminded me of my scrambling days in the UK hills as Felipe's vague outline disappeared into thick mist ahead of us. In these situations, it's traditional for someone to say that you could be in Scotland – and, sure enough, Angus didn't disappoint us.

'It feels like the Cuillin Ridge.'

But this was going too far. Even by Scottish standards, the Cuillin Hills on the Isle of Skye are renowned for weather formed in Neptune's closet. I had been there, and it had rained barrels every day for a week. It was so wet that my 'waterproof' GPS device didn't function until I got back home again and warmed it for days by the radiator.

The following year I went to an outdoor shop in the Cairngorms, an area of Scotland not known for blissful sunshine, to buy a rain cover for it.

'The GPS is waterproof,' the assistant said. 'It disnae need a rain cover.'

I told him my story from the Isle of Skye.

'Ach, you didnae tell me you needed it for Skye,' he replied.

It was a dry mist here on Pichincha, nothing at all like the soggy cloud soup we get in the UK, where your outer layers soak up water like a sponge. We carefully copied Felipe's movements as he stretched crab-like across the black rock, which had been much eroded by the tramping of boots. Not a scrap of vegetation sprouted from these slopes and we scrambled blindly onwards.

I was just starting to get into it when we suddenly emerged onto a small summit platform marked by a cairn. Pichincha's infamous clouds swirled all around us. Bouguer and La Condamine would have had difficulty triangulating a Toblerone here. But as we sat on top and ate our sandwiches, brief breaks in the cloud gave us views across to Guagua Pichincha. The mountain wasn't breathing gas as far as I could tell, but its broad profile, with a distinct depression in the middle, gave the impression of a summit with a vast crater.

'That depression in the middle is *prima facie* evidence of volcanic activity, isn't it?' Tony said, looking at me.

'It's what?' I replied.

'Never mind.'

Guagua Pichincha would probably be a more remarkable mountain to climb, but there was no denying Rucu Pichincha's accessibility, and our journey up in the cable car had been memorable.

It was hard to imagine how Bouguer, La Condamine and Ulloa had managed to spend 23 days up here in a tiny hut. The temperature was tolerable for us, but the swirling cloud and barren rocks gave the place a joyless feel. With sub-zero temperatures, thick snow and howling wind, they must have felt quite vulnerable.

The sandy slopes that had been such a slog on the way up came into their own on the way down.

'Are you ready for a run?' Felipe said.

I took out my trekking pole, and before I had time to

extend it, he had already hurtled down, dust clouds rising in his wake. Angus wasn't far behind him. I chased after them. It took only a few minutes to reach the bottom. I looked back and Ruth was right behind me.

'That was fun,' she said.

Further up the slope, Tony was descending more gingerly, which gave me an odd glow of satisfaction. Back in the 1730s these slopes would have been grassy páramo. They had been converted to desert by the steady tramping of boots, an example of human impact on the environment.

We returned along the broad ridge, beneath the clouds once more. The contrast between nature and civilisation could not have been more conspicuous. Here we were in wild grasslands, yet the city sprawled over the plains beneath, homes and tower blocks as far as the eye could see. We even watched a large passenger plane gliding over the buildings below us and coming in to land at the international airport.

Thierry met us back at Cruz Loma, and we descended to the city. The station was bustling; we had to queue for a long time to board the cable car. We soon discovered why. For some reason, it took three times as long for the cars to descend as they had taken to go up. Perhaps they were pedal-powered, and the operators had to work harder when there were more people. I had visions of half a dozen men on exercise bikes sweating away in a room behind the ticket office.

Whatever the reason, there was an added moment of comedy when we reached the bottom – or when *I* reached the bottom. I was in a car ahead of the rest of the group, and everything came to a grinding halt a few seconds after I got out. I turned around to see my companions dangling helplessly a few metres away. Had the pedal operators gone for a tea break, I wondered? Or perhaps a chain had fallen off, the gears were skipping, or they were applying some WD-40 to get the thing cranking into motion again.

I laughed, but 10 minutes later they were still hanging there and clawing at the windows in frustration. Eventually the team in the back room started pedalling again, and my friends completed their ascent of Rucu Pichincha by drifting the last few metres down to the base station.

'Imprisoned without trial,' Tony said when he climbed out and approached me.

'You should consider litigation,' I replied.

He opened his mouth to respond, but thought better of it, and said nothing.

'There was soft paja grass a few feet below our car,' Felipe said. 'If the doors had been open I would have jumped.'

So ended my first volcano climb in Ecuador. It was by no means a classic, and a very different experience to what the early explorers had to put up with, but I realised that Pichincha was an asset for Quito to have. A zoom up the cable car and a brief scramble to the summit was an easy way for climbers arriving in Ecuador to acclimatise before heading out to grander mountains.

It's difficult to travel any great distance in Ecuador's Central Highlands without coming across the name of Edward Whymper, the British wood engraver who came to Ecuador in 1880 and bagged first ascents of many of the country's peaks. His expedition was a feast of virgin peak deflowering that just isn't possible now that most of the world has been explored.

Whymper and his companions, the Italian guides Louis and Jean-Antoine Carrel, weren't always successful. For example, on Iliniza Sur (5,248m), the peak that Pierre Bouguer had observed from the coast in 1740, they abandoned their first attempt for a highly unusual reason: they encountered a serac wall 60m high. A serac is an unstable block of ice that forms between crevasses on a glacier. In his account of the climb Whymper described looking up and seeing that the summit was 'garnished with a cornice of a novel and very embarrassing description'.[2] Those of you who have a puerile imagination may be able to form an idea of what it looked like, but for those who don't, Whymper even drew an illustration and included it at the start of the relevant chapter of his book. I'm perhaps a little innocent, because to me it looks like a mushroom, but Whymper clearly thought it gave the summit the appearance of a giant bellend. Whatever its appearance, it was frightening enough to make the men turn back.

The two Carrels are generally regarded as having made the first ascent of Iliniza Sur a few months later. Jean-Antoine provided proof of this ascent in the form of a rock from the summit. How the two guides made their way up the giant snow phallus was never fully explained, but they did report to Whymper that it had 'developed prodigiously'[3] since their first attempt (as phalluses tend to). When they took Whymper back there, he noticed that it was garlanded in shafts of ice up to 50ft in length that occasionally snapped off and rolled down the ascent line. This was too much for him, and he retreated a second time.

This scary ice formation on the summit of Iliniza Sur has not been reported since, or at least not in the manner that Whymper described.

On our mountaineering objective, Antisana, however, Whymper reigned supreme. Of the four big glaciated volcanoes in Ecuador, Antisana is the one that's least frequently climbed, and this is one of its attractions. It is more remote and has no climbing hut at its base. It's also more technical, a steeper ascent that sometimes involves steep ice sections. It is guarded by a maze of crevasses. Unlike Cotopaxi and Cayambe, it's not suitable for novices. Finally, Antisana is located on the east side of the Avenue of the Volcanoes. It's one of the first peaks to get clouds from the Amazon. There is more rainfall, and you sometimes have to wait for clearer weather.

Antisana is considered dormant. It last erupted in 1802; its crater is now filled with ice and no longer visible. Otherwise it has the usual hazards for a snow-capped peak. In 1831 the French botanist Jean-Baptiste Boussingault attempted to reach the summit with Colonel Hall, an officer in Simón Bolívar's liberation army. They aimed for the saddle between the main and south peaks. Boussingault used his mineralogical hammer to cut steps. These days such slopes can be climbed easily using crampons, but crampons as we know them did not exist in the 1830s – early examples were crude and insecure. In those days the only safe way to ascend steep slopes was by cutting steps in the snow. This is exhausting enough if you happen to be carrying a shovel (most mountaineers don't). With a hammer it must have been more difficult; hammers are generally used for banging in nails.

Perhaps fed up by his companion's constant tapping, Colonel Hall retreated after a few hundred feet. But Boussingault continued upwards until he reached an ice cliff, which he believed to be no more than the height of a house beneath the summit. According to his barometer he had reached 5,381m. There's still no agreement on the exact altitude of Antisana's main summit, but one of the most commonly cited figures is 5,753m, so it must have been some house.

They climbed Antisana in cloudy conditions, but

occasionally the sun broke through, producing 'a glare too intense to be endured by the eyes'.[4] Their eyes agreed with this assessment, because later that evening, after returning to a nearby hacienda to sleep, both men awoke to snow blindness, and had to be led back to Quito on mules the following day. Snow blindness is basically sunburned eyeballs, caused by the sun's reflection off snow in the thin high-altitude air. These days you can prevent it by wearing sunglasses. What Boussingault should have done was reduce the glare from the glacier by wearing a scarf around his head, so that his eyes were peering through narrow eye slits. This would have made him look sinister to onlookers, but as long as he remembered to take the scarf off before wandering into a bank, it wouldn't have caused too many problems.

Antisana was eventually climbed for the first time by Whymper and the two Carrels in 1880. After an unsuccessful first attempt, during which Whymper made the same blunder as Boussingault and ended up snow-blind, they set off again on 9 March. Whymper had noticed that in Ecuador the sky over mountains was often clear during the night and early in the morning, but it clouded over as the day progressed. He didn't think they had any way of finding a route through Antisana's maze of crevasses in cloudy conditions, but if they set off early enough then they stood a chance. Even under the light of the moon and stars, the dark lines of crevasses would be clearly visible on pale snow slopes.

They established a campsite at 4,900m beside the moraine beneath Antisana's glacier, and set out at 5.30 the following morning. They made quick progress to begin with, by following the tracks they had made two days earlier, but at 7.30 they could already see clouds forming over the summit. Like Boussingault, they aimed for the saddle between

Antisana's main and south summits, but before they reached it they found themselves in a labyrinth of crevasses, some half a mile long. One snow bridge was so wide that, despite having long spans of rope between them, all three found themselves crossing it at the same time. Had it collapsed as they were crossing, all three would have fallen into the same crevasse.

Fortunately, the snow bridge held – but they didn't feel at all safe. They heard ominous cracking sounds and believed the slope above them was about to avalanche. Not for the first time as climbing partners, Whymper and the older Carrel, Jean-Antoine, got into an argument about tactics. Carrel wanted to traverse the slope, slanting upwards to gain higher ground, but this ran parallel to cracks in the ice that Whymper thought carried a risk of avalanching beneath them. As leader of the expedition, Whymper overruled him, and they went directly up the slope instead.

The rivalry between Whymper the employer and Jean-Antoine Carrel the guide is one of the great tales of antagonism in mountaineering history – sometimes cordial and sometimes not. If they were characters in a modern Hollywood movie, then they would probably have ended up shagging. In the 1860s they were rivals in the race to make the first ascent of the Matterhorn. For most of this race they were collaborators. Many guides considered the Matterhorn to be unclimbable, but Whymper noticed that Jean-Antoine Carrel was a little more determined than most; the kind of guide who could find a way past difficulties that would stop lesser men. Carrel considered the Matterhorn to be his mountain. He wasn't going to let anyone make the first ascent if he didn't take equal share in the glory.

In 1865 Whymper won the race to be first to the top of the Matterhorn on the same day that Carrel was leading a party up by another route. On the summit, Whymper decided to take gloating to a new level by jumping up and down, whooping, and throwing rocks down at Carrel's party a few hundred metres below them. This, I believe, was the Victorian equivalent of mooning. Tragically for Whymper, he was about to experience immediate karma. A rope snapped during his descent and four members of his party fell to their deaths. The incident gained notoriety in the same way that major tragedies on Everest do today. For Whymper, it cast a shadow over his life for several years afterwards.

By 1879 this rivalry between Edward Whymper and Jean-Antoine Carrel had been forgiven, if not forgotten. When he organised his expedition to Ecuador, Whymper knew he would stand a better chance of climbing glaciated volcanoes if he had a couple of experienced mountaineers with him. Whatever his thoughts about Whymper, for Carrel I guess a job was a job. A chance to be paid for a year of exploratory mountaineering in the Andes would have been a bit like Gordon Ramsay being paid to think up rude words for a year. It was a highly successful partnership. There were frequent disagreements, but Whymper knew what he was letting himself in for when he hired Carrel: they shared a measure of mutual respect, and Whymper's frequent anecdotes about Carrel's tantrums are written with a spark of affection.

But I'm digressing. We left the pair – and Carrel's younger cousin Louis – somewhere beneath the summit of Antisana. They reached it at about ten o'clock. Whymper had been hoping to look east into the boundless rainforests of the Amazon basin, but he was thwarted by the usual clouds that had descended over the mountain. On their way back down, the sky cleared sufficiently for them to see they had indeed been standing on the highest point of the mountain.

There were more fun and games in store for Whymper on the way down. He was travelling in the middle of the rope when he fell through a snow bridge into a crevasse and found himself dangling over a cavernous space between polished walls of ice. The two Carrels made several attempts to get him out by pulling the rope in opposite directions, rather like a child's twirly-whirly toy – perhaps they were hoping he might ping out of the top of the crevasse and land on the edge, like a piece of toast flying out of a toaster. But each time his head appeared above the parapet, more of the snow bridge fell away. Eventually Jean-Antoine leapt over the crevasse and joined his cousin on the other side, and between them they were able to haul Whymper out like a harpooned fish.

After our ascent of Rucu Pichincha, we continued our expedition by climbing progressively higher volcanoes, until we were considered sufficiently acclimatised to tackle Antisana. On Pichincha it was easy to feel that we hadn't really left Quito. We moved further afield and stayed in two pleasant haciendas in the high páramo surrounding Cotopaxi. We climbed Rumiñahui, an extinct volcano with three distinctive summits in the shape of a letter 'W'. We camped at 3,900m on the side of the Ilinizas, and climbed Iliniza Norte (5,126m).

Meanwhile Tony the good-looking lawyer was becoming a little more endearing on account of his forgetfulness. He had gained a reputation for mislaying his cap, putting it down whenever we stopped somewhere, then forgetting where he had left it. It was usually somewhere obvious. On one occasion it was lying on a stone a metre in front of him. Sometimes we were delayed because he had to go back and look for it. One time he returned in a foul temper.

'My bloody hat, where the hell did I leave my bloody hat?'

Simultaneously, we looked at the crown of his head and he raised his hand.

'I'm wearing it, aren't I?'

On Iliniza, I was wandering around the campsite after a rainstorm when Felipe stopped me and pointed to a patch of paja grass some distance from our tents.

'Mark, is that yours?'

There, neatly perched on a tuft, as though it had been hung deliberately to dry, was Tony's hat. It was soaking wet.

'Your hat, Tony, your hat,' I shouted through the fabric of his tent.

'I've bloody lost it again,' a voice came back. 'I've been looking for the last hour, but it's nowhere to be seen.'

'I'll let you know if I see it,' I replied, returning to my tent.

I decided not to tell Tony that Whymper had emerged from a crevasse on Antisana minus a cap, which had fallen off while he dangled over its depths. Tony might consider the story an omen.

As I read Whymper's account in a pleasant hacienda after our ascent of Iliniza Norte, I was intrigued by his description of the last section before they reached the summit.

The snow still rose on our left, and we bent round to the north, and after a few hundred yards it fell away on that side. Then we bore north-west, west, south-west, south, south-east and round to the north again, always keeping the rising snow against the left shoulder. At last we could perceive no tendency to rise and fall in any direction, and came upon a nearly level plain of snow, lost in mist on all sides. This was the summit.[5]

I mentally tried to draw a picture on a map. If these directions were correct there were two possible conclusions. Either they were spiralling around the mountain like a corkscrew, or – perhaps more likely – going round in circles.

Unlike Whymper, we had the benefit of a guide. In fact, we had several. On the drive to Antisana we stopped in a small town called Pintag, on a hill above the plains below Quito. There was a small square with a colourful painted church, and the ice-clad cone of Cotopaxi could be seen rising above a ridge. Here we met two more guides, Ramiro and Domenica, who would be helping Felipe to get us up Antisana. The bespectacled Ramiro was a lively character; Felipe told us he was a famous poet, though he denied it. Domenica was one of Ecuador's only female mountain guides. She was also cheerful, and spent much of her time laughing at the other two, especially when reference was made to Ramiro's poetry.

The road above Pintag became increasingly rough. We drove beside a long black lava field, then rose into the wide grasslands of the páramo. It felt wilder and more remote than other areas we had been to. Pheasants and ibises grazed beside the dirt track as we drove deeper into the heart of the páramo. Antisana appeared on our left, an incongruous mound of white above the green grasslands. It was no simple snow cone like Cotopaxi, but a tumbling mass of crevasses and pressure ridges. Approaching from the west we saw two obvious summits. The main summit on the left was a broad plateau, but the plateau itself was protected by overhanging cornices. To reach the summit it would be necessary to make for the broad saddle between the two peaks, as Boussingault and Whymper had done.

We stopped an hour short of camp to get out and walk. It

was scenery to calm the nerves, get the heart pumping in a more leisurely fashion, and take the mind on a long journey away from the stresses and strains of modern life. Back home in Britain, the landscape would be described as wild moorland. There were stranger plants than the endless banks of heather I was used to, but the orange-flamed chuquiragua and red fingers of lycopodium were becoming familiar.

Thierry found this profusion of flora endlessly fascinating. He had a penchant for taking arty shots, and wild flowers were among his favourite subjects. Not only did he photograph them from every angle, but every posture he could contort his body into: down on one knee in the marriage-proposal position, on his front filming at ground level, or lying on his back to snap a flower from underneath. Every so often he disappeared from view, and I glanced behind me to see him in another ungainly posture. I couldn't help chuckling.

Camp was at 4,500m, at a point where the grasslands ended and the moraine fields left behind by Antisana's glaciers began. The movement of the glacier meant that the route up the mountain changed from season to season. Felipe had been up Antisana many times, but it was his first time this season.

Later that afternoon, I emerged from my tent to see Felipe and Angus looking up at the mountain and discussing the route.

'Where do we go?' I asked.

'Up there, you go to the left, you go to the right, go to the left, go to the right, you miss the crevasse, you go to the left, you go to the right again, and then you pop up over the big open crevasse, and there you go,' Angus said.

'Thanks, Angus. That's really helpful.'

I found Whymper's route description a little easier to follow.

Though Antisana was completely clear, Cotopaxi was being battered by dark storm clouds 40km across the open moorland behind us. More clouds reached our camp later in the afternoon and Antisana disappeared from view.

We didn't have much time to rest. We were due to wake up at stupid o'clock, which was eleven o'clock Eastern Standard Time, the time zone in Ecuador. That wasn't even tomorrow. Antisana was a mountain of amazing ice formations and a profusion of crevasses spanned by snow bridges. As Whymper had observed, it also tended to be clear at night and cloud over later in the morning. We needed to climb through the night before the ice started melting and the clouds shrouded the route from view. But, honestly, eleven o'clock? I was tempted to stay in the dining tent partying all evening, but we only had orange juice.

This wasn't the only bad news. Ruth was ill with symptoms of altitude sickness. She didn't want to risk climbing, and decided to retreat to a hacienda near Quito. Antisana was the mountain we had all come to Ecuador to climb, but Angus the intrepid ice warrior behaved like the consummate gentleman that he was, and abandoned his climb to keep her company.

I couldn't believe it. I thought back to the story he'd told us about the Ama Dablam T-shirt. To my mind, this wasn't just refusing the young lady's offer of her own T-shirt, but ripping off his custom-designed Ama Dablam one and presenting it to her on a velvet cushion.

'If I had a wife, there's no way I would abandon my Antisana attempt just because she was ill,' I said to Thierry as we sat in the dining tent with coffee at midnight, psyching ourselves for our climb.

'Perhaps that is why you don't 'ave a wife,' he replied.

Outside, the sky was almost clear. The moon was only a few days from full, and we could see the whole outline of

Antisana above us. Despite the clear sky, it was surprisingly warm, with just a thin crust of frost on the surface of the tents.

We left at 12.30. The steep scree bank above camp levelled out into a wide, boulder-filled plain. At 1.45 we reached the start of the glacier, where we roped together after putting on harnesses and crampons.

The departure of Ruth and Angus meant we had one guide each. This had many advantages, and one big disadvantage. Thierry, the most experienced climber, was paired with Felipe, the lead guide – clearly the dream team. Tony, the big guy, was paired with Ramiro, the poet and also the biggest guide. There was a certain logic to this. If Tony were too big to pull out of a crevasse then at least Ramiro could read him poetry until one of the other rope teams arrived to help. Meanwhile I was paired with little Domenica – at barely half my size, I hoped she was twice as strong. If not, then I'd just have to make sure I didn't fall into a crevasse.

The first part of the glacier was easy, on hard ice with a light dusting of snow. Climbing a glacier at night has an otherworldly feel. You are in a black-and-white world with nothing but the crunch of snow beneath your feet and the darkness beyond. It's easy to drift into a trance until the occasional voice of your companions brings you back to reality.

We made good time, and by four o'clock we had reached 5,100m, around half our ascent. Then things got difficult, and Whymper's route description started to make sense. Crevasses, snow bridges and seracs riddled the glacier – and finding a route to the summit was like finding a way through a maze. Dead ends barred by unbridgeable crevasses forced us to backtrack. To save time, we split up. Felipe and Thierry went off in one direction, Ramiro and

Tony in another, and Domenica and I in a third. We called out if we found a way through, the other pairs turned, and we regrouped. It was a bit like searching for Easter eggs but without any chocolate at the end.

An orange moon lit up the horizon behind us and pale clouds painted the sky in many shades of blue. As dawn began to break, Domenica found a bamboo wand left by previous climbers to mark the route. This was the signpost we needed; from this point we managed to keep to the trail.

But while the route finding became easier, the climbing became harder. We weaved in and out, traversed under ice walls, angled from side to side up steep traverses, and climbed across elevated snow bridges. One 30m vertical section was steep enough to warrant facing in to the slope and front-pointing up with our crampons. This technique involves walking up steep ice by kicking in the front-facing spikes on the toe of each crampon, driving your axe into the face above to steady yourself.

There was no protection except the rope between us. Domenica kept it short and tight. If I slipped and fell then I would pull us both off – unless she had managed to whack her axe far enough into the ice to hold us in place. Tiptoeing up on front points is agonising on the calf muscles, and mine felt like I'd been kicked from behind by Vinnie Jones in a two-footed challenge. Unfortunately I didn't have the option of rolling on the floor and shouting, 'come on, referee, you blind bastard'. I had no choice but to endure the pain and struggle on up. I arrived at the top gasping for breath, and Domenica showed her appreciation by cutting me a seat in the snow with her ice axe. A true gentleman would have offered it to her first.

'That's great, thank you,' I said, flopping into it.

It was six o'clock now. Dawn had broken over the Avenue of the Volcanoes. Below us, with the rock wall of

Antisana's south summit as a backdrop, Ramiro and Tony appeared over a brow. It was as if we could see all of the mountains in Ecuador from this lofty seat. Ramiro began to recite them, like he would a poem. But I knew this open landscape of free-standing mountains now. I interrupted and named them myself.

Cotopaxi's cone of ice dominated the view about 40km away, and the ripple of dark hills to its right had become familiar. Sincholagua, Rumiñahui and the two Ilinizas stood in a receding line to the right. Pasochoa, Corazón and Atacazo lined up to the right of these, while Pichincha lay half-concealed behind a serac.

The more distant mountains south of Cotopaxi were new to us, but a giant snow dome towering above the clouds, higher than any point on the horizon, was unmistakeable. It could only be Chimborazo, 400m higher than any other mountain in Ecuador. Domenica identified some of the others for me: Altar, a rocky razor blade; Tungurahua, a jet-black island above the clouds; and Quilindaña, a prominent blade of rock. All of these mountains peeped above a blanket of cloud. But perhaps the most interesting was the farthest one, which we could hardly see. Sangay erupted the previous year and was still very active. Every few minutes it revealed its whereabouts by bellowing a cloud of gas so far into the sky that it dwarfed the surrounding mountains.

We continued to criss-cross up steep traverses, above and below walls of ice, until we emerged below Antisana's heavily corniced summit ridge. There was no direct route up this formidable obstacle, so we traversed beneath it, crossing a mass of broken blocks of ice, evidence of a fallen serac. Domenica stopped from time to time and looked around, grinning like a Cheshire cat. She seemed to be as enthralled by the intricate route as I was. It was a much more interesting ascent than I'd expected.

'I have been here nine times,' she said, 'but we only reached the summit once.'

'Hopefully this will be the second time,' I said.

She nodded with a smile. We were confident now. A few minutes later we emerged onto the summit ridge between the main and south summits through a ramp in the cornice. Now we turned left towards the top. Felipe and Thierry, the dream team, were sitting and waiting for us on wide slopes just beneath the summit. We made our way up the final few steps together, and at just past 7.30, after seven hours of climbing, we made it to the top. I'd found the climb exhilarating; looking at the others I could see they shared my elation, and we were all in good shape. It probably wasn't much for serious climbers, but for me it was the most intricate summit route I had ever experienced.

The summit of Antisana was a huge snow plateau, big enough for penguins to play football on. Few mountains peered above its near horizon even though we'd seen many on the way up. Only Chimborazo, Iliniza and ever-present Cotopaxi were prominent, but a new mountain had emerged to the north: Cayambe. It wasn't quite the perfect volcanic cone like Cotopaxi, but it was pretty close. To the east, the land dropped away to the endless expanse of the Amazon basin. We couldn't see the green of the rainforest, only a blanket of cotton wool clouds, but otherwise the sky was clear. Whymper never got to see this view.

No crevasses intruded on the summit plateau, so we unclipped the ropes and walked around taking photographs. I started filming a summit video just as two heads appeared above a brow. Ramiro and Tony had dropped behind us during the ascent, but now here they were.

Ramiro was sprightly as ever, but Tony stooped behind him on the rope, rather like the *Homo erectus* figure in an anthropological drawing of evolving humans. He looked exhausted, but he had kept going.

I shook hands with them when they reached us.

'I finally got here and I'm knackered. But happy, very happy,' Tony said.

It took him a few moments to register that I was pointing a camera at him.

'You're not bloody videoing me, are you? That would be a cruel thing to do to a man who's at his lowest but highest.'

The silhouettes of Ramiro and Tony arrive on the summit of Antisana

The weather had been perfect, and I felt privileged to be there. I had read so much about Ecuador's cloudy weather, but I had no complaints about the weather on this, my first big Ecuadorian volcano. I hoped there would be many more like it.

My elation evaporated during the descent. A mild night had become a sweltering morning and the sun beat down relentlessly. The crisp snow was melting to powder, and it slid beneath my feet with every step. Snow bridges were in danger of collapsing; we needed to be careful as we crossed them.

When we got to the steep section that we had ascended using our front points, I tried to descend it facing forwards, which would have made for a much quicker descent, but Domenica gave a gasp behind me.

'Be careful, be careful, don't do it that way please.'

I turned around, faced into the slope, and carefully descended on my front points again while Vinnie gleefully booted me in the calves. It was painful and slow; I had been confident descending on my feet, but Domenica was right. The slope was steep and I was a lumbering rhino compared to her graceful form on the other end of the rope. Had I slipped then we would both have fallen.

The final section of diamond-hard ice dragged on. The dream team disappeared into the distance ahead of us. I tried to follow them, but Domenica was wary of a possible fall and wisely kept the rope tight between us to slow me down. It was like a dog and its owner wrestling with a lead. But at least I was polite enough not to stop and have a pee against a rock.

I staggered onwards in the unbearable heat. If Tony had been *Homo erectus*, I was now looking like the ancestor of a Precambrian baboon.

Relief washed over me when we reached solid ground at the end of the glacier. We stopped, rested and removed our crampons. I limped into camp at 11.30 after 11 hours of climbing, and spent the remainder of the day asleep.

My first big Ecuadorian volcano had been an unforgettable experience, but there was more to come. The following morning we descended from our campsite and walked across the páramo. The sky was clear and the land rose and fell in waves ahead of us. I could faintly see

Chimborazo on the far horizon, too – but these were minor background details in the scene. One feature screamed for attention.

The perfect cone of Cotopaxi stood proudly ahead of us. Its snow line was sharply defined, like a road marking. It shone like a beacon among the three stripes of blue, brown and green that defined the rest of the landscape. It was my next project.

3 COTOPAXI

'I'm sorry, but I don't drink alcohol any more,' Javier said as I offered to open a beer for him. He looked serious.

'That's OK, no need to apologise,' I said. 'I'm sure you have a good reason.'

It was a throwaway statement, made half in jest. I didn't expect him to start telling me what the reason was. But he did.

'Yes, I do. I have a very good reason.'

There was a pause, and I thought he'd finished speaking.

'Angus, a beer?'

'Oh, go on then,' Angus said. 'That is, if Javier doesn't put me off.'

'I used to drink a lot when I was younger,' Javier said. 'A lot. Then one evening when I was drunk I decided to climb a church tower.'

We laughed.

'You don't have to give up drinking just because of that. It's much better to give up climbing instead,' I said.

'Or perhaps just climbing when drunk,' Angus said.

'I haven't finished,' Javier said. 'I managed to climb the tower, no problem. If I had stopped there, then everything would have been OK, but the alcohol had consumed me. There was a big cross on top of the tower, and I tried to

54

climb that too.'

We stopped laughing and listened to the next part of the story with open mouths. It felt like he was describing a scene from a Hitchcock movie. I imagined lightning flashing across the sky and rain clouds as Javier's figure slowly made its way up the cross, silhouetted against the moonlight.

'There was a loud crack, and the next thing I knew I was falling from the tower with my hands still clutching the cross. I woke up in hospital. Most of my body was in plaster. I was in a bad way. I swore that if I ever recovered from the accident then I would give up alcohol.'

There was silence. We were speechless. Ecuador is a strongly Catholic country. I didn't know whether Javier was a religious man, but if he was, then there could be few more symbolic examples of divine providence than the story he'd just told.

It was Angus who broke the silence.

'That's quite a good reason.'

This released the tension, and we roared with laughter. Javier Herrera was the owner of Andeanface, the Ecuadorian expedition outfitter which had arranged the logistics for our trip. He was a laconic individual with a dry sense of humour lurking beneath the surface. It wasn't always easy to tell when he was joking and when he was serious. I reflected that the whole story about the church tower could very well have been made up, but I couldn't be sure. Luckily he didn't seem to be upset by our laughter.

In any case, we were on slippery ground, so I decided to change the subject.

'Tell us about Chimborazo, Javier.'

'Ah, yes, Chimborazo,' he said, moving on to the next slide.

We were in the sitting room of Javier's flat in a luxury tower block on one of the hillsides above Quito. He had invited us over for a slide show of the various volcanoes we would be climbing.

Tony and I intended to stay in Ecuador for a few days after the others left, to climb Chimborazo, Ecuador's highest mountain. It would be considerably more challenging than anything else we would be climbing, but because there were only two of us, and the others were all focused on Antisana, it felt like an afterthought, a postscript to the main climb. Nothing could be further from the truth.

But there was a problem. Chimborazo wasn't in good condition that year, and may not be safe to climb. The next slide showed a red dome of rock, crowned by a thick glacier. On the left side of the dome, the glacier spilled copiously across the red rock face, but the meagre ice to the right looked streaky, like it had been flicked from a paintbrush in a Jackson Pollock painting. It was a classic example of a glacier that is drying out and receding over time.

Javier pointed to the left side of the dome, where the ice was thicker. The dome extended to the left and eventually became a ridge of dark grey rock. The contrast with the red rock of the face was sudden. There was a clear line below the glacier where the rock changed colour. The route Javier traced with the mouse pointer was almost exactly along this line, but fractionally on the red part. The route joined the glacier just above the end of the dark grey ridge.

'This is the Normal Route up Chimborazo,' he said. 'As you can see, this year it is very dry. There has been a six-month drought, and the route is now menaced by black ice. It is very dangerous. There is a lot of rockfall. It is possible, but Felipe is your guide. He is UIAGM-certified. It will be up to him to decide whether it is safe.'

UIAGM, also known as IFMGA, is the international body representing all of the world's mountain guide associations (mountain guides are very good at guiding people up mountains, but they're not very good at acronyms). UIAGM-certified guides are to guiding what Calvin Klein is to underpants – that little logo above the trouser waistline to say that what's under here is really top notch. Their training places a strong emphasis on mountain safety, including assessing rockfall and avalanche risk. There were around twenty UIAGM-certified guides in Ecuador; Felipe was one.

We looked his way.

'It is possible,' he said. 'We can try.'

I smiled. 'How possible? Fifty per cent, seventy-five per cent, or more like ten per cent?'

Javier and Felipe looked at each other, but didn't speak. Neither of them was smiling. It was Javier who answered.

'The usual success rate on Chimborazo is twenty per cent.'

'Twenty per cent? The *usual* success rate. You mean like in a normal year?' I replied.

Javier nodded.

'And this year isn't a usual year. It's much more dangerous?'

He nodded again.

'So basically you're saying we have bugger all chance of getting up?'

Javier's face remained expressionless. 'I didn't say that. But you British people have a nice way with words. You have a better way of describing things than we do.'

I looked at Tony, and he was laughing.

'Do you fancy climbing Cotopaxi, Tony?'

He shrugged.

'No, I'm serious. If Chimborazo is in shit condition then why not climb Cotopaxi instead? It's a decent mountain, a great alternative in fact. I'd love to climb Cotopaxi one day. Why not this time?'

'Fine with me,' Tony said. 'I don't really care. Actually I'd prefer Cotopaxi, especially if Chimborazo could be a liability.'

We glanced at Javier, and he looked visibly relieved.

'I think it is better if you climb Cotopaxi. As you say, Chimborazo is...' He paused for a moment of dramatic effect, '...How did you say it? In "shit" condition. But there is no problem with Cotopaxi. It is in much better condition, and it is an easier climb. Felipe will still go with you. You can stay in the hut and climb the next day. If you are strong and the weather is OK, then you have a good chance of success.'

And so it was decided. Cotopaxi was already a mountain I knew more about than Chimborazo. I had seen the slide show. I still hadn't seen the summit, but I knew to avoid eating guinea pig. If I could get up Antisana, then in some ways Cotopaxi would be an even better objective to look forward to. It was certainly much more widely known.

Cotopaxi (5,897m) is better known for its eruptions than its climbing history. It has often been described as the highest active volcano in the world, though that claim is debatable on many levels.

As we sat in Javier's living room in December 2009, Cotopaxi's last confirmed eruption had been in 1940. It was considered to be active. The much bigger 6,739m Llullaillaco in Chile (a mountain that no Welshman has ever been able to pronounce) last erupted in 1877, but was considered to be dormant. I won't attempt to tell you how these volcanoes get classified, as I'm not a vulcanologist, but in layman's terms Cotopaxi can best be described as an active volcano that likes to take a few naps.

About 4,500 years ago an enormous lahar – a devastating

river of mud, rock and ice – formed on Cotopaxi's northern slopes. It ripped across the Limpiopungo Plain, directly north of Cotopaxi, diverted either side of Pasochoa, a 4,201m volcano rising above the southern end of Quito, then raced across the area now occupied by the towns of Cumbaya and Tumbaco, close to Quito's international airport (which luckily wasn't there then). The lahar travelled over 300km to the north-west – where it ended up in the Pacific Ocean – and 130km east into the Amazon basin. Evidence of this devastating event can still be seen clearly today.

Written accounts of eruptions on Cotopaxi go back a long time too. In 1534 the Spanish conquistador Pedro de Alvarado witnessed ash clouds from Cotopaxi as his army marched across the Andes. In 1742, Bouguer and La Condamine witnessed the first of a series of eruptions while climbing Guagua Pichincha. As they were descending, Cotopaxi exploded 50km away. The eruptions lasted for two years and destroyed the town of Latacunga. La Condamine wrote that 'cataracts of fire pried open new routes down the mountainside, where avalanches of half-melted snow barrelled down the mountain into the plains below'.[6] In 1768 Latacunga was again destroyed by lahars after another huge eruption.

In 1803 the German scientist Alexander von Humboldt witnessed a short eruption of Cotopaxi as he was waiting in Guayaquil for a ship to take him to Mexico. There were several minor eruptions between 1853 and 1866 before a major period of activity began in 1877. A huge eruption on 26 June produced a lahar on the north side that reached Esmeraldas on the Pacific coast, and one on the south that again destroyed Latacunga. This latter flow was reported to have reached the town in just 30 minutes. You don't need to be a maths genius (and believe me, I'm not) to calculate that if Latacunga is 35km away then this wall of mud must have been flowing at a speed of at least 70km/h. Colonel Hall described Latacunga as a 'city of ruins'[7] when he visited it with Boussingault in 1831. He saw a church that looked like it had been blown up with gunpowder. Latacunga is now a thriving metropolis of around 100,000 inhabitants. It's not the safest place, but on the plus side there is a nice view of an active volcano.

Edward Whymper witnessed another major eruption as he and the Carrels made an ascent of Chimborazo in July 1880. There was another large eruption in 1903, and smaller eruptions continued until 1940. There is a bizarre claim that it erupted in 1942 but nobody saw it because of the clouds. Cotopaxi had been snoring gently since then. It had been climbed many times safely, and Tony and I weren't expecting to be blown away.

I made my first close acquaintance with Cotopaxi when we climbed Rumiñahui, an extinct volcano 14km to the north-west, the day after our ascent of Rucu Pichincha.

To reach Rumiñahui we drove across the Limpiopungo Plain, right beneath Cotopaxi's base. Alexander von Humboldt, who visited in 1802, described Cotopaxi as 'the most beautiful and the most regular of all the colossal peaks of the upper Andes'.[8] A more quintessential view of a volcano would be hard to find. A dirt road led across a wide, grassy plateau towards a perfect cone framed under clear blue sky. Cotopaxi's gently tapering lower slopes were a sea of brown ash, featureless but for the deep gullies where you could imagine its terrible lahars had once flowed.

The top third of the volcano was a continuous sheet of ice, apart from a single dry spot at 5,500m, just below the summit, where a sheer cliff broke through the glacier. This black rock was the outer wall of the crater and was known as the Yanasacha Wall. There were ice cliffs directly above it that I hoped we wouldn't have to climb. On the eastern side the ice was a crumpled mass of seracs and crevasses, but on the north-west part the ice was smoother and looked like it would be a safer climbing route.

Between the park gate and the volcano, the wide expanse of the Limpiopungo Plain was sparsely vegetated, but there was enough to feed the herds of wild horses who clustered freely. Most eye-catching though were the giant boulders that littered the plains – some the size of fists, others towering like houses. It was easy to imagine where they came from. These were the bombs of volcanic rock that Cotopaxi had fired out during eruptions.

One of the first to have a go at reaching the summit of Cotopaxi was the German scientist Alexander von Humboldt in 1802. He didn't get much higher than 4,400m, which is lower than Cotopaxi's car park is today. Humboldt said it was 'extremely difficult' to reach the lower edge of the snow line, and he asserted 'with some degree of certainty'[9] that it would be impossible to reach the edge of the crater. Humboldt was a clever chap who got many things right. He was one of the first people to group plants by their climate zone and surrounding environment, rather than by their shape and characteristics. He invented isotherms, and discovered that the Orinoco and Amazon rivers were connected. He was one of the first people to observe and document man-made climate change (a concept some people have difficulty with even today). But on climbing Cotopaxi I can state confidently that this is one of the things he got wrong.

If you've been following the climbing history of Ecuador's volcanoes so far, you're probably expecting me to say that Cotopaxi was first climbed by Edward Whymper along with Jean-Antoine and Louis Carrel in 1880. They made the first ascents of pretty much every other volcano in Ecuador, after all, so why not Cotopaxi? Well, I'm going to surprise you. Those three men did do something rather special on Cotopaxi, but it wasn't that.

Inspired by Humboldt, two German geologists Wilhelm Reiss and Alphons Moritz Stübel travelled to Ecuador in 1868 with the explicit intention of studying its volcanoes. If I had my time again (and I was a bit cleverer) then I would probably try to become a vulcanologist or a glaciologist, two branches of science where you have a pretty good excuse to climb a mountain for work purposes. Of these two, being a vulcanologist probably has the edge, because not only do you have a good excuse to climb some way up the side of a mountain, but you're actually compelled to reach the summit so that you can look down into it and study the crater.

During his observations of other mountains, Reiss had taken the opportunity to study Cotopaxi from all angles for possible lines of ascent. By 1872 he had been in Ecuador four years and observed how the snow came and went in cycles. There was a point on the south-west side where he had noticed the black lines of old lava flows creeping up above the ice. Sometimes they disappeared under snow, but they eventually reappeared again after a dry spell. He hoped these narrow black trails would provide him with a possible route to the summit. Reiss bided his time, and after a period of dry, hot weather in November 1872 he saw the trails reappear. He decided to make his move.

Reiss made his ascent on 28 November with his Colombian butler Angel Escobar. Famous Colombian

Escobars include the drug lord Pablo Escobar and footballer Andres Escobar, who was heinously murdered after conceding an own goal that knocked his team out of the 1994 World Cup. In my humble opinion, Angel Escobar deserves to be just as well known as these two. Not only was he the first Colombian to make a first ascent of an Ecuadorian volcano, but almost certainly the first butler to make a first ascent anywhere.

They crossed a lava field that had been left behind by an eruption in 1854. It was five years before the devastating eruption of 1877, and they could see fumaroles (small wisps of volcanic gas) rising out of the vertical cliffs above them that formed the *outer* walls of Cotopaxi's crater. Reiss was well acclimatised after the years he had spent in Ecuador's volcanic highlands; he even felt well enough to smoke a cigar while climbing. But as they climbed higher and had to take more frequent rests, he decided it would be a wise move to stub it out.

As Reiss climbed higher on Cotopaxi, his route alternated between icy snowfields and loose volcanic sand. He had started the climb with 13 porters, but when he stopped for a rest at 5,700m, only his dog and butler were still following. The dog was howling in pain but didn't want to leave its master. They ascended into the clouds and thought there was still a long way to go as cliffs rose above them, but suddenly they arrived on the summit and found themselves staring down into the crater.

Reiss noted that the crater was elliptical, and he estimated it to be 500m deep. Dense white clouds of volcanic gas rose out of it, but he was a scientist, which meant he couldn't just take a couple of summit photos and head back down again. He had to do something silly while he was up there. He sat side-saddle on the rim of the crater, investigating the deposits from the fumaroles, while Escobar held his hand to stop him falling down into its bowels. There was a sudden gust of wind that blew sand impregnated with sulphuric acid into his eyes. His eyes immediately became inflamed and he was virtually blinded. He could perform no more observations, and the only thing on his mind was to descend as quickly as possible. Their situation wasn't improved by a snowstorm on the way down, but luckily their porters were still waiting for them and assisted them back to camp.

The following year, Stübel repeated Reiss and Escobar's (and the dog's) ascent of Cotopaxi by the same route, accompanied by four Ecuadorians. It seemed there wasn't much left on Cotopaxi for Whymper and the Carrels to do.

Or was there?

The following day was Christmas Day, and we chose to celebrate it with some ice axe practice on the flanks of Cotopaxi.

From 3,800m on the Limpiopungo Plain, it's possible to drive up featureless slopes of dusty red sand to a car park at 4,600m. I've not visited all of the world's car parks, but in terms of setting I'm going to stick my neck out and say that this one is up there with the best of them. The view is northwards across a broad plain scarred by devastating lava and lahar flows. The plain is bounded by three extinct volcanoes: rocky, W-shaped Rumiñahui on the left; the flatter, greener Pasochoa at the end of the valley; and the pink dragon-back of Sincholagua to the right. On a clear day (which, as you are beginning to understand, does not occur so often in the Avenue of the Volcanoes), the snowy peaks of Cayambe and Antisana are also visible across the páramo, the first peering coyly behind a shoulder of Sincholagua, and the second rising above wide grasslands further to the east.

Refugio José F. Rivas, the mountain hut that is the starting point for climbs of Cotopaxi, is 200m above the car park, at 4,800m. Located just below the level of the 'permanent' (though receding) snow line, it was opened in 1971 and is named after a Catholic priest, Padre José Rivas, who supported one of the local climbing clubs and helped to raise funds to build the hut. More eccentrically, he held a mass on the summit in 1979. I expect his congregation spent much of the service praying there would be no eruption.

We put on our big mountaineering boots, packed our climbing equipment, and started plodding up a clear path that zigzagged up scree slopes. The hut's proximity to the car park made it a popular spot for day trippers who had driven up from Quito and the surrounding towns and villages. They came in all ages, shapes and sizes. Not all of them were active outdoor types – indeed, most probably weren't. Some struggled with the altitude, and none more so than a crying baby, carried on its father's shoulders. At 4,600m there is only 58 per cent of the oxygen there is at sea level. The hapless parent didn't realise that his child was suffocating.

Angus raised his camera for a photo of the hut, only for a young woman in a pink shell suit to walk into view. He hastily lowered it again.

'I must be back in the eighties,' he said. 'I'm not taking mountaineering photos with these chavvy locals in them.'

Some people were more stylish. I walked behind Tony, and noticed that several inches of his boxer shorts were showing above the waistband of his trousers.

'I don't want to embarrass you, Tony, but I can see your underpants,' I said.

'Stop dissing me, man,' he replied. 'Don't you know it's the fashion these days?'

'Can I lend you my climbing harness to stop your trousers falling down?'

We walked past the hut to a tongue of glacier a short distance beyond. Here we put on our crampons and harnesses before heading onto the ice. We had all climbed on snow and ice before, but we had different levels of experience, so Felipe gave us a short refresher on ice-axe and crampon technique for climbing different gradients of ice. It sounds simple – and sure enough, after a bit of practice, it is – but by using the right technique for the right ice slope you can save yourself a lot of effort. The techniques included walking up a gentle slope with our feet pointing outwards like Charlie Chaplin, walking sideways up a steep traverse by keeping our feet parallel and lifting them one over another, and climbing a steep ice face using the front points of our crampons and the pick of our axes in the ice above us.

It was basic stuff, but Felipe was a good instructor, and he found it useful to assess our abilities before assigning rope teams. We ended the session by practising our technique for ice-axe arrest. This is useful if you fall on a steep snow slope and don't want to slide all the way down to the bottom crying 'weee!' Or if it's a really big mountain like Cotopaxi, 'weeeeeeeeee!'

'Hold the head of your axe like a dagger,' Felipe said, 'and stick it into the ice as hard as you can, like you're stabbing someone in the chest and you really want to kill them.'

'Is it better to imagine it's someone you know,' Tony said, 'like Mark?'

'If I die on Cotopaxi then I have prima facie evidence that Tony is the culprit.'

I said the words 'prima facie' in the voice of a baby.

'No you don't,' Tony replied.

I moved along the line and positioned myself between

Thierry and Ruth. The French and the Scots consider themselves to be lifelong enemies of the English, but in this case I believed them to be more peaceful people to stand beside.

'When I shout "Fall!", I want you to throw yourselves onto the ice in the arrest position,' Felipe said. 'It could happen any moment, so I'm not going to give you any warning.'

'Hang on a minute,' I said, 'I just want to take a photo.'

'Fall!'

We belly-flopped onto our stomachs. I managed to get two hands on my ice axe without dropping my camera, but I don't remember how. We repeated this exercise several times, attracting a small audience of Ecuadorians, who had wandered beyond the hut to investigate the commotion and found it so entertaining that they stayed to watch. Every time we fell over on the ice there were whoops of joy and peals of laughter. This actually made things easier. Being the idiots that we were, we started playing to the gallery, throwing ourselves to the ground with a roar, and making Tarzan noises. I never thought ice-axe arresting could be so much fun. It didn't occur to any of us to mimic a real-life situation by screaming in terror.

Our audience was still there when we finished our session and wandered off the ice. Some of them asked to have their pictures taken with us, as if we were climbing celebrities. All we'd been doing was buggering about on the ice.

'What's it going to be like if we climb this thing next week?' Tony said. 'I expect we'll be signing autographs.'

A light snow began to fall as we removed our crampons, so we retreated to the hut for some hot soup. The place was crowded with locals enjoying a short Christmas excursion. Some of them were carrying huge chunks of ice they had chipped from the glacier to take back home and chill their Christmas drinks with.

It was a jolly scene, but the hut hadn't always been a place of refuge. On 7 April 1996, 13 people died when a large section of ice broke off the glacier directly above and triggered a colossal avalanche that buried the hut. It was Easter Sunday, and there were more tourists than usual – people who, unlike mountaineers, were unaware of the risks that mountains hold. Most of those inside the hut survived the avalanche and were able to escape with the help of rescuers, but day trippers on the slopes outside were not so lucky.

Three men who would have been acutely aware of the risks were our old friends Whymper and the Carrels. They were true alpine climbers. They had many friends who had perished in the Alps climbing new routes; four of Whymper's climbing partners had fallen to their deaths descending from the Matterhorn. If ordinary climbing hazards weren't enough, they climbed Cotopaxi in 1880, three years after the great eruption of 1877.

They could increase their chances of survival if they climbed quickly and came down straight away. But that wasn't Whymper's way. Cotopaxi had already been climbed by seven people and a dog. Whymper wanted to do something special, and Cotopaxi was the mountain to do it on. His excuse for travelling to Ecuador had been to investigate the effects of high altitude on the human body. Their first climb in Ecuador had been the highest mountain, Chimborazo, which they had climbed virtually straight off the boat. They all suffered from altitude sickness and needed to descend quickly.

By the time they climbed Cotopaxi they had been in Ecuador's highlands for several weeks. Whymper wanted to test if they were becoming accustomed to the altitude, a process now known as acclimatisation. They would do that by climbing Cotopaxi and spending a night at nearly 6,000m. Spending a night and day on Cotopaxi's summit would also give them more time to peer down into its crater. Its gurgling, bubbling crater that had exploded violently three years earlier. They knew what they were letting themselves in for, but what the heck; they were climbers.

They started testing their acclimatisation early by pitching their camp at 4,600m. They set off at 5.20am on 18 February and climbed from the north-west side by following a ridge that projects slightly in the direction of Rumiñahui.

The snow line started at around 4,700m, but it stopped abruptly 300m from the top, because the slopes just below the summit crater were still covered in ash. Much of this would have come from the 1877 eruption, but Whymper noted that fine particles were still being ejected. The ash slipped from underneath them, making for a laborious ascent, but they found firmer footing on occasional streaks of ice.

The climbers arrived on the summit rim at around midday. Being well organised, Whymper had a plan for if the volcano erupted while they were up there. Admittedly, it wasn't very sophisticated, but it was easy to implement: namely, abandon all equipment and comrades, and bugger off down as quickly as possible, every man for himself.

Jean-Antoine Carrel believed the mountain was alive, and he called it the 'animal'.

Just a few minutes after they arrived they felt a roar from deep within.

'When we heard the roar, there was an "it is time to be off" expression clearly written on all our faces,' Whymper said.[10]

I bet there was.

A cloud of cool steam enveloped them, but things seemed to be safe after they'd given it a few minutes to settle and they decided to stay. They pitched their tent a little way down from the summit on the outside of the crater. The ash was unstable, and it took them a long time to dig a platform flat enough to accommodate it. They must have opened the door in the morning with a certain amount of trepidation, hoping they hadn't slid all the way down to the bottom.

Some time after nightfall, they fixed a rope, and Whymper went for a look down into the crater. He lay on his stomach while Jean-Antoine kept hold of his legs. Beneath the steam clouds he could see fire bellowing. Like Reiss he observed the crater to be elliptical, and he estimated it as 700m north to south and 500m east to west. Parts of the inner walls were snow-clad, while others were encrusted with sulphur. A network of fiery cracks surrounded a circular spot, right at the bottom 350m down. The spot was incandescent with glowing lava and flames flickered all over its surface. There wasn't much that scared Jean-Antoine Carrel, but had it winked at them, then I expect he would have shat himself.

Every half hour the crater belched steam that came over the rim and engulfed them. Although it didn't feel thick, by morning their tent was covered in a black film. That morning they made some observations and left the summit after midday, having remained on the top for 26 hours. They had suffered no ill effects from the altitude, and Whymper had made an important discovery about acclimatisation.

Two months later, while they were camped on Cayambe, they saw a huge quantity of steam ejected from Cotopaxi, 90km away, which travelled towards them and passed overhead. By the time it reached them, it was a continuous body of cloud, and Whymper estimated there were 90km^3 of gas being emitted. Had it not issued from a vent, and instead found its passage barred by rock, then, as Whymper observed:

> *The whole continent might have quivered under an*
> *explosion rivalling or surpassing the mighty catastrophe at*
> *Krakatoa.*[11]

They knew what they were letting themselves in for. You could describe their ascent of Cotopaxi as something special, but there are other adjectives too. 'Bonkers' is one that springs to mind, but fair play to them.

Climbing Cotopaxi was a very different experience to Antisana, and the main difference was the number of people. On Antisana we had an entire mountain to ourselves; we'd driven up to a remote part of the páramo, and could see for miles across open grasslands. There wasn't another sign of human habitation anywhere in that broad expanse: no people, no vehicles, no houses. We'd trekked up to our camp and enjoyed a peaceful evening, watched only by the stars. When we climbed up to the summit the following day, there were no other climbers – it was only us.

A few days later, Felipe drove us up to the car park on Cotopaxi. It was much busier than it had been when we visited on Christmas Day. Dozens of cars were parked in neat lines, and the trail up to Refugio José Rivas resembled a dusty version of Oxford Street.

Inside the hut, things were no better. Hundreds of day trippers were crowded in, as well as thirty or so climbers who would be staying the night. There was a noisy buzz of people crammed onto benches and tables. Overhead in the dormitory, climbers clomped around on the wooden floorboards in their boots.

We found a spare corner of table and settled in.

'I don't know how I'm going to put up with this,' I said to Tony.

He was unpacking the copy of Whymper's *Travels amongst the Great Andes of the Equator*, which I'd lent him to help pass the time. He looked up.

'Think what it's like for me,' he said. 'Each time I hear your voice, I'm afraid you're going to tell me another one of your awful jokes.'

This helped to release the tension. I got my own back by telling him some of my worst ones. Even so, I found the hut claustrophobic and stressful. It wasn't the best preparation for an overnight climb, and I yearned to be camping again. Even at busy campsites the privacy of a tent can be a welcome retreat. The noise went on throughout the afternoon, and I wore earplugs to provide some measure of peace.

Happily, the noise began to die away at five o'clock as the day trippers left to return home. We escaped from our cramped corner when Felipe found a table in the warmer main room attached to the kitchen. He cooked us a nice soup and stir-fry for dinner, and I began to feel confident again. Since the day we drove to Antisana, we had experienced six good days of perfect weather in a land renowned for clouds. It was almost too much to hope for, but we just needed the perfect spell to last a day longer.

At 7.30 we went upstairs to the bunks to try and get some sleep before our midnight start. In those days the José Rivas hut had two big dormitories with triple bunk beds that appeared to have been made from Meccano. I slept on the top deck of a huge metal contraption of around a dozen beds. This unwieldy beast was constantly changing its centre of gravity. Every time somebody rolled over – especially those of us on top – the entire thing swung from side to side. I lay in fear of a bolt springing loose and the flimsy metal girders pinging us through the air to land in a pile of wriggling sleeping bags like a squirm of maggots. I wore my earplugs and wasn't bothered by the noise, but the vague sense of being in a prolonged earth tremor didn't help ease my mind. I managed to grab two or three hours' sleep until 10.30 when people began to get ready for their overnight ascents. From that moment on, further sleep was impossible.

I rose at midnight. As soon as I removed my earplugs I could hear the wind outside, and I knew it would be colder than on Antisana a few days earlier. Outside, however, it didn't feel so bad. Aside from the wind chill, the ambient air temperature was still quite mild.

Tony, Felipe and I went downstairs to the dining room for hot tea and granola. At one o'clock we left for the summit. Of the 30 climbers aiming for the top that night, we were pretty much the last to leave, but we expected to overtake a few of them on the way.

We could see a trail of head lamps high on the slopes above us. Some of them had left more than an hour earlier. The trail headed straight up from the hut in a series of zigzags, and to begin with we made steady progress. The snow line on Cotopaxi was much higher than on Antisana. By the time we reached it at 2.15, we had already climbed 400m and were at 5,200m.

We roped up, put on crampons, and moved onto the glacier with Felipe at the front, Tony in the middle and me at the back. It's normal to put the smallest person in the middle of the rope in the interests of balance. Felipe opted for a different model this time, and put Tony the big guy there. If Antisana had been any indication, he was the one most likely to tire first, and therefore most at risk of falling into a crevasse. On the back of the rope he would be likely to jerk us both backwards like the anchorman in a tug-of-war team. But with me behind him, at least I could keep an eye on him and react more quickly. That was Felipe's theory, and from an early stage in the climb it looked as though Tony intended to prove him right.

The trail headed more steeply up a ridge, and I had to turn sideways to make progress. After an hour of climbing we stopped for a rest.

'How are you feeling, Tony?' I said out of politeness.

'Fuck me, I'm fucked,' he replied. 'Fuck my fucking stomach.'

He put down his pack and took out some water.

'What did you say?' Felipe asked.

Tony was leaning over and taking his time to respond, so I helped him out.

'He said fuck him, he's fucked. Fuck his fucking stomach,' I replied.

Before he joined us to climb volcanoes, Tony had travelled extensively in Ecuador, visiting the Galapagos Islands and then the Amazon region. After returning from the Amazon and linking up with us, he had been ill for nearly a week. He seemed to be better on Antisana, and in the hut the previous day he had been in good form, despite the unnecessary protests about my jokes. But we were only three on the rope, and if one of us needed to turn back, then we would all have to.

'You're doing good, big man. You can do it,' I said to him.

'Don't worry, there will be no unfair dismissal. I'll make it up all right. I'll just feel shit.'

His use of a legal term reassured me that his condition wasn't too serious yet, and we continued. Tony was true to his word. His pace slowed from time to time, and he frequently asked Felipe to stop and rest. His face was as white as the ice of the glacier, and he kept apologising. But he kept going.

The route wasn't as intricate as it had been on Antisana, but it became more so as we climbed. We wove around the side of some gaping crevasses, and passed to the right of the Yanasacha Wall. A complex formation of steps crowned by a giant ice mushroom rose above us in daunting fashion. There was a distinct smell of sulphur.

'Have you farted, Tony?' I shouted. 'Remember, I'm behind you on the rope.'

'It's sulphur. It's a bloody volcano, you idiot.'

Dawn broke as we traversed across a precipitous face of ice. The long drop to our left, too steep for any chance to hold a fall, made our route perilously exposed. Thankfully, the large number of people passing this way had left a clear trail in the snow a metre wide, like a road hewn into a sheer cliff. I wasn't in any danger of falling off anything a metre wide, but how about Tony in his present condition?

Before I had much chance to dwell on it, another problem loomed ahead of us. A protruding pillar of snow, like a castle buttress, appeared directly across our path. The metre-wide channel climbed vertically upwards to get over this obstacle. Just as I was thinking we had an easy walk to the summit and all Tony needed to do was keep plodding, it seemed that we would have to do some climbing after all.

Felipe turned around.

'Stay here. Don't move until I say "climb",' he said.

'What?' Tony replied.

Felipe stepped towards him with anger in his eye, like an irate schoolmaster who had just spotted a pupil on the front row picking his nose and flicking the bogey to try and make it stick to the blackboard (didn't we all try to do that at some time?)

'I said stay where you are and don't move until I say "climb",' Felipe said again, glaring at Tony and pausing over every syllable.

Felipe uncoiled the rope to make it longer between him and Tony, then headed up the buttress on his front points. Tony turned around and looked bewildered.

'What did I do?' he said. 'I guess I'm being a pain in the arse.'

'Don't worry. He's UIAGM-certified,' I said, which seemed a fair explanation for what had just happened.

A short while later we heard Felipe's voice.

'Climb.'

Tony lumbered up the vertical channel in ungainly fashion, his legs wide apart like a desperate man trying to struggle up a snowman's back passage. I would have looked away, but I was attached to him by a rope and he was in danger of falling on top of me. I had no choice but to watch. Fortunately, I discovered that Tony could be very determined in these situations. I watched him straddle the buttress and ease his way around it, disappearing from view.

'Well done, you're safe now,' I heard Felipe say from the other side.

I followed them, and found myself on a firm path again, traversing high above the páramo with views of Quito and beyond. There was another steep snow slope, a couple more twists and turns, and we stepped onto the summit at 6.45. Despite the stops, we had made good time, and wouldn't have wanted to be there much earlier.

It was a much smaller summit than Antisana's, and this time we had to share it with 20 other people, but we didn't mind. I was elated to be there, and the weather had been kind to us again. We could see all the volcanoes we had climbed in the previous days: Pichincha rising above Quito, Rumiñahui just below us, the twin peaks of Iliniza to our left, and the snow-clad mass of Antisana across the páramo to our right. More distant peaks were visible too. We were midway between Cayambe and Chimborazo. Each of these two domes of snow was clearly visible 100km away on opposite horizons. I knew I would have to return and climb them some day too.

But the crowning glory of Cotopaxi's summit was not the 360° panorama of isolated volcanoes, but the gigantic crater directly below, a gaping chasm of chocolate-brown rock, framed by a shining ring of snow and ice. It was too deep to see into the bottom. We were perched on a platform of snow a little above, and to look into its depths would have required me to lie on my stomach and peer over the edge of the ice, like Whymper had done while Jean-Antoine Carrel held his legs. I was worried that if I asked Tony to do the same then he would think it funny to let go. I was more than satisfied with what I could see already. It was perhaps for this reason that it didn't occur to me that the crater was still active, and somewhere down there a beast was sleeping.

Cotopaxi gave us another perfect day and another magical summit, but it was cold and windy, and Felipe expressed his concern about a bottleneck at the snow buttress. After 20 minutes on top of the second-highest mountain in Ecuador, we headed back down again.

Directly below us as we descended, on the blanket of cloud between ourselves and the Ilinizas, the black triangle of Cotopaxi's shadow cast a striking profile. Somewhere in that shadow our figures moved. And the next time I returned to Ecuador, there would be a new figure in that silhouette.

Cotopaxi's summit crater, framed by a shining ring of snow and ice

4 CHIMBORAZO

Exotic locations often have dubious superlatives applied to them, sometimes with little or no attempt at verification.

How often have you travelled to a place and found somewhere claiming to be the highest, the biggest, the oldest, the longest, the deepest? In Ladakh, India, I once drove up the world's highest motorable road. Until then, I hadn't even known that *motorable* was a word, and I've since been higher in a car. At the top was a place calling itself the world's highest souvenir shop, which raises a question: who on earth measures the altitude of all the world's souvenir shops? The newsagent of a place called Tomintoul in Scotland had a sign in the window advertising 'The highest chance of winning the National Lottery in the country'. Which is ridiculous. It's perfectly possible to carry the winning ticket to the summit of Ben Nevis and wait up there till they announce the draw.

There are some claims that can be proved more easily. You only need to spin a globe to see that there aren't many high mountain ranges on the equator. It's therefore easy to guess that at 5,790m, Cayambe in Ecuador is the highest mountain directly on it (which it is, by a long way in fact – only 5,199m Mount Kenya comes close).

Other claims are proved mathematically after years of

scientific discovery. The purpose of the French Geodesic Mission to Ecuador (which really should be listed in the *Guinness Book of World Records* as the longest maths field trip in history) was to confirm that the earth bulged around the equator. This fact had one profound meaning for Chimborazo, the highest mountain in Ecuador.

It meant that Chimborazo wasn't just the highest mountain in Ecuador. It could justifiably claim to be the highest mountain in the world.

'Piss off,' I can hear you saying. 'Everyone knows the highest mountain in the world is Everest. Chimborazo? Of course it is. And cucumbers are purple.'

But not so fast. It's a strange world we live in. If the earth bulges around the equator, then it means that places closer to the equator are further from the earth's centre than places close to the poles. Much closer, in fact. Mountains in Ecuador are around 2km further from the earth's centre than mountains in the highest part of the Himalayas.

More specifically, Chimborazo is 2,168m (give or take a few metres) further from the earth's centre than Everest. In fact, Chimborazo is the *highest mountain in the world when measured from the centre of the earth*. There's even a chap on the internet who has proved it by means of an enormous mathematical formula.[12]

In fact, for a long time Chimborazo was believed to be the highest mountain in the world, full stop. Its written history began with the Incas and the Spanish conquest of Peru, when two important battles were fought on the mountain's slopes. In 1525 two brothers, Atahualpa and Huáscar, quarrelled over their inheritance. In 1532 they fought a battle near Ambato, on the north-eastern slopes of Chimborazo. Atahualpa, the King of Quito, eventually defeated his brother and became the supreme ruler of the Incas, but his reign didn't last long. The following year he was captured, imprisoned and executed by the Spanish conquistador Francisco Pizarro.

In 1744, Bouguer and La Condamine calculated Chimborazo's height to be 6,276m, pretty close to the most widely accepted height today of 6,310m. It wasn't until 1827 that a higher mountain, Sajama (6,542m) was measured in Bolivia. As for all the giant 8,000m peaks in the Himalayas, nobody had a clue just how whoppingly gigantic they were until the Great Trigonometrical Survey of India started the work of measuring them in the 1820s.

So when he made the first proper attempt to climb Chimborazo in 1802, the German scientist Alexander von Humboldt may have thought he was climbing the highest mountain on Earth.

It was a beautiful, cloudless start to the morning as our guide Romel Sandoval drove us south from Quito on the Pan-American Highway.

'Look, I think I can see Cayambe,' Edita said as we peered out of the window.

And so we could. To borrow a cliché from the marketing people I've just been sneering at a few paragraphs ago, the drive south from Quito has to be one of the more memorable stretches of road on planet Earth: the defining portion of the aptly named Avenue of the Volcanoes. There are peaks on either side, one after another, like neatly planted palm trees lining a boulevard. To give you some idea of just how remarkable this stretch of road is, imagine a dozen volcanoes the size of Mount Fuji – some snow capped, some breathing fire – lining both sides of the M4 between London and Bristol. Imagine an active volcano wedged on the ring road between Reading and Slough, another one popping up just south of Swindon. That's what it's like leaving Quito on the road to Ambato.

On our left we had clear views of three of the big four. It was another chance to study them all, contemplate some memorable climbs, and think about the remaining one that was still to come.

Cayambe was the most distant, but it was fresh in Edita's mind because we had climbed it with Romel the previous day. It had seemed more straightforward than my ascents of the other two – no maze of crevasses to find a way around, no lumbering lawyer breaking wind on the rope in front of me. From the summit we looked across a vast plain of white cloud, like a calm sea rippling in a light breeze, with the higher peaks of Ecuador rising above the water like mountainous islands. It was a view I had become attuned to, but to Edita it was new.

Now Cayambe was a glistening upturned bowl, and we could see there had been fresh snow overnight. While our ascent had felt easy, you sometimes don't realise how much these climbs take out of you. We intended to climb Chimborazo the next day. Our climb of Cayambe could be a positive or a negative factor, but that depended on how much recovery time we needed. We had just been to 5,790m and would be well acclimatised. There was a chance we could breeze up the mountain, but if we were still tired, then it could easily turn into a death march.

To the right of Cayambe and a little closer to Quito rose Antisana, a more crumpled peak with multiple snowy summits. This had been the hardest climb of the three, but also the most enjoyable, snaking between crevasses like a slalom skier weaving between flags (though a little more slowly). I remembered our camp, overlooking the peaceful grasslands of the páramo, with the perfect cone of Cotopaxi on a distant horizon. I'd not seen wise Felipe or cheerful

Ramiro again, or little Domenica, the pocket rocket who had managed to remain calm as I staggered along behind her.

I had a pocket rocket of my own now. Edita Nichols – or, to give her maiden name, Edita Uksaïte – was like a little bulldog, faster, stronger and more energetic than me, always leaving me struggling to keep up. I considered this a good thing. After Cotopaxi I climbed some bigger mountains in the Himalayas. I joined expeditions to several of the world's 8,000m peaks, and succeeded in climbing Everest. I met Edita on one of these expeditions, to 8,516m Lhotse, and we started dating. She had led a far more adventurous life than I had. Born and raised in Lithuania, she left home after finishing school. Over the next 15 years she lived in France, Canada and the United States – where she was married and divorced again – then finally settled for a few years in Italy.

In Edita's case the word 'settled' was relative, because her job took her all over the world. She worked in emergency response for an international humanitarian organisation. The phrase 'tough cookie' doesn't even begin to describe her, unless the cookie is made from a kind of edible steel. While I tend to get flustered if a bartender takes my glass away while there's still half a centimetre of beer in the bottom, Edita could turn up in a developing country with badly damaged infrastructure within hours of a major disaster – the sort of place where the security guard carries an assault rifle and there's a poisonous creepy-crawly hiding under the toilet seat – and get on with the job of saving people's lives. For her, this meant arranging complicated logistics to ensure that survivors had enough food.

Difficult tasks seemed quite simple for her. In 2013 she became the first Lithuanian woman to reach the summit of Everest. While my own Everest summit day had been fraught with danger and I considered myself lucky to get down alive, hers was trouble free, the main hiccup being that she held the national flag upside down in her summit photo (red at the top, then green, then yellow – good grief).

'I want to climb that one next,' she said, bubbling with excitement as Cotopaxi's perfect profile rose up behind the lower hills. 'When can we do it?'

'It's closed,' Romel said. 'We don't know when it will open again. Maybe not for many years.'

We discovered this when I asked Javier to arrange the trip for us. I knew he could arrange pretty much anything in Ecuador for us, but it turned out that he was hopeless at stopping an erupting volcano. On 14 August 2015, Cotopaxi emerged from its 75-year nap and did the same thing many people do after emerging from a long sleep: it let rip.

At 10.50am local time, a giant ash plume blasted 8km above the summit crater. There were five more explosions that day, some producing lava flows. These were a concern, because history had shown that Cotopaxi's most deadly hazards were not, arguably, the explosions themselves, but the devastating lahars that occurred when the glacier ice melted into floods that gathered ice, rocks and mud from the surrounding terrain.

But over the next two weeks, the ash emissions that rose 2km above the crater and drifted to the west were the principal hazard. For a week they were more or less continuous. Those most badly affected lived in the towns and villages the other side of Rumiñahui. It was an area of high population density. Residents had to wear masks and carry out regular evacuation drills. Four weeks after the first eruption, Ecuador's Institute of Geophysics estimated that over 630,000m^3 of ash had been emitted.[13] To give you an idea of just how much ash that is, imagine 9.7 million backpacks stuffed full of it. If the ash fell evenly to a depth of 10cm, then you could pitch around 2.1 million two-person tents on its surface. That's about 24 Glastonbury Festivals.

Am I making myself clear? It's a lot of ash.

The ash was certainly an annoyance and an inconvenience, but by the time we were planning our trip initial fears of a more explosive eruption and deadly lahar flows had died away. By December, the government state of emergency had been lifted and Cotopaxi National Park was about to be reopened for tourism. But this didn't include climbing. There were still minor eruptions, and the volcano continued to emit ash and steam – along with clouds of potentially lethal sulphurous gas. Gone were the days when bowler-hatted explorers could swan up the mountain with their alpine guides, spend a night on the summit and peer into its active crater.

We could see that its western side was still black with ash. What set Cotopaxi apart from other mountains of its size was its crater: the chocolate abyss with a glistening ring of ice. But Romel said that was gone now. I wondered if anyone of my generation would get to see that sight again.

Romel told us about the eruption four months earlier.

'We knew it was going to happen,' he said. 'In about February, it started smoking, and then there was a strong smell of sulphur. Later, the inside of the crater started filling with water from the melting ice. I climbed it in June, and was climbing Cayambe when it erupted in August.

'Everyone was scared. The eruption went several kilometres into the air. People were worried about the lahars. There were lots of scare stories in the media, but nobody knew what would happen. The government always has plans for evacuation, but everyone ignores them. There are over a million people in this valley where all the ash was settling, but where can they go?'

Romel swept his arm across the mountains on the right of the avenue ahead of us – Atacazo, Corazón and Iliniza.

'Everything around here was covered in ash, but wind

and rain eventually cleaned it all again.'

It seemed that Edita would have to wait a long time before she could climb Cotopaxi, but I had just one of the big four volcanoes left to do. Chimborazo was substantially higher than any of the others. It exceeded Cotopaxi by more than 400m. I knew that it was going to be a good deal tougher to climb, and that was before the added difficulty of the route we had chosen.

When we arrived in Quito the previous week, Javier came to our hotel to discuss the route. He confirmed that the Normal Route was not in good condition, but an alternative was the west ridge, beneath a crag of rock called El Castillo. This route would take us above the rockfall danger that plagued the Normal Route and caused us to abandon our plan of climbing it on my previous visit.

But there was a problem. We would need to climb from Refugio Carrel, the lower of the two mountain huts at 4,800m. We were looking at 1,500m of ascent on summit day. That's a lot of mountain in any part of the world, but on Chimborazo, as we have seen, we were further from the centre of the earth than anywhere else. This meant there was more land below us than at any other point on the planet. I thought back to my physics lessons at school, and realised that the pull of gravity must be stronger. It would be like that time Domenica was on the rope behind me, pulling me back like an irate dog owner. Only worse, surely?

I wasn't sure if my science was entirely accurate (it wasn't; it was silly), but I did know one thing. It was going to be a long day. Or more precisely, a long night and day.

Better scientists than me had attempted Chimborazo. In his lifetime, Humboldt was one of the most famous scientists in the world. He is now better known as an explorer, almost entirely due to one great expedition to Latin America that embraced five years of his life from 1799 to 1804. By the time he made his attempt on Chimborazo, Humboldt had already climbed several volcanoes.

In Ecuador, he made a fairly lame attempt on Cotopaxi, but climbed Pichincha three times in April and May 1802. Pichincha was still bubbling away then, although there hadn't been a major eruption since 1660. He lay on a rock and peered over the edge of the crater, where he saw bluish flames and nearly choked on the sulphur fumes. Like La Condamine's, his description evoked scenes from the underworld.

'No imagination would be able to conjure up something as sinister, mournful and deathly as we saw there,' he wrote.[14]

He had never visited Scotland when he wrote this, or he would have known about bagpipes.

How high Humboldt climbed on Chimborazo has been the subject of much debate. It's fairly certain that he didn't climb to 5,878m, as he claimed. If he did, then he would have been surrounded by glaciers, and would have been climbing one for some distance. He described ascending a knife-edge ridge, in fog, which was 'only spotted with a thin layer of snow here and there'.[15] His party arrived at a 120m ravine that proved an insurmountable barrier, and turned around. Their route has since been identified as a ridge on the southern side where, even today, after two more centuries of erosion, the glacier extends down to 4,800m. To have climbed so high without spotting a glacier underneath them would have been rather like wandering along the Brighton sea front without noticing the salty spray and tide lapping against the beach. His descriptions of altitude symptoms are also puzzling. Few mountaineers will recognise the bleeding from the lips, gums and eyes that he described, unless they'd been in a high-altitude fist fight.

In 1831, fresh from their tussle with snow blindness on Antisana, Boussingault and Hall also made an attempt on Chimborazo. Boussingault claimed to reach 6,004m. His account contained a little more detail than Humboldt's, but not enough to satisfy Edward Whymper when he made the first ascent of Chimborazo in 1880. Whymper the wood engraver would have made a good physics teacher. He scolded Humboldt the master scientist for failing to provide any bearings to identify his location. He was also pretty sure the eminent polymath had made some monumental cock-ups with his altitude readings.

Among many puzzled questions, he had this to say:

There were matters in their relations that I did not understand; particularly, the divine speed with which they descended.[16]

In Boussingault's case Whymper came out with a one-liner laced with a dry wit that Winston Churchill would have been proud of:

Boussingault says the descent was wearisome. It seems, however, to have been lively.

We will never know for sure how high Humboldt and Boussingault climbed, but Whymper analysed their climbs in detail after visiting the south side of Chimborazo. He concluded that both men reached roughly the same height, at the 'foot of the Southern Walls'[17] at around 5,600m. In Boussingault's case this may have been true, but in Humboldt's case, given the absence of glacier in his account, Whymper was being generous. Boussingault's route description is vaguely recognisable as the south-west ridge, now known as the Whymper Route. He described 'a prism of trachyte, whose top covered with a cupola of snow, forms the summit of Chimborazo'.[18]

This is a somewhat flowery description of what the summit looks like from that side, crowning the Southern Walls. We were about to see for ourselves.

Above Ambato, a city of 165,000 people on Chimborazo's north-east side, a smooth metalled road climbed into a landscape of wild, rolling grasslands that wouldn't have looked out of place among the denuded and sheep-cropped moorland back home in Britain. We drove higher still, and the views opened out as we came to a high plateau. We could see for miles across a featureless landscape. The terrain became increasingly arid – grass gave way to sand as we arrived on the Gran Arenal (or 'The Great Sand'), a vast desert plain on the west side of Chimborazo. We knew the mountain was up there somewhere to our left, but it must have been feeling shy. While the sky was blue overhead, a stubborn shroud of white clouds kept Chimborazo hidden from view.

Not quite so shy were the vicuñas. These are the rarest members of the South American camelid family (which includes llamas, alpacas and guanacos). They were slender and long-necked, a metre high, with tawny coats that blended with the ground. The Arenal seemed to contain nothing to eat but a few tufts of grass and the occasional chuquiragua bush, but the vicuñas were thriving there. We could see many by the roadside, some individuals as well as small flocks of half a dozen.

The road across the Gran Arenal is the highest in

Ecuador, rising to 4,300m at the Chimborazo park gate. It was fast and straight with very few curves, and it felt like we were crossing the roof of the world as we circled Chimborazo from north to west.

I'd given up any hope of seeing the mountain that day. On a long stretch of desert highway, a cluster of lonely stone buildings stood by the side of the road. It was the park gate, a tiny complex with a restaurant, toilet block, checkpoint, and a small car park. We passed beneath an archway and began climbing a dirt track to Refugio Carrel. It was a road that would eventually take us to 4,800m.

As I braced myself for a bumpy ride, the unthinkable happened. A gap started to appear in the clouds, like the curtains parting across a stage. Little by little, Chimborazo was revealed – and it wasn't what I expected. I had imagined a snow mountain, with tumbling glaciers down its sides, but what we saw was a red smear of rock spreading from north to south in two long ridges. We were approaching from the south-west, so these were the west and south ridges of Chimborazo. I could see that the south ridge sported two substantial outcrops of rock like minor peaks. The lower one ended abruptly in a cliff; it seemed a likely candidate for the gap in the ridge that ended Humboldt's climb, but it was towards the bottom of the ridge, and not even close to the 5,878m that he claimed to have reached.

The south-west ridge projected towards us, and was indistinct from the angle that we approached. Directly above it rose the red rock of the south-west face, Whymper's Southern Walls, and above the face was the Veintimilla summit – Boussingault's cupola of snow. The main summit, known as the Whymper summit, lay just behind the Veintimilla summit to the right.

Whymper and the Carrels climbed Chimborazo soon after getting off the boat in Guayaquil and ascending through the Andes.

They had their first view of the mountain across the Gran Arenal from Guaranda. Two things surprised Whymper. First, there were far more glaciers than he was expecting. Second, Chimborazo had not one but two summits (in fact, there are five, but he could only see the two highest ones from the west side). It wasn't easy to tell which summit was higher. He thought it might be the eastern one, a little to the right and behind the first one (in this they were correct, for the Whymper summit, as it is now known, is about 40m higher than the Veintimilla summit).

He and the Carrels concluded that the east summit couldn't be tackled directly, because the glaciers beneath it streamed over vertical rock faces. They did identify two practical routes to the west summit though. The first was the south-west ridge, which led straight up from the Gran Arenal, and the second was the northern skyline, which appeared to be a single long snow slope free from any impediments. They chose the south-west ridge for their first attempt, because they believed it must have been the route taken by Humboldt and Boussingault. There was one point on the ridge that they thought might present a difficulty, but if they could get beyond it, then the rest of the ascent to the west summit looked possible too.

A few days later they crossed the Gran Arenal and took their mules all the way up to nearly 4,900m before Jean-Antoine Carrel established a camp beneath a wall of lava at 5,079m. This was higher than any of them had ever been before, and they were all suffering from altitude sickness of a much more familiar form than Humboldt's bleeding eyes and gums:

> *We were feverish, had intense headaches, and were unable*
> *to satisfy our desire for air, except by breathing with open*
> *mouths. This naturally parched the throat, and produced a*
> *craving for drink, which we were unable to satisfy.*[19]

Less familiar was their cure for altitude sickness. This was a time when many travellers were beginning to explore the Himalayas, experiencing high altitude for the first time, and nobody really knew what to do about it. They were experimenting with novel methods. Whymper tried some 'chlorate of potash' on the advice of a doctor who had been part of an expedition to Yarkand in Central Asia. This is known today as potassium chlorate, and is used, among other things, to make firelighters and detergent. It comes in the form of a white powder, but instead of snorting it like certain other white powders, Whymper and his companions dissolved 10 grains into a wine glass of water.

Everyone, that is, except Jean-Antoine Carrel, who stubbornly refused to take 'doctor's stuff'. He had a far more effective cure of his own, that could be used for everything from dysentery to lack of air. Namely, red wine. Clearly, he would have been able to sympathise with Whymper's 'craving for drink'. Funnily, it's a substance that has proved far more enduring as a cure for illness than potassium chlorate (I wouldn't recommend drinking detergent, even for treating dysentery).

They spent their first day at the camp resting and recovering – or as we'd call it nowadays, acclimatising. Whymper's description of that day makes uncomfortable reading.

> *Eating would have been impossible, and to talk or drink*

was difficult. We could only gasp ejaculations, or a few
words at a time, and efforts at conversation were cut short
by irrepressible, spasmodic gulps.[20]

It's difficult to know what to make of this, but I expect I would also find conversation difficult if I found myself ejaculating in a tent with other men.

Their camp was somewhere towards the bottom end of the south-west ridge. Whymper described both the view to the east, up the ridges and valleys that Humboldt may have ascended, and to the north, across the newly named Vallon de Carrel (or Valle Carrel as it is now known). At the head of the valley, the Thielmann Glacier came down from Chimborazo's west summit. This was named after Max von Thielmann, a German scientist who had explored Chimborazo and made the fourth ascent of Cotopaxi two years earlier. If there's ever going to be any consolation from the hell-sprung apocalypse that is global warming, it's that all the world's glaciers are going to vanish, thus thwarting these knobbers who thought it would be nice to name geographical features after themselves. But anyway, at the end of the glacier was a 'long and serrated ridge which terminated the view in that direction'.[21] This was the west ridge, now known as El Castillo – a place I'd soon become very familiar with.

Looking up the south-west ridge, Whymper noted that they could climb to 5,250m without touching snow. Above this were jagged blocks and pinnacles of lava that needed to be skirted on either side of the crest. They established a high camp on a small platform at 5,268m, in the shelter of one of these pinnacles on its eastern side. It took them several days to ferry loads up to this camp and establish a base for their summit assault.

After a day's delay, caused by the discovery of some

putrid ox cheek in their expedition supplies, they set out at 5.35am on 3 January, as soon as there was enough daylight to see by. They immediately crossed to the west side of the ridge and looked up towards the summit. A large pinnacle of rock barred their way on the crest of the ridge. They would have to pass beneath its left side. Beyond the pinnacle, the ridge rose gently on snow until it reached the first of two cliffs. This was the point which, when they studied the mountain down in Guaranda, they agreed would be likely to present some difficulties.

Above the first cliff was another snow slope, then a second cliff that was crowned by the thick glacier of the western summit dome. This second cliff looked like it could be skirted to the left by keeping on snow and ice. Whymper's skill as an artist and engraver meant that he didn't need to exhaust too many words on description. He produced a sketch of the view from the point where they crossed to the west side of the ridge, and stuck it in the appropriate place of his book. Entitled *Chimborazo, from a Little Above the Third Camp*, it's one of the most evocative sketches in the book (along with one of a damsel in Cayambe village pouring a bucket of slops over a minstrel beneath her balcony). It perfectly illustrates the complete route up the south-west ridge to the west (Veintimilla) summit.

Whymper named both sets of cliffs the Southern Walls of Chimborazo. It took them about two hours to ascend the ridge to the base of the lower one.

'Thus far and no farther a man may go who is not a mountaineer,' Whymper said.[22]

He recorded the altitude as 5,647m. If Humboldt or Boussingault did go that way – and Boussingault may have done – then Whymper did not believe they could have climbed any higher.

There was a small breach in the lower wall, where ice had

formed in the cracks and allowed a passage up at an angle of 50°. The Carrels set to work forging a route up with their axes. They made good progress until a fierce wind whipped up. Realising they were not going to reach the summit that day, they deposited their equipment and retreated to camp.

They set off again at 5.40am on 4 January. By following their tracks of the previous day, they were through the breach in the Southern Walls by eight o'clock. Here they angled left on snow until they reached the upper part of the Thielmann Glacier, which led all the way up to the west summit.

Without knowing for certain which summit was the higher, their initial idea had been to skirt underneath the west summit to reach the saddle between the two, then head to whichever summit was the highest. When they saw that the saddle was more like a plateau about a third of a mile wide, they decided to head straight to the closer west summit first. But long before they reached it, they found themselves sinking up to their necks in soft snow. They could only progress by beating the snow down and crawling through the resulting hollow on all fours, like some sort of giant high-altitude mole. It would have been unbelievably hard work – but, on the plus side, gardening would seem like a piece of cake when they got home.

To reach the west summit, it took them over four hours of this snow 'floundering' (a lovely descriptive word that should be used more often for this sort of thing). But Sod's Law was in operation. Guess which summit was higher? The east one, of course. They could see immediately that they would need to continue.

Luckily, when they reached the final summit dome, they found that the snow was firm and they were able to arrive on the summit at 3.45pm, 'standing upright like men, instead of grovelling … like beasts of the field'.[23]

Imagine crawling to the summit – you would feel such a wimp.

In 1880 no one dreamed of climbing a mountain without taking some good old-fashioned scientific observations, in the same way that fancy restaurants can't seem to serve anything, even a fried egg, without putting a little bit of parsley on top. Despite the late hour, they remained on the summit for over an hour and a half, which meant they had to complete much of the descent in darkness. They got past the difficult section through the Southern Walls as the last rays of sun disappeared beneath the horizon, and reached their camp on the south-west ridge after nine o'clock. It had taken them an exhausting fifteen and a half hours.

Take note of this time. It will crop up again.

Whymper had been surprised by the number of glaciers, but what surprised me as we drove up to the hut was the absence of them. There was a substantial expanse of ice terraces beneath the Whymper summit, but on the Veintimilla summit I saw just a thin sliver, like icing on a cake. Likewise, the Thielmann Glacier, which formed the left-hand skyline, looked more like a narrow ice ramp. As for Whymper's 'Southern Walls' – so named because there were two of them, steep rock bands breaking through the snow – his use of the plural would no longer be appropriate. The whole of the south-west face appeared to be one single mass of red rock.

'Is it always like this?' I asked.

This might sound like a stupid question to ask about a mountain – Is it always like this? Of course it's always like this; it's a sodding mountain – but Romel understood what I meant.

The south-west face of Chimborazo, with the El Castillo
ridge on the left and Whymper Pinnacles on the right

'It's very dry this year,' he replied. 'There hasn't been much snow.'

Refugio Carrel was a neat red-roofed building at the top of the road. Like on Cotopaxi, there was a car park for day-trippers a few hundred metres away, but as climbers who would be staying overnight, we were allowed to drive a little further and park right beside the hut.

We passed a sign saying 'Chimborazo Refugio Hermanos Carrel'. This had me scratching my head.

'Who's Hermanos Carrel? I thought they were called Jean-Antoine and Louis.'

Romel laughed. 'In Spanish, *hermanos* means "brothers", but that is also wrong.'

This time I laughed. 'They weren't brothers.'

'No, they were cousins,' Romel said. 'Jean-Antoine was about twenty years older than Louis. The person who made this sign did not know his history.'

The car park meant that, once again, I found myself in a hut full of day trippers on the afternoon before a climb, but it was much smaller and not as noisy as the hut on Cotopaxi. We found a trio of empty bunk beds upstairs and left our bags. Then, while Romel went to find a table in the dining room, Edita and I stepped outside to study the mountain.

We were in a wide bowl bounded by the west and south-west ridges. The features in Whymper's descriptions and engravings were immediately recognisable. We were right underneath the south-west face, which I could now see was a swirling mix of bloodshot reds, ochres, greys and blacks, shaped like an eye. It felt like I was staring into the Great Red Spot of Jupiter.

The most obvious features on the south-west ridge were the Whymper Pinnacles from Whymper's iconic engraving, thrusting up from the crest like a shark's fin. The ridge led up at a gentle angle until about 5,500m, but then it appeared to merge with the face. Above that, it looked like a route for rock climbers only, right up to the crust of ice a few hundred metres thick that crowned the face beneath the Veintimilla summit. Whymper was impressed to be able to get up to 5,250m without touching snow, but now it looked closer to 6,000m. There was no sign of the slope of snow and ice that enabled Whymper and the Carrels to traverse left onto the Thielmann Glacier.

We turned our attention to the left-hand skyline – the route we would be taking. The west ridge looked long and gentle, but guarding its top was a series of rocky towers like the battlements on a castle wall. This 'long and serrated ridge' of Whymper's description formed the feature appropriately known as *El Castillo*, or 'The Castle' in English. Romel told us that it too had been covered in a glacier until as recently as 15 years ago. Tomorrow we would be skirting underneath the battlements until we reached the snout of the

Thielmann Glacier which, from where we stood, appeared to rise all the way up to the Veintimilla summit at an angle of no more than 30°.

The Normal Route, which Javier now considered too dangerous, led up one corner of the Red Spot until it met the skyline between El Castillo and the Thielmann Glacier. It went right up the red rock of the face on slopes that looked as parched as a sun-dried tomato. We hadn't discussed it as an option. It was easy to see there would be a lot of rockfall.

After lunch in the busy dining room we retired to our upstairs dormitory for a snooze. It felt surprisingly peaceful to begin with. Although there were 12 bunks in our room, we were the only people there – until four o'clock, that is, when a large group arrived. They were thoughtful, and kept their speech to whispers as we dozed. My language skills aren't great, but I thought I heard Russian voices.

When we went down to dinner at 5.30 I saw a familiar face. It was Luda Korobeshko, a tall Russian who was co-owner of the Russian mountaineering operator 7 Summits Club. She had been my guide on Elbrus in the Caucasus Mountains three years earlier and I'd not seen her since. One of my abiding memories of that climb was her husband Alex Abramov handing around a bottle of vodka at dinner time before our summit night. Each time he came to me, I put my hand over the glass.

'No, Alex, I can't. We have to get up to climb in a few hours.'

'But you must. It is good for acclimatisation,' he said in his deep, booming Russian voice. It was a voice that I could not refuse.

These Russians seemed a quieter bunch – or perhaps Luda was more restrained when Alex wasn't around. We had a brief conversation, and I learned that they were leaving for the summit the same time as we were. After pork chops and rice for dinner we headed for our comfortable dormitory to get a couple of hours' sleep before another stupid o'clock start.

I dreamed I was standing on the side of a mountain watching a fabulous sunset, with the lights of a city far below. Was I back on Cayambe again? A faint pink glow bathed the ice of the glacier, and the sky to the west burned with an amber flame. I spent countless peaceful minutes looking across a landscape coloured like Arabian sand. Later, I was on a golden ship being swept across the sand. I smelled the sweet scent of jasmine in the air.

Suddenly the blaze of the sun expanded to an infinite size and I blinked until my eyes adjusted to the glare. I woke up in a poky room with a number of bodies who looked as confused and dishevelled as I was. Somebody had switched the light on; it was time to get ready for our climb.

Edita was still fast asleep, so I leaned over to stroke her arm. She sat up immediately.

'What time is it?' she asked.

I glanced at my watch.

'Nine thirty.'

Then, not quite believing what I'd said, I said it again with more emphasis.

'It's nine sodding thirty.'

And so it was. This made it the earliest start I had ever made for a summit climb in my life. It was still the evening before the night before. It was so early, the bats were still getting dressed.

I can't lie to you: I detest night-time ascents. I detest having half a night's sleep, waking up in the dark, and getting dressed by the beam of a head torch. At least this time somebody had put on a light, though my gratitude for this generous action hadn't yet manifested itself.

I can't imagine many of you have tried eating breakfast at 9.30pm, just a brief flick of a lamb's tail after you've had dinner, but it's a bit like attending back-to-back concerts by Justin Bieber and David Hasselhoff. You can have too much of a good thing. I invariably have to push my boiled eggs and pancake aside, knowing full well that I'm not yet ready for that level of excitement in my day.

I detest waiting around in the cold night air for my companions to get ready, knowing that valuable sleep time has been frittered away like dollars on a Big Mac. I despise trudging for hours in the pitch blackness and seeing nothing at all of my surroundings. That's the reason I haven't paid for a haunted house theme park ride since I was a small child. If you're going to fly halfway round the world to climb a mountain, it seems to me that one of your main priorities should be to ensure that you can see it.

And while virtually every other form of physical activity invented by mankind involves starting cold and steadily warming up, with night-time ascents the opposite happens. You start cold and get steadily colder as the night progresses, until just before dawn when you know what it feels like to be a snowman with only buttons for a coat and a nose as hard as a carrot.

Your photographs of the ascent are largely meaningless, unless you're fortunate to have taken one as a bat flew past and provided a splash of colour by pissing into the scene. On the coldest ascents you can't even have photos when the sun comes out, because you find that your camera has turned into an ice cube. Some climbers even take the precaution of carrying a disposable 'fun' camera to use in the event of frozen-camera syndrome (or 'fun, my arse' camera, as I have sometimes called it).

Your only consolation is to descend these mountains during daylight, and discover what you missed on the way up. But the final indignity of a night-time ascent is having to sleep for the rest of the day to catch up on the sleep you so recklessly tossed away when you woke the previous evening.

You may be wondering why on earth people climb mountains at night. It's a fair question.

On some alpine routes, you need to climb before the sun hits the slopes and melts the ice. Once the sun is up, there's an increased risk of rockfall, avalanches, and crevasses opening up. In some parts of the world, days start crisp and clear before clouding over some time in the morning. In these places it's good to reach the summit early before the views disappear into cloud.

Sometimes an ascent is so long that it might be impossible to complete entirely during daylight. In these situations it may be better to climb in darkness at the start of your ascent, while you are still fresh, rather than at the end, when you are tired. Some people like to watch the sunrise from the top of a mountain (they must feel silly when they get down and discover people watched it from the bottom as well).

Sometimes none of these conditions apply, but people still get up early and climb during the night. This often happens on popular, guided peaks, where climbing at night has become the norm, and reaching the summit is considered more important than enjoying the experience.

In Ecuador, getting up and setting off at midnight has become so common on the big glaciated volcanoes that I wouldn't be surprised to walk past someone climbing in pyjamas. There is some justification. Rockfall, crevasses and cloud cover are risks on all of them. But I am also certain the guides love it. They love shaking their clients awake when they are at their maximum grumpiness; they love force-feeding them potato soup while their stomachs are still blissfully snoozing. I believe there is even a practical test in the UIAGM examination to set an alarm clock for some time in the past. I play my part in this performance by trying to be as grumpy as possible.

We put our boots on and stomped down to the dining room for breakfast. We had only eaten dinner a few hours ago. It seemed ludicrous to be having breakfast long before midnight, but I knew I would need all the energy I could get. As we have seen, I'm useless at eating in the middle of the night. However, I used to be good at eating a kebab on my way home from the pub. It was closer to that hour of the day, and I had no difficulty wolfing down a good-sized bowl of granola, fruit and yoghurt.

There were about twenty people heading for the summit, and most were leaving at around the same time. A few minutes before eleven o'clock, we hoisted on our backpacks, then stepped out of the hut and into the darkness.

Our climb started with a short walk along a flat, dusty plain to reach the base of the west ridge. It was a slightly tedious way to start a summit climb, but we were surprised when we heard a vehicle revving up behind us. Headlights shone across our path a few minutes later as a car drove past.

'I bet that's the Russians,' I said.

'How do you know?' Romel said.

'Did you see the tall Russian lady at breakfast? I know her. She was my guide on Elbrus a few years ago. She arranged for one of those tracked snowcat vehicles to take us from the huts at 3,800m all the way up to 5,100m on summit morning.'

'You climbed Elbrus in a tracked vehicle?'

'Some of it, yes. So I'm guessing it's the Russians in that

car.'

It took us little more than 10 minutes to reach the foot of the west ridge, where the track steepened over rocks and any motorised cheating became impossible. Romel climbed at an easy pace. For the next few hours we trekked steadily up the ridge, ascending hundreds of metres without breaking sweat.

A cold north wind bothered me for a little while, but Romel seemed unconcerned. He was right. At the top of the ridge we traversed beneath the rock towers of El Castillo, which sheltered us from the gusts. In the darkness it felt like an exposed scramble, with a wall of rock to our left and an unseen drop to our right.

We caught up with other climbers at the far end of El Castillo. The altitude was 5,450m; although we had not yet reached the glacier, they were putting their crampons on in the shelter of the rocks. We stopped to do likewise.

'Hello, Mark,' I heard a voice say in the darkness.

It was Luda.

'I thought you were behind us. You didn't take a car, did you?' I said.

'Yes, that was us,' she said.

'Is that cheating?'

In the darkness she couldn't see me smiling.

'No, I don't think so. We took a snowcat, remember.'

Which was a good enough answer for me.

Romel roped us together and led off, with Edita in the middle and me at the back. The first section had been easy. It didn't prepare us for what happened next.

We stepped out onto an exposed, dusty ridge and the wind hit us with a whirl. Dirt whipped up and struck me in the face, as though an annoying child on a beach had thrown sand over me. I panted with exertion as we fought our way along the ridge. Grit blew in my eyes and I found myself swallowing a mouthful of sand.

'This is the worst restaurant I've ever eaten in,' I screamed at Edita in front of me. She held a gloved hand over her face; clearly she was finding it as unpleasant as I was. It was still pitch dark and much too early to put on our sunglasses.

Soft and crumbling pebbles rolled beneath our feet. It was like walking on marbles, but our crampons helped us to gain purchase. Luckily the exposed section of ridge was only short and soon we found ourselves beneath a rock wall. Romel scrambled up and we followed behind.

But now we had a new problem. The stone was so soft that it crumbled in my hands as I made my way up. Rock faces aren't so easy to climb when they have detachable handholds. We were directly above the Normal Route, and I could understand how rockfall had turned it into a firing range.

'This is like climbing a crumbly old cheesecake,' I said.

'Why do you keep talking about food?' Edita replied.

'It's OK, we'll soon be on the ice,' Romel said.

'That will be the icing on the cake.'

But the wind whipped up again, and I didn't hear Edita groan.

When the ice began at 5,650m, it was probably the most atrocious ice I had encountered in my life. Like the rock, it was dry, crumbly and steep, a type where you couldn't trust to arrest yourself in the event of a fall. If the British Army had designed this mountain as an assault course, they couldn't have done a better job. I expected at any moment to come across a cargo net. In the darkness it felt dangerous, but we pressed on. We would have to worry about the descent when the time came.

The steepness and crappy ice conditions were relentless, but daylight's arrival at six o'clock offered a measure of relief. Now I could see how dry the glacier was. It must have been a few weeks since it last snowed, and the powdery surface was like grey ash. I couldn't recall ever having seen such dry snow. The clouds were far below us, and the twin summits of Iliniza appeared on the horizon to our left. Chimborazo's summit cast a vast shadow across the Gran Arenal behind us.

We crossed a nasty section of *penitentes* as we approached the Veintimilla summit. These ice stalagmites are so-named because they are supposed to resemble a procession of penitent monks. They come and go with the seasons, and are formed by the action of sun and wind on newly fallen snow. Contrary to their name, they are far from penitent. They stood in our way like a troop of doormen at a nightclub, refusing you entry because you're wearing the wrong shoes. My La Sportiva boots were bright yellow, which wasn't promising.

'You're having a laugh – you can't come in here with those on your feet,' I heard one of them say to me. Or did I imagine it?

Most of the pinnacles extended well above our heads, and the passages in between were narrow. We frequently had to climb up onto ledges to find a way across into parallel passages – awkward when tied to teammates.

It was tiring work, but just before 7.15 we met a team coming the other way. This is always an encouraging sign on a busy mountain, as it usually means that you're not far from the top.

Their guide congratulated us on our successful ascent.

'He's a bit premature, isn't he?' I said to no one in particular as we continued past them.

A few moments later, we stepped onto the Veintimilla summit.

Chimborazo's second summit was not very obvious. The

ice dropped slightly on the other side to a dip that you might describe as a saddle, but it was only a few metres, and it rose again to the obvious higher point of the Whymper summit a short distance away. There was a magnificent view north to the three distinct volcanic cones of Cotopaxi, Cayambe and Antisana rising in a line above the clouds. Cayambe – where we had stood two days earlier – was the more distant, peeping timidly between the other two.

The impenetrable maze of penitentes covered both summits completely. I was already worn out, and I hoped the trail to the main summit would be easier than the approach to the Veintimilla.

We stopped for a rest. Another rope team arrived, and again the guide held his hand out to congratulate me.

I must have looked bemused. 'But we're not there yet,' I said.

The guide turned around and walked away from his group.

'What's going on?' I said to Romel. 'Why is everyone congratulating us? The ref's not blown his whistle yet. The summit's over there.'

I pointed to the Whymper summit, a black shadow curving above the penitentes field.

'Most people are stopping here,' he said.

'But why?'

He let out a short burst of laughter, more like a cackle.

'You guys are the strongest people here. It's OK. Have a snack and then we will continue. It's not going to be easy.'

It suddenly made sense why Chimborazo only had a 20 per cent success rate. It should really be far higher, but there we were on the Veintimilla summit. It was only 7.30; the Whymper summit was just a short distance away. It seemed evident that guides were bringing their clients up to the Veintimilla without any intention of going higher, and telling them that they'd reached the summit.

Romel was cut from a different cloth. We didn't consider stopping for one moment. The job was not yet done, and it was inconceivable to turn around so close to the top. We unroped for the final section, and Romel led the way onwards, with Edita and me following behind.

We soon came to a dead end. I was surprised to see there were no wands marking the route between the two summits. It looked as if nobody had been to the Whymper summit for a long time. Romel beat a route between the penitent monks, treating them with varying degrees of roughness: a shoulder barge here, a charge there. One was trampled on, and another pushed over. One poor chap even had his arm sliced off with an ice axe. But we were following the wrong procession, and after a few moments we arrived at the edge of a 5m cliff.

'We'd better turn around,' Romel said. 'I don't think we can climb down there.'

I biffed a monk's head off and we jumped up on its neck so that Romel could get past. We backtracked a short distance, and Romel was joined by another guide whose client had seen us proceeding. We let the guides get some way ahead to avoid following them down another blind alley. It was demoralising, seeing the maze ahead of us and knowing that we might have to retrace our steps at any moment.

The sun beat down on us, sapping our strength, if not our resolve. Little by little, Romel and the other guide made progress. Soon a line of about half a dozen climbers appeared behind me as I followed Edita, following us as we followed Romel across the saddle. I thought about asking the one behind me to grab my waist so that we could conga to the top. We crossed the saddle and climbed more steeply towards the summit. The penitentes became a catacomb of ice, picturesque and intricate. The walls of snow were softly melting in the sun, and several times I leaned against one only to see a piece of it break off. At one point we had to squeeze through an archway and climb onto a shelf, as though we were exploring some ruined monastery.

Among the penitentes on Chimborazo,
with the Whymper summit up ahead

Then I heard Romel give a whoop, and suddenly we were there, on an elevated platform above icy trenches. It felt like we'd been engaging in mountain warfare; I had lost all track of time.

'Congratulations. Now you are really here – the true summit of Chimborazo.'

We hugged, cheered, and then I slumped down on the ice for a long-deserved rest.

'I'm knackered.'

By contrast, Edita was lively, exploring the summit and purring with excitement as she clicked her camera in all directions.

'Wow, I feel like I'm floating,' she said.

I already had a good idea what the view to the north was going to look like. Most of the land around us would be hidden by a sea of grey cloud. Cotopaxi, Cayambe and Antisana were probably rising above it like islands. I knew that view was amazing, and I would enjoy looking at it again, but first I needed a rest. I had forgotten that Cayambe had been the first of the glaciated volcanoes Edita had climbed. She wasn't going to wait to get her breath back.

As I rested my back against the ice, I summoned the energy to take out my GPS and measure the altitude. It was time to stir the pot of controversy. Nobody can ever quite agree on Chimborazo's height. The most commonly quoted figure is 6,310m, but some people prefer the figure of a British survey team, who measured the height at 6,268m in 1993. Others claim this team only reached the Veintimilla summit in foggy conditions and stopped there (a story I would have been more inclined to believe after our experience that morning). At one point, Chimborazo's Wikipedia page even listed the altitude as 6,263.47m, a figure which is crassly precise given that the depth of ice changes every year – a centimetre could have melted off by the time someone finished editing the page.

The GPS fluctuated up and down, then came to rest at 6,284m.

That should end the debate then.

I had got my breath back, and was able to stand up and take a look around. The wind had carved Chimborazo's summit snow into a series of fragile ice sculptures. The peaks to the north were now familiar to me, but for the first time I could see three new mountains to the east. I say 'new', but they were only new to me. The highly active volcanoes of Tungurahua and Sangay were classically conical in shape.

Neither of them was erupting at that precise moment, but both were still active, belching out frequent ash clouds that I guessed might be partly responsible for the dry ice conditions we encountered here. The third peak, El Altar, was long extinct, and rose above the clouds like a jagged rock fortress.

I started shooting a summit video.

'Here we are on top of the highest mountain in Ecuador,' I cried above the wind.

'No, it's the highest mountain in the world,' Romel said.

'We are closest to the sun,' I heard the other guide say.

We remained on the summit for half an hour, and it was becoming warmer. This caused problems as we returned to the Veintimilla summit. It was comfortable enough descending off the Whymper, but soon we were fighting through penitentes in sweltering heat, struggling back *up* to the Veintimilla.

I was glad to get that bit over with, and I flopped down in the snow. It was ten o'clock, and it had taken us nearly three hours to traverse between the two summits.

'Now I see why everyone stops at the Veintimilla,' I said between gasps.

'It's only thanks to you that anyone reached the Whymper today,' Romel said.

'You did most of the work. In any case, it was never an option. The ice was awful, but the weather's great. We'll never get a better chance.'

I steeled myself for the descent. For I was buggered, and I knew it was going to be tough. We were the last team to leave the summit; the other climbers had left us trailing in their wake. Perhaps we were still tired from Cayambe two days earlier, but it took us three whole hours to descend the Thielmann Glacier. I trod carefully at the front, but not carefully enough for Edita, who was still clearly strong enough to tug on the rope as she followed behind. It reminded me of Domenica on Antisana. Did she want to be a mountain guide too?

'Slow down!' she cried. 'This is dangerous.'

'It's OK, I have you held,' Romel said at the back of the rope. 'You can go quicker.'

'I can go quicker, my arse,' I replied.

The difficulties didn't end at the bottom of the glacier, where I slumped onto solid ground. A sequence of slapstick comedy followed when we took off our crampons and continued down the red, pebbled surface. First I, then Edita, then Romel fell on our backsides. I got up, then almost immediately fell down a second time, emitting a loud 'oof!' as I caught the contents of my rucksack in the curve of my spine. The slope was about 40° and I felt like I was starring in some comedy game show where you have to run across an avenue of marbles. I swear I heard Stuart Hall laughing uncontrollably in my ear.

'I think I'd better put my crampons on again,' I said.

'Good idea,' Romel said. 'Let's all do that.'

I felt a bit silly wearing crampons to descend gravel, but it worked and I felt more stable. Then, just as we were descending Cheesecake Wall – as I had christened it on the way up – a rock slipped from beneath Edita's feet and hurtled down the mountain. She lost her balance and gave a startled cry as she stumbled down behind it. I was standing below and turned sharply as she fell into me. Luckily my feet were stable and I was able to catch her in my arms.

There isn't much that fazes Edita, but I saw a troubled look in her eye as I held her tightly and she took a few deep breaths.

'Don't worry,' I said. 'We're going to be slow and careful, but we'll get down safely, no problem.'

I said this loudly so that Romel could hear me too. He

was standing calmly at the top of Cheesecake Wall as if nothing untoward had happened, but I could see from the position of his feet that he had been ready to brace. He must have been wondering how many more hours it would take, and whether we were going to need an epic rescue. But I was still confident. We were tired, but in no danger.

We reached the end of the pebbled ridge and took our crampons off to traverse beneath El Castillo. This section felt exposed in the darkness, and although a fall would have been nasty, the path was broad and easy. Romel went ahead and we found him sleeping on a rock below El Castillo.

Now it was Edita's turn to look after me as I staggered down the remainder of the ridge, stopping frequently to take off my pack and rest. We were beyond all danger now, and we let Romel return to the refuge, his duty done. But Edita stayed with me, occasionally walking in front, but always looking back and waiting if she saw me stop. Bless her. She must have been bored stupid. If I'd had the latest issue of *Tortoise Owner's World*, I would have lent it to her to read.

We finally hobbled home at 2.30pm. It had taken fifteen and a half hours. That, you will remember, was the same time it took Whymper and the Carrels on the first ascent, when they had floundered belly-deep through powder snow and spent an hour waving a barometer around on the summit. It was also 4 January 2016 – exactly 136 years to the day since that great ascent.

I felt like the walking dead, but I also felt a warm sense of satisfaction. I had stood on top of all four of Ecuador's big volcanoes. I had climbed both of the highest mountains in the world, depending on how you measure them. And so had Edita. I loved Ecuador, its open landscape and wide views. But with the main peaks done, I didn't expect to be returning soon.

I was wrong again.

PART TWO

THE NORTH COAST 500

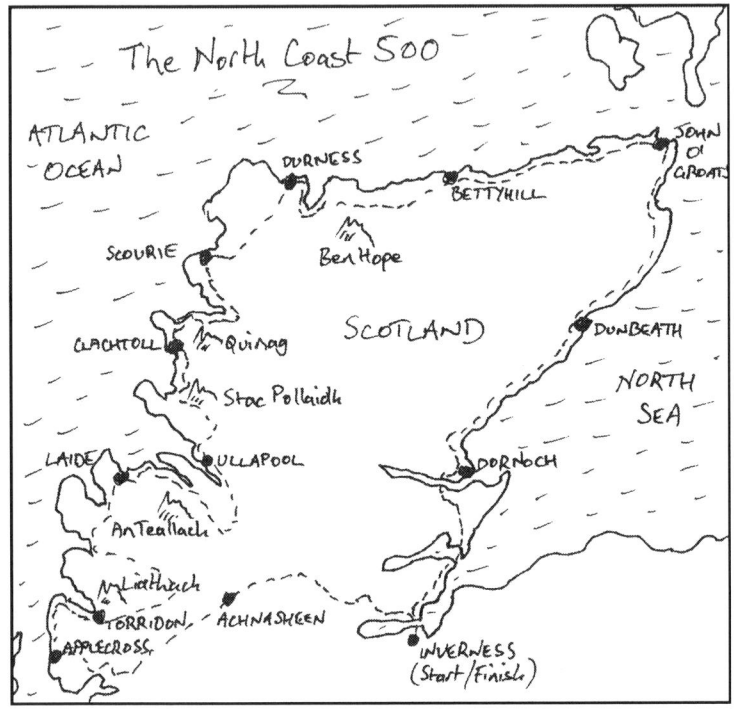

5 A WHEELY GOOD ADVENTURE

Barely four months after our ascent of Chimborazo, Edita was sitting in a guest house on its eastern side, sharing stories with Javier about their previous adventures.

'It was epic,' Javier said. 'It was my cousin Pablo's idea, and his friend Steve. They asked me to organise a bike ride starting from Pedernales on the Pacific coast. We would cycle all the way to Cotopaxi, then climb it. Steve believed it had never been done before. It would be the first ever Cotopaxi sea-to-summit.'

Edita had quickly decided that Ecuador was her new favourite country, replacing Nepal, her previous favourite, after two disagreeable experiences there. The first of these was the expedition to Lhotse in 2014 when I first met her. A strike by Sherpas led to the expedition being abandoned before we had a chance to start climbing. Climbing Sherpas are like railway workers in one respect: if they decide to go on strike, then nobody's going anywhere. On the positive side, we found ourselves back in Kathmandu with time on our hands, so we started dating.

I'd had enough of 8,000m peaks, but Edita was more determined than me. She decided to return to Nepal and climb Lhotse again the following year. She was joined by her friend Margaret, who had also been with us the year before.

This time something rather more dramatic happened. While Edita and Margaret were at Everest Base Camp, a 7.8-magnitude earthquake rocked Nepal. It triggered an avalanche that wiped out much of base camp, killing many climbers. Around 9,000 people died across Nepal; hundreds of thousands lost their homes.

Unless you've been in a war zone, it's hard to imagine how terrifying it must have been. The avalanche missed Edita's tent by little more than the length of an ice axe, and she emerged to a scene from the apocalypse. For many days she was stranded at camp as aftershocks continued. Everest Base Camp is surrounded by mountains, and everyone was on edge each time the ground shook, wondering if another avalanche would come down.

While most of us would return home traumatised after such an event, Edita is made of sterner stuff. She had an opportunity to remain in Nepal and help people after the tragedy. She was a specialist in humanitarian logistics, and her employer, the United Nations World Food Programme (WFP), needed to get vital supplies to people in remote areas. With much of Nepal's infrastructure destroyed, Edita was put in charge of managing WFP's porter programme. Around 20,000 porters were employed to carry supplies across the mountains to people in need.

Every dark experience produces light, and for Edita the light burned like a flame, but neither she nor Margaret wanted to return to Nepal for a third attempt. Instead, Edita persuaded Margaret to go to Ecuador with the idea of climbing Chimborazo by an untrodden route on the northern side.

And that's how they found themselves sitting at a table in a guest house with Javier and a group of his friends, drinking a glass of Chilean Merlot and having a conversation about Cotopaxi. The guest house was called

Posada la Estacion and it stood on a quiet stretch of road opposite Urbina station. The station was a handsome and historic whitewashed building, famous for being the highest stop on the Trans-Andean railway line. Behind it, the eastern summit of Chimborazo rose above emerald-green fields, a single giant dome crowned with ice.

'So what happened?' Edita said.

'Well, five of us started the journey,' Javier replied. 'Three Ecuadorians, one American and a Dutchman. It took us four days to cycle from Pedernales to Tambopaxi, a lodge in the national park, and then a day to trek to the hut. I was feeling ill that night, and two of the others had already quit. But Pablo and Steve climbed all the way to the summit. We think it was the first ever recorded ascent of Cotopaxi from sea level without the use of motorised transport.'

'You must be very proud,' Margaret said, putting her wine glass on the table with such force that the table started rocking.

It continued rocking.

There was a rumbling sound and the ground began to shake. It was a familiar feeling for them. Edita knew what was happening immediately, and so did the mountain guides who were in the room. But Margaret was a little less clear about what was going on.

'Terremoto!' someone shouted, and they all stood up.

'Quickly, Margaret, we have to go outside,' Edita said.

The floor was rotating rapidly now, and although the walls remained firm, pictures in frames started to sway like clock pendulums. As the ground continued to shake, they wondered how long this could continue before the walls collapsed. Nobody wanted to stay and find out. They stampeded out of the door and ran across the road in the direction of the station.

'Where is my camera?' Margaret said.

'Don't worry about your camera, Margaret,' Edita replied. 'As long as you are safe.'

'But I must see the train.'

'Train? What train? Margaret, it's an earthquake.'

Like Edita, Margaret had been at Everest Base Camp when the earthquake struck. But the human mind is a complex organ, and it's funny what things the memory recalls. In her childhood she had lived opposite a railway line, and whenever a train hurtled past, the walls would shake. These events were so powerfully ingrained in her memory that when the walls started shaking in Urbina, Margaret's immediate recollection was not the earthquake in Nepal, but a train passing on the track.

'Oh my god!' she cried.

But by then the ground had stopped rotating – the earthquake was over. The building was still standing, and there appeared to be no damage. By one of those strange twists of fate, this particular earthquake had an identical magnitude, 7.8, to the one they had felt at Everest Base Camp. This time the epicentre was far away, down by the Pacific coast at a place called – that's right – Pedernales: the very place Javier had just been talking about.

Up in the Andes, the sky was dimming. On the other side of the station, the bell shape of Chimborazo could only be seen in outline. They remained outside for a few more minutes until they felt it was safe to go back in. I don't know what was going through Margaret's mind as they re-entered the lodge. Had I been in her shoes, then perhaps I would have been wondering if my glass of wine was still on the table.

But Edita had her mind on something else.

'Javier,' she said, 'has anyone ever climbed Chimborazo from sea to summit, like your cousin Pablo did on Cotopaxi?'

Javier scratched his head. 'There are a lot of people in Ecuador who cycle and climb, but I know most of the best climbers, and I would probably hear about it if someone had.'

He paused for a moment, then continued.

'I don't think it's ever been done. It would be a world first.'

Like a journey down the Amazon, life's path meanders in unexpected ways. And while there are hazards along the way, you're almost always better off following the turns and seeing what's around the corner than reversing course and fighting the current.

In my previous book, *Seven Steps from Snowdon to Everest*, I talked about how two career setbacks sent me on a different path to the one I was expected to follow. It was a path that ultimately took me up the highest mountain on Earth.

When I heaved myself onto a bed in Refugio Carrel after my fifteen-and-a-half-hour summit day, like a drowning sailor hoisting himself onto the deck, I have to be frank with you that I had no intention of climbing Chimborazo ever again. That was the mountain ticked as far as I was concerned. The view from the summit was amazing, but the glacier that was drier than a Mormon dinner party, the red rocks that were the texture of an apple crumble, and the night of monotonous plodding in the dark were things I would miss like a liver-and-Marmite sandwich.

I'd been more exhausted on a mountain, but when you climb them for enjoyment, sometimes you have to consider whether the view justifies the effort. We all have our preferences in life. I don't want to criticise anyone else for theirs (unless they watch celebrity baking shows). Fine art has always been one that puzzles me. Queueing for two hours and paying $50 to peer at a dead fish may be a good analogy for how some people feel about mountain climbing. Chimborazo had cost rather more than a $50 entry fee. As I rested in Refugio Carrel, two words came to mind. The words were *this* and *sod*, not necessarily in that order. I was done with Chimborazo.

Or so I thought, but I wasn't the first to go through those emotions, and I certainly won't be the last. After winning his fourth Olympic gold medal at Atlanta in 1996, the oarsman Steve Redgrave rowed to the edge of the lake and gave a live television interview, during which he announced his retirement from rowing.

'That's it. I've had enough. If anyone sees me go near a boat ever again, they have my permission to shoot me,' he said.

Happily, nobody took him up on this invitation. Just two days later he changed his mind, and four months later he resumed training. After four years he won his fifth gold medal at the 2000 Sydney Olympics.

It takes a special type of person to do something like that. A special type of idiot, perhaps you're thinking?

So if you'd told me that barely two years after climbing Chimborazo I would be heading up it again, this time pedalling a pushbike, I would have laughed uncontrollably. And then, when I'd realised that you weren't joking, I would have asked you to pass me the gun so that I could shoot myself.

To climb it for a second time was one thing, but to cycle up it? I wasn't even a cyclist. How on earth did that end up happening?

You're probably already starting to guess.

Edita's second expedition to Chimborazo didn't get far. They climbed ankle-twisting grassy slopes in drizzly rain to get to their base camp. Cold and wet, they spent three miserable days there as the rain played piano on the tent roof. A brief lull on the second evening enabled them to launch a summit attempt, but they'd only reached the snout of the glacier and started roping up when they realised they might as well have Stevie Wonder as first man on the rope for all the chance they had of navigating a route in the darkness and the fog. They returned to their tents and abandoned the expedition.

When Edita got back to Quito, she found an email from her employer, WFP, instructing her to remain in Ecuador to help organise the logistics for the earthquake response. By then I was living in Rome, where WFP are based. I had managed to get some work there, and we thought it would give us an opportunity to spend more time together. After she returned from Ecuador, Edita was sent to Chad in central Africa and I hardly saw her for much of the next year. Things weren't working out as we planned them (they hardly ever do).

'We could quit our jobs, go on a big trip, then come back and look for work in London,' I said tentatively one evening when she was back in Rome.

For many people, quitting their job is a big decision, but not for me. I did contract work, and was used to taking time off after a project to travel and write. Edita's job as a humanitarian aid worker was even more colourful. She completed short missions all over the developing world.

Even so, I expected her to hesitate – but her eyes lit up.

'Good idea. I've always wanted to live in London. But where shall we go for our big trip?'

I wasn't expecting such an immediate decision, so I didn't have an answer prepared. Hence I ended up saying something stupid.

'Um… How about that Chimborazo sea-to-summit challenge that you told me about?'

'Great idea – let's do it.'

But we couldn't possibly do it. It involved bicycles: silly things that wobble as you ride them, and fall over if you stop. Although I can ride a bike, I hadn't done so for about twenty years, and I'd never enjoyed it much. My legs were finely honed for walking.

'Or we could climb another 8,000m peak?'

'No, let's do the Chimborazo sea to summit.'

'We could walk the Great Himalaya Trail?'

'Let's do the Chimborazo sea to summit. I've always wanted to do a big cycle ride.'

'But you're not a cyclist,' I pointed out.

'I've always wanted to be. I can ride a bike.'

It seemed that she had always wanted a lot of things, but she was right about being able to ride a bike. So could I. Did that make me a cyclist? I didn't think so.

'We could stay in Rome for a little longer – see if things work out with our jobs?'

It was no good. It was as if I'd stood in the world's most persistent dog turd, and nothing I could do would ever wipe the stain off my shoe.

To be frank, I was terrified. For some of my childhood, I had ridden a bike with stabilisers. When I progressed to two wheels – I called it 'downgrading' – I discovered that, unlike walking, it was physically impossible to cycle in a leisurely manner. If the wheels were rotating too slowly then I had to go down a gear and pedal faster; if they were rotating too quickly then I would go up a gear and the bike would accelerate. Soon I would be hurtling along again. Even in the highest possible gear, if there was a little too much resistance in the wheels, nothing felt more pressing than to counter the resistance by rotating the pedals faster. There was no speed that was just right.

Consequently, I couldn't cycle any distance without getting exhausted. On one occasion I was sweating so much that I had to take my coat off and drape it over the handlebars. I had barely pedalled a metre before the bike stopped moving with the suddenness of a bullet from a gun. The next moment I found myself hurtling through the air like Superman, and came to rest in a ditch.

Hills were a particular problem. If they were longer than half a mile, then I could only get to the top if I got off to push. I might as well have been riding a wheelbarrow. I had only ridden bikes with fewer gears than a car, and assumed the problem was with my legs. How could I develop more powerful leg muscles for cycling? Only by riding a bike, and that involved more cycling – an unpleasant task for a walker. It was a vicious circle, and there seemed no way out.

Worse than any of this, cycling seemed unspeakably dangerous. In my early twenties I lived for a year in Cambridge, which at the time seemed to be the cycle capital of Great Britain. In those days if you didn't ride a bike in Cambridge then you were considered a delinquent (though I think in Cambridge they used the word 'scoundrel'). I was young and keen to impress, so I conformed. Through no fault of my own, in the space of a year I was knocked off my bike twice by vehicles, and once by a pedestrian on a cycle path. I also had a collision with a tree, but that was probably more my fault than the tree's.

When I moved to London the following year, I had no intention of riding my bike ever again. That was in the 1990s, when double-decker bus drivers competed to be Ayrton Senna on streets without cycle lanes. I no longer gave cycling a second thought, but in the intervening years, the city became a lot more cycle-friendly. A few years later, there were so many bikes that they were impossible to ignore, and in a fresh twist, it seemed to me that the danger had been transferred to pedestrians. Bikes had become terrifying. In rush hour, there could be 40 at once, all going at different speeds. Judging a gap to cross the road was like threading a needle while sitting on a tumble drier. It was no longer safe to cross at a green light without a cyclist hurtling through and missing you by a hair's breadth.

If I were to start cycling again, then could I bring myself to point my front wheel at a pedestrian and shave their eyebrows as I steamed through a red light?

That was the pedestrian's perspective, but now I intended to complete an extreme cycle challenge that had never been done before. It was time for me to start looking at things from a cyclist's perspective again. It didn't look good. While a visible minority of cyclists ignored red lights, biked through pedestrian crossings, cycled the wrong way down one-way streets, or cycled on pavements, a quick browse of the cycling media convinced me that perhaps being a pedestrian is safer after all.

I read about a phenomenon known as car dooring, which involves smashing a cyclist in the face with a car door by opening it at the precise moment they are steaming past. Cyclists are advised to lessen the risk by adopting the 'primary position'. This is not a sexual position, though many injured cyclists may have considered adopting one of these on the driver responsible; it instead means to ride in the middle of the road. Other situations I remembered from my Cambridge days included drivers turning in to side roads across a cyclist's path, or overtaking cyclists on narrow roads when traffic is coming the other way.

It's easy to believe why some topics are controversial,

such as politics, religion, and the growing of beards without their requisite moustaches, but cycling? More sinister than these accidents – which seemed attributable to driver incompetence – was a disturbing tendency for motorists to demonise cyclists on social media, born from a belief that they had more right to use the roads than the cyclists who slowed them down.

'Cyclists. In Lycra. The left-wing, vegan, mixed-gender toilet supporting, ISIS-sympathising scourge of modern-day Britain,' I read in the comments section of a popular media website.

They forgot to mention the shaven legs, which are surely just as offensive. But why the aversion to mixed-gender toilets? I imagined the writer peeing in a plant pot because his wife had just used their one and only bathroom.

'Poor London, first immigrants and now cyclists,' read another comment.

This person must have been livid when Chris Froome won the Tour de France for Britain after being born in Kenya. More disturbing was the following comment, which illustrates where any form of hate eventually leads.

'I hate the cyclists who I can't knock over without being prosecuted.'

And there were more parochial comments peculiar to the situation in Britain.

'As soon as you pay more road tax you can have more of the road.'

'Cyclists think they own the roads. We pay taxes – move over.'

In the UK, taxes seem to play a disproportionate part in any discussion about cycling. This is because you have to pay tax on a motor vehicle, but not on a bike. These arguments puzzled me – you also have to pay *more* tax on a gas-guzzling vehicle that spews a haze of soot and carbon into the atmosphere to rival the output of a coal-fired power station, but this doesn't give these vehicles a right to barge other, cleaner vehicles onto the pavement in a fit of entitlement.

What I thought about these comments didn't really matter. The fact remained that a number of different vehicles were permitted to use our roads, but not all road users felt they had an equal right to be there. Hatred of cyclists was a thing. It was obvious that, to have any hope of completing the Chimborazo sea-to-summit challenge, I needed to spend more time on a bike to gain a cyclist's perspective and train my cycling legs. But how to do this? I've never been a big one for training. In any case, there simply wasn't time.

Edita agreed to contact Javier to coordinate the logistics in Ecuador. She had the easy job. Although she was a specialist in logistics herself, all she really needed to do was agree the dates and Javier would do the rest. We agreed upon September, just after the rainy season in Ecuador. Meanwhile, I set about arranging a warm-up for us in a less exotic location.

I hit upon the idea of a two-week cycling holiday somewhere in the Scottish Highlands. I remembered how Ecuador's open landscape of free-standing volcanoes reminded me of Assynt, a region in north-west Scotland where miles of peat bog and tiny lochs were punctuated by dramatic, isolated peaks. It was a place I'd last visited 20 years ago, and it brought back fond memories. I also remembered how Angus had compared Rucu Pichincha, our very first Ecuadorian volcano, with Stac Pollaidh, one of the Assynt peaks.

If I took Edita cycling in that part of Scotland, it could potentially kill a number of birds with a single stone. Number one, it would help to turn my spindly walker's chicken legs into big, powerful Mark Cavendish-style thighs that could be used for leg wrestling a rhinoceros (I couldn't think of a scenario where I'd use them for this purpose, but you never know). I would gain confidence on the roads, overcome my fear of motorists, and adopt the primary position at least as frequently as the submissive one.

It would also give me an opportunity to revisit a place that I enjoyed. If we took our hiking gear with us, we could even combine the cycle ride with our love of hill walking. Edita had never visited Scotland. By climbing a hill in impenetrable hill fog (as she surely would), she would understand why I kept saying 'we could be in Scotland' whenever we encountered mist.

I found a bike-hire specialist in Inverness called Ticket to Ride, who rented out touring bikes for two weeks or more, and even came to pick you up at the end if you needed it. I had no idea how far we could cycle in two weeks, so I tentatively arranged some dates in August and a pickup at the end from somewhere north of Ullapool, a fishing village 75km from Inverness. Neither did I have any idea what type of bike to hire, so I booked a pair of hybrids, based on a statement on their website. It said 'The hybrid (or "trekking") bike is ideal for a cycle tour of the Highlands', which is what we seemed to be doing. I didn't know what a hybrid was, but I had a vague notion that if I couldn't pedal up a hill then I would be able to switch on the electric motor. I was disappointed to discover that a hybrid bike is not like a hybrid car. It's called hybrid not because it's partly electric, but because it's a cross between a road bike and a mountain bike.

By June our bike trip was only two months away, and I was no nearer working out an itinerary – but with no idea how far we could cycle in a day, I had no clue where to start. I flew back to London to vote in the 2017 general election that had been called a month earlier, and we attended a mountaineering lecture at the Royal Geographical Society on behalf of the Himalayan Trust, the charity that Sir Edmund Hillary set up after making the first ascent of Everest. By chance, one of the trustees of the charity was Angus, who had climbed in Ecuador with me all those years ago.

We bumped into him in the bar before the lecture, and I told him about our Chimborazo sea-to-summit challenge.

'Wow. You must be training pretty hard for it,' he said.

'Er... we've not really started yet.'

'But you said you were doing it in September.'

'Yes, but we've hired some bikes from a shop in Inverness. We're going to cycle around north-west Scotland, maybe climb some hills too. The only problem is, I have absolutely no idea where we're going to go, or how far we can cycle in a day.'

'No problem. I can do an itinerary for you.'

I nearly dropped my beer. This was the most fortuitous meeting imaginable. Angus was Scottish (though you would never guess from his name). He had been to Ecuador. He was a climber too, but the most pertinent fact was one that I had completely forgotten until now: he was also a keen cyclist. I had bumped into exactly the right person at exactly the right time.

Despite his seemingly generous offer, Angus had no intention of working out an itinerary for us. He thought it was the beer talking, and he didn't believe for a minute that I was going to follow through with our plan.

This didn't matter, though. He gave me the only information I really needed.

'How long have you hired the bikes for?' he asked.

'Two weeks.'

'Then you should have plenty of time to cycle the North Coast 500. There are lots of hills on the way round that you can climb up.'

6 THE BEALACH NA BASTARD

No wonder I hadn't heard of it. Two years earlier, there had been no such thing as the North Coast 500, but it was already well on the way to becoming one of Scotland's most popular tourist attractions after Edinburgh Castle, Ben Nevis and the Loch Ness Monster.

The North Coast 500 – or NC500 as we would soon be calling it – is an 830km road trip loosely following the coastline around the far north-west of Scotland. It was invented by the North Highland Initiative (NHI), an organisation set up by Prince Charles as a way of boosting tourism in the Scottish Highlands (and keeping him busy until his mother is ready to let him take over the United Kingdom). The NHI markets the NC500 as 'Scotland's answer to Route 66', not because it crosses the length of the United States in a 2,500km sweep, had a song written about it, and was a major migration route for families escaping the great American dust bowl of the 1930s, but because it's… well, a road that you can drive around, I guess.

I can tell you that it's called the NC500 because it's 516 miles long and NC500 sounds a bit cooler than NC516. While most people drive around it either in camper vans or on Harley-Davidsons (and other vehicles, too), the route has become something of an extreme challenge for endurance cyclists. In August 2015, the freakishly talented endurance cyclist Mark Beaumont christened it as a bike trip by cycling the whole thing in the ludicrously outlandish time of 38 hours. The former professional cyclist James McCallum then chopped an extra 7 hours off Beaumont's record by pedalling it in a barely human time of 31 hours. To prove that it's a challenge not only for endurance cyclists but crap cyclists too, I intended to follow in their slipstreams by completing it in… well, just by completing it without ending in a crumpled heap (though the last part of this resolution could prove ambitious).

I didn't have the legs to match the achievements of Mark Beaumont or James McCallum (or a bike with a jet engine), but we hoped that 14 days might be enough. By coincidence – and with serendipity that mimicked the parallels between the NC500 and Route 66 – on the day we started our bike ride around north-west Scotland, Beaumont would be 38 days in to an attempt to cycle round the entire world in 80 days. As thousands of people around the globe were eagerly tracking his progress on social media as he whizzed across Central Asia, approximately bugger all people (with the possible exception of my dad), would be tracking my progress as I crawled through Scotland. To give myself credit, I would also be accompanied by the first Lithuanian woman to climb Everest, so there remained a chance that our trip might at least raise some eyebrows in Lithuania.

But before we could get on our bikes, we still had some preparation to do. There was an official North Coast 500 website that we hoped to glean information from, but it appeared to be funded by selling NC500 membership (whatever that meant) and memorabilia. It didn't seem possible to read their cycling itineraries without popping in your credit card details and purchasing an NC500 sporran or similar item of branded merchandise. That wasn't much use to us, as the sporran would probably dangle too close to the brake cables, but we did manage to download a guidebook listing some of the sites to visit along the route.

Rather more helpful was the Walkhighlands website, a resource that you can disappear into for so long that if you're not careful they will need to call mountain rescue to get you out again. I identified four peaks that we could hike up from the NC500. These were Liathach, An Teallach, Suilven and Ben Loyal. I was familiar enough with Scottish weather to know that the chances of them being clear of cloud on the day that we happened to ride past were only slightly higher than finding Sean Connery waiting at the start to serenade us with bagpipes, but you never knew.

To avoid booking accommodation, we decided to camp (we both loved camping). Finally we had to decide what equipment to take with us. The camping and hiking part of our agenda was no problem. We had all the equipment and clothing we needed from countless previous adventures, but I was woefully ill-equipped with the tight Lycra that every cyclist had to wear in order to look even vaguely competent. Two days before we were due to start, we visited a Decathlon store in London to buy the full uniform: cycling shorts, groin-hugging long trousers, short- and long-sleeve shirts with pockets at the back, fluorescent jackets and ponchos.

For some reason the long trousers came equipped with a pair of shoulder straps which, had I been carrying a few extra pounds, would have made me look like the wrestler Big Daddy. It was a little disconcerting to ponder upon why the item needed shoulder straps. Did the trousers slip down while riding? To be honest the shorts were a bit of a shock too. They had built-in padding in the seat because, I was told, all cycle tourists can expect to get sore hindquarters after a few hours on the bike. A bigger shock was some special cream the shop assistant recommended us to buy. He said we could ease the discomfort by smearing it onto our buttocks every morning before getting on our bikes. This raised other questions that had been lurking at the back of my mind. I had no idea that cyclists had to smear cream on their buttocks every morning, but I did know that they shaved their legs. Would I need to do that too? The thought made me decidedly uncomfortable.

Phew. We had given ourselves less than two months to plan the bike ride and make all the arrangements, and we had done it. I was a happy man when we arrived in Inverness one Tuesday morning in early August. It took us a little while to find the bike hire shop, Ticket to Ride. Google Maps pointed us towards the middle of a small square called Bellfield Park, but when we got there the only building we could find was a public toilet. We walked round it three times and couldn't find a bike shop anywhere. We were mystified, and a little nervous. Had a customer hated their bike so much that they decided to label a public convenience with Ticket to Ride on Google Maps? Only on our third circumnavigation did somebody emerge from a side door wearing cycling shorts. We followed his trail and found ourselves in a tiny workshop the size of four toilet cubicles, where two men were busily repairing bikes.

'Ah, you must be Ticket to Ride. We've come to hire a pair of hybrids.'

We were introduced to Lindsay, whom I had exchanged emails with. He explained that the park was a conservation area, and they weren't allowed to put up a sign.

'But there's a sign on the door of the ladies,' Edita helpfully pointed out.

'Aye, but I think that's allowed, to stop people peeing in the bushes.'

He took us outside to a bike rack a short distance away

from the building.

'These are your hybrids. They have puncture-resistant tyres, but just in case you do have a puncture, there's a wee repair kit with a tube under the seat here.'

I liked the sound of the puncture-resistant tyres. One of the things that put me off cycling as a child was that my father always made me repair my own punctures. It literally used to take me hours. I'm haunted by memories of perching my bike upside-down on the freezer, using fork handles to prize off the tyre and inner tube, and running a bath to try and locate the puncture by looking for air bubbles. Without the forks, freezer and bathtub, I didn't stand a chance of repairing a puncture on the road. Besides, we didn't have that many spare hours in our itinerary. Hopefully the wee repair kit under the seat was just a precautionary measure.

'Do you have any more questions about the bikes?' Lindsay said.

I didn't want to sound like a complete knobber, but I realised there were a few basics that would be useful to know.

'Er… actually, can you explain how the gears work?'

'OK, no problem. The shifter on the left handlebar controls the front plates. It basically just has a low and a high ratio. Most of the time you'll be in one or the other. You can use the low ratio when you're on hills and the high ratio if you're pedalling fast.'

'So I'll just keep it in low ratio all the time, then.'

'Not necessarily,' Lindsay replied, quickly moving on (he probably thought I was joking). 'The shifter on the right handlebar has eight speeds. You'll be changing these most of the time. Use the lower gears when you start pedalling or on hills, then work up the gears as you gain speed.'

I think he was starting to realise who he was dealing with. 'Then we have the brakes,' he said. 'Apologies if you know this already, but right is the front wheel, left is the back.'

His apology was unnecessary. But I didn't want him to think that he was lending his bike to an idiot, so I didn't ask him which of the two brakes I was supposed to use. I had a vague memory from my school days of someone saying that you're not supposed to use the front one because there's a risk you'll go flying over the handlebars if you stop too fast.

I also asked Lindsay to adjust the saddles to a height we considered suitable. I had no real idea of the optimum height for a bicycle seat, but I did remember spending a weekend lying in agony when I lived in Cambridge, after pulling a muscle in my back. I believed this was because I had the saddle far too high, and had to stretch to put my feet on the ground when I stopped at traffic lights (I was a good boy, and believed that cyclists should stop at red lights). I therefore asked him to set my seat fairly low. If you're an experienced cyclist, you will probably be shaking your head, because you will know that I had just made my job a little harder.

The panniers were our biggest concern. Each bike had a pair of saddlebags on the back, and each pair had a total volume of 56 litres. Would it be enough? I was a bit worried, and had emailed Lindsay a couple of days earlier to see if we could hire extra panniers should we need them.

'You'll be wanting this beast,' he emailed back with a file attachment. I opened the attachment. It was a picture of a large yellow trailer.

'What do you think?' I asked Edita.

'Let's hope we can get everything in the panniers. I don't fancy pulling a trailer all the way around. Unless we can rent a tractor too.'

With some relief we discovered that everything fitted neatly. The only thing we needed to strap on to one of the racks was the tent. Shortly after eleven o'clock, we were ready to embark on our very first cycle tour.

'Far to go today?' Lindsay asked just before we left.

'Only to Achnasheen,' I replied.

The first two days of the North Coast 500 involved cycling across country from Inverness on the east coast to Applecross on the west. While there were campsites aplenty on the more touristy coastal sections, there was a dearth of accommodation (or indeed, villages of any sort) on these first two days while we cycled from coast to coast. After much googling I had unearthed a hotel in a place called Achnasheen, about halfway across, which advertised camping in its garden. It was 65km from Inverness, which according to Google Maps would take just three hours and thirty-eight minutes on a pushbike.

Clearly Lindsay didn't agree with Google.

'Oh, that's a fair ride then,' he said.

Bugger. As things turned out, reality didn't agree with Google either, though this was partly due to our own poor decision-making.

Things started positively, almost leisurely. We took a route out of Inverness that followed the River Ness, mostly on cycle paths. North of the city, we had to climb our first hill across the Beauly Firth on the 1,056m Kessock Bridge, which spanned the water on high concrete supports. It carried the busy A9 trunk road north, but I was relieved to see a narrow cycle path on the left, separated from the four lanes of traffic by a tall metal barrier. One thing Google Maps hadn't accounted for was that there might be a man in an electric wheelchair coming the other way who, as common decency dictates, must take priority over two cyclists with broad saddlebags. If you're wondering how long it takes for an electric wheelchair to traverse a 1,056m road bridge, I can tell you that it's quite a long time.

Edita crosses the Beauly Firth at Inverness

We had a pleasant ride along the north shore of the Beauly Firth on a single-track road, stopping for sandwiches as we enjoyed the last of the morning sun. After lunch we reached a main road, and made much quicker progress, covering the 10km between Muir of Ord and Contin in just half an hour.

It was here that we made our first tactical error. While researching alternative routes for cyclists, I had come upon a blog post on the North Coast 500 website that described a 10km diversion on quiet forest trails, avoiding a busy section of winding main road where lorries and camper vans were known to hurtle past. It sounded appealing. We were here to enjoy pleasant countryside, but there was a catch. The article made it clear that the route was 'only suitable for more lightly loaded touring bikes, and mountain bikes with tyres which have a good tread'.[24]

'What do you think?' I said to Edita when we reached the turn-off. 'Apparently these forest trails are quite rough, and not really suitable for heavily loaded touring bikes like ours.'

I blame myself for what happened next, for I knew perfectly well that Edita likes a challenge.

'Let's do the forest trails. They can't be that bad,' she said.

What the article hadn't spelled out was that the forest trails were far from flat ('undulating gently with one reasonable hill' was the phrase it used to describe the mountainous treat that followed). Within minutes of leaving the main road I had come to the lowest of the low gears, and there were no more gears left. I had pins and needles in my arms from rattling up the rough gravel track. My buttocks had not been spanked so freely since my schooldays. I had hoped to complete at least one day of the cycle ride without getting off to push, but it wasn't going to be this first one. My legs were buckling under the strain; I realised I would have to dismount before I started rolling backwards down the hill.

We rattled along, and the trails became increasingly rough. At times I wondered if the bike had square wheels. In one section the gravel was as sharp as glass, and I had to get off just to spare my tyres. There was a stream to ford; we crossed on stepping stones while wheeling the bikes beside us. Just when I thought things couldn't get any worse, the heavens opened and angels started peeing in their masses. We took our ponchos out for the first time. Edita showed me a technique for keeping our legs dry by hooking the poncho over the handlebars. It kept my legs dry all right, but within minutes I was carrying a small pond on my lap. I wondered if ducks would swoop down and start paddling there.

By the time we rejoined the main road at Garve, two hours had passed since we left it, yet we were just 9km further on. We were sodden, battered, had sore arms and sore legs, and we'd tried our damnedest to defy the puncture resistance of our puncture-resistant tyres. We'd barely cycled 16 of the North Coast 500's 516 miles. It was a little early for such an ordeal, and I didn't need to remind myself there were still 500 miles left. A word of advice for any other cycle novices: if you're going to pick a stupid variation to the route, try to do it closer to the end.

We were at a low ebb when we passed a sign that said 16 miles to Achnasheen (about 26km). It was four o'clock. Tired and wet, we stopped for a snack in a lay-by. If we were going to have weather like this every day then perhaps I should have brought my swimming trunks.

We were running out of energy. Peanuts and Mars bars helped to recharge us, and with no more forest trails we made good progress thereafter. We pedalled rapidly along a smooth road in a wide valley, our ponchos hissing in the breeze. The hills were bleak and featureless, but it was gentle moorland rather than forbidding mountains. A railway line accompanied the road a hundred metres away to our left. Lakes intervened at regular intervals and patches of pine forest broke the monotony. In some ways it was a typical Scottish Highland scene. I was much happier now that we were eating up the miles, but I was having to stop often to nurse aches and pains in my buttocks and shoulders. I felt pins and needles in my forearms, and had to keep swinging them like a monkey to get the blood circulating (or, at least, a monkey who knew how to ride a bike).

Achnasheen turned out to be a handful of houses near a roundabout where the main road branched up a side valley. We reached it shortly after six o'clock, approximately three hours later than Google had predicted. I felt conspicuous as we cycled into the grounds of the Ledgowan Lodge Hotel, with its red stone walls and bay windows standing proudly among a cluster of pine trees. I took my cycle helmet off before walking into the carpeted reception area, expecting to be grabbed by the ear at any moment by a bow-tied and kilted Highlander, then tossed out into the forecourt with a '…and don't come back, you scruffy English bastard'.

But these were the Highlands, not Glasgow during an Old Firm derby. A cheerful young man greeted me.

'Aye, you can camp up on the garden there. It's a wee bit damp, but the grass is nice and soft. You may have some trouble with the wee bastards in the morning, but that's the time of year, you know. You can use the toilets in the hotel to wash. Will you be dining in the restaurant? It's nice and warm, and ye can have a wee pint of ale.'

Does it rain in Scotland? Yes, we'll be dining in the restaurant, I told him. We leaned our bikes against a picnic table on the highest part of a freshly mown lawn that sloped gently down to a curtain of pine trees guarding the road.

'We seem to be the only people here,' Edita said as we erected our lightweight two-person tent. 'Where are the kids?'

'The kids? I don't understand.'

'He said we may have some trouble with the wee bastards.'

I roared with laughter. 'Stay still for a moment.'

'I can't,' she said, swatting the air with her arms. 'These damn flies. How do you live in a place like this?'

'I didn't tell you about the midges. Those'll be the wee bastards he was referring to. Let's get the tent up, jump inside, and zip it up behind us.'

'Midges? Javier mentioned midges.'

'Javier? He's from Ecuador. What does he know about midges?'

'He's been to Scotland. I told him we were coming here for a training ride before our sea to summit, and he said "watch out for the midges". He told me they were like mosquitoes, but these things are more like black flies.'

'Maybe, but the only good thing I can say about them is

they're not going to give you malaria. They're worst in June and July. I was hoping they'd mostly be gone by now, but it looks like there's still going to be plenty of them around.'

Midges tend to be found in warm, wet areas with plenty of rainfall. This makes the peat bogs of north-west Scotland prime habitat, where the warm currents of the Atlantic Gulf Stream meet the coast of Britain. It's a little-known fact that only the female *Culicoides impunctatus* (or Highland midge) bites humans, and she does so not because she has a craving to eat human flesh, but as part of her reproductive cycle. Male midges, on the other hand, have a vegetarian diet and feed on harmless plant juices. The average midge lives no longer than a month, but most Scotsmen will tell you that's 30 days too long. The biting season lasts for about 10 weeks, but it happens to coincide with prime tourist season – hence why occasional visitors from Ecuador have an abiding memory of them.

There is no guaranteed repellent for the Highland midge, though many people have a favourite technique. Some have reported that skin creams such as Avon Skin So Soft, designed to turn wizened human flesh into something resembling the texture of a baby's bottom, can be effective; meanwhile more manly types recommend maximum-strength DEET insect repellent that you can use to oil a car engine. In my experience there is a more effective method, however. Attractiveness to midges is a quality that has not been studied much by scientists, but it's certainly true that some people get eaten more than others. The best way to repel midges is to go hill walking with someone who makes for a tastier meal than you do. This was Edita's first time in the Highlands, and her midge susceptibility was untested, but the fact that she'd noticed the pesky blighters before me was a promising sign. For me, at least.

Nothing focuses the mind on erecting a tent more than

the Highland midge. They seem to be as attracted to tent fabric as they are to peat, and line the outside of tents like a coating of tar. Within minutes, we had ours up. We removed the panniers from our bikes, threw everything into the tent and dived in behind. It was satisfying to have the first day behind us. There had been a few aches and pains, but that was to be expected.

In the hotel bar a little later, I overheard a group of Italians ordering some Highland whisky.

'Does it have peat in it?' one of them asked.

Peat was something I knew I would be introducing Edita to during the hill-walking part of our trip. There are few hills in the Scottish Highlands that can be climbed without wading across a peat bog: layer upon layer of damp, mushy earth containing the remains of grass, mosses and tree roots that have rotted and compressed over centuries. Midges love the stuff, but hill walkers despise it with a vengeance. It slows them down, browns their trousers, and even claims the odd boot if they're not laced up tightly enough. Hikers have nightmares about sinking into the peat, like quicksand, and dying a slow death by drowning – a single hand clawing to the sky as the mists swirl across the moorland and midges attack their flesh.

It's easy to dismiss peat as pointless, but it actually has a couple of uses. In earlier times, crofters used to cut it into bricks, dry it out, and burn it to heat their homes. Some Highland bothies still have peat stacks to fuel the bothy fire. Until relatively recently in the Scottish Highlands, 'peat cutter' was an actual job, though you may not find many on LinkedIn.

Peat is often used in the whisky-making process. Although they don't actually put it in the whisky (that would be disgusting), they burn the peat to give the finished product a distinctive smoky flavour.

In any case, the barman, who was the same gentleman who had greeted us in reception, misheard the question.

'Have I peed in it?' he said.

I decided to have beer that evening. Although a delicious lamb shank helped to restore some of the energy I'd used up on the bike, we both regretted declining the hotel's offer of an £11 breakfast with the other guests. The porridge that we cooked up over the stove the next morning left us both feeling hungry. This wasn't the case for the midges, who had a feeding frenzy as we packed away the tent.

Apart from the section along forest trails, the first day had been relatively flat. We knew the second day would be very different, for in the afternoon we would be crossing the dreaded Bealach na Ba. In Gaelic, a *bealach* is a pass, and the name translates as the 'Pass of Cattle'. This particular one rises to 626m, or 2,053ft, which makes it the highest point on the North Coast 500. If my theory was correct, that I would gradually develop a cyclist's leg muscles as I pedalled around, then doing this particular section on our second day was not a good time. In Britain (if not the rest of the world), 2,000ft is classed as a mountain.

It was too early to worry about any of this as we set out that morning. I decided that the worst-case scenario was that I would end up wheeling a loaded bicycle up 626m in thick mist. I felt confident I could do that, but I must have looked laboured as I led off, as Edita soon overtook me.

'Let me break wind for you,' she said as she passed.

'Break wind for me? I think I had enough porridge at breakfast to do that on my own.'

'No, silly. Follow my back wheel. It will make things easier.'

It may not sound like a romantic gesture when your partner offers to break wind for you. It took me a moment to realise that Edita wasn't offering to fart on my behalf, but suggesting that I follow in her slipstream like cyclists in a peloton. Immediately behind her back wheel was an area of lower air resistance where the air was moving at a speed close to that of her bike. It meant that she would be doing more work, and I would, to a certain extent, be pulled along behind her. It might have worked in theory, had I been able to keep up with her.

The first 30km to Lochcarron were fairly easy. We started in the same broad valley we had followed to Achnasheen the previous afternoon – wide moorland between bleak rolling hills, with lochs every few miles and not many trees. The valley gradually narrowed as we approached the coast, becoming more enclosed and forested. There were a few gentle uphill gradients, but the downhills compensated for them – we could take a rest from the pedalling by freewheeling down the hill. The hills also provided opportunities to rest our sore buttocks by standing up on the pedals. In this respect I discovered that a few easy hills were not to be feared. On the contrary, they could even be a blessing.

We entered Glen Carron on a section of single-track road. On our left, the motionless surface of Loch Dùghaill reflected like a mirror. The lake looked peaceful, but still water means only one thing in the Highlands of Scotland at this time of year.

'These damn midges,' Edita said when we stopped for a butt rest (as Edita liked to call it in her American English) and wandered down to the lake shore for a photograph. 'Let's keep cycling.'

The land flattened out, and we reached the west coast at the sea loch of Lochcarron at 11.30. We passed a lochside café next to a golf course. Knowing that we were going to need all the energy we could get to cross the Bealach na Ba, we stopped for an early lunch. The setting was wonderful, and it was warm enough to sit outside, with the sea loch lapping the shore a few metres away. Just enough of a breeze kept the midges away.

But it wasn't the midges that had me trembling with fear. Above one of the tables inside the door was an aerial photograph of a road snaking up a snowy combe in a series of severe zigzags. Dark clouds above a loch at the bottom of the combe – or *corrie* in Scottish terminology – added an air of foreboding.

'That must be the Bealach na Ba,' I said to Edita. 'It looks like a bastard of a climb.'

'Try not to think about it. We've just got to do it,' she replied.

It was sound advice. If you're heading to the gallows, it's worth remembering that there are no hardships until the trapdoor drops. I clung to this thought as we left the café at one o'clock, and had a leisurely cycle ride through the village of Lochcarron. It was a peaceful village with a single long promenade of whitewashed houses against the loch shore. My memories of it would have been pleasant had there not been a fiendish hill at the far end. One minute I was pedalling along happily, the next it felt like there was a large elastic band attached to my back wheel. As my legs rapidly weakened I felt that any moment I would be pinged back down to the village.

We struggled up 200m, rattled across a cattle grid, and reached open moorland, where I was dismayed to find a long downhill section on the other side. This wasn't the Bealach na Ba, but a mini Ba – a warm-up, if you like (I didn't like). We whizzed down it, losing those hard-earned 200m in a matter of minutes. We were crossing a small peninsula, and soon we reached another sea loch on the other side, Loch Kishorn; across it we could see a road rising up a hillside. The striped dome of Sgùrr a' Chaorachain (a mountain, not a lung condition) rose dramatically in grassy tiers. We rested at the turn-off to Applecross and shared a can of Coke. It was two o'clock, and the moment of truth had arrived. I still felt full of energy, but I wondered how long it would take for the Bealach na Ba to knock that out of me like the stuffing being knocked out of a cold chicken. Could I cycle all the way up without getting off to push, or would a band of angels riding golden unicorns sweep me up and carry me to the top?

In fact, Scotland's idiosyncratic single-track roads gave me some useful assistance. These roads aren't wide enough for two cars to pass one another; most aren't even wide enough for a car and a bike. Every few metres there are little bays where the road is wider. If it isn't already obvious what the bays are for, each one has a tall metal signpost marked with the legend 'Passing Place'. These are not for urinating against, but for stopping to wait for traffic coming the other way. I used them like a diver coming up for air, and stopped in them at every opportunity, even though I wasn't obliged to. An article on the North Coast 500 website had prepared me for the etiquette of cycling along single-track roads. The unwritten rule was that whoever got to the passing place first had to stop and wait for traffic coming the other way. But not all motorists believed this rule applied to cyclists.

'Occasionally, you meet a driver who either doesn't understand the conventions of using passing places, or doesn't consider that cyclists have the right to use the road,' the article read.[25]

In these situations I was supposed to adopt the primary position, which of course meant cycling in the middle of the road while the fractious motorist hurtled towards me. Obviously one of us would need to stop (or, as we say in English, *blink first*) to prevent a head-on collision.

'Hopefully the driver will understand this message,' the

article continued.

Yes, indeed.

We made good progress to begin with. There were steep sections, but flatter bits too, enabling me to exert less energy on the pedals. We rested in passing places and leapfrogged each other as we took it in turns to take photos. We each cycled at our own pace, rarely able to build up a rhythm, and quite unable to break wind for one another.

It was certainly a picturesque bit of road, climbing parallel to Loch Kishorn, with views south-east across the water to the mountains of Glen Shiel. But I knew from the photo in the café that the worst was yet to come. The road turned inland and steepened towards the pass. Somewhere up there were those fearsome zigzags. As the gradient increased, so did the frequency of my rest stops.

I can't remember exactly when I decided to call this bit of road the Bealach na Bastard, but by the time Edita tried to take some video footage, it had certainly been renamed. I was too tired to play the part expected of me.

'Are you ready to set off?' she said as we rested in a passing place.

'No, I'm fucking fucked. I've got to wait for that fucking thing,' I said, pointing to yet another car that had appeared around a corner.

'Watch your language, please.'

'I'm sorry, but I'm too tired for this.'

Eventually, I could only cycle for 10-20m at a time. The panniers felt like lead balloons. My leg muscles were too weak to keep pumping. We had climbed around 400 of the 626m when we reached a long, straight section that ascended up the side of the corrie. Loch Kishorn had disappeared around a corner, and ahead I could see the dreaded zigzags. They weren't far away, but the angle of the slope had become too much for me. It was no use; I had to get off and push.

In Greek mythology, King Sisyphus annoyed the gods and was condemned for eternity to push a large rock up a steep hill. Each time he approached the top, the rock rolled back down and he had to start all over again. There is a similar character in Lithuano-Scottish mythology. I'm going to call him Marcus, a court jester in black cycling tights, who was condemned to push a bike with heavy panniers up a steep hill while being filmed on somebody's GoPro.

Pedalling up to the Bealach na Bastard

Drivers beeped at me, and gave thumbs-up signs that they presumably believed might encourage me along. I knew they meant well, but I'm not much of an exhibitionist, and I never wanted to be a court jester. Towards the top of the hairpins, an ancient Volkswagen camper van spluttered past, coughing furiously. I was almost as quick as it was, and felt certain it was going to roll back onto me like Sisyphus's rock.

At the top of the hairpins, the road straightened. It was enough encouragement for Edita – who was pushing too now – to get back on her bike. But I was dismayed to see the road continue onwards just as steeply. I kept pushing until the last quarter of a mile, where it flattened out. This flattening enabled me to get back on and cycle into the car park at the top of the pass, so that it looked like I'd pedalled all the way.

We reached the Bealach na Ba at 4.30. A cylindrical cairn looked across a silver sliver of water to the Isle of Skye. Grey clouds hung over the Cuillin Hills, but we could see their tops. Other cyclists came over to talk to us.

'Respect to you guys, cycling up here with those great big panniers,' one of them said.

'Er… we might have got off to push a little of the way.'

One of them had cycled around Skye and was now doing the North Coast 500. His wife was supporting him by driving around in her car, stopping to give him water and food.

'This is the hardest cycle ride in Britain,' he said. 'The Bealach na Ba is on every cyclist's bucket list.'

I was tempted to argue with him. It hadn't been on mine, and it still wasn't.

'He's cheating,' Edita said after he left. 'How can you get your wife to carry all your things for you?'

'But we'll be supported in Ecuador, won't we?'

'That's different. It's Ecuador.'

I couldn't argue with that.

We slumped against the summit cairn and tucked in to our snacks. I was exhausted and happy, and for half an hour we didn't move.

Our reward for cycling up the Bealach na Bastard was still to come. It had taken us two and a half hours to come up, and I knew we had just as far to descend that evening.

Little did I imagine that barely half an hour later I would be steaming into the campsite at Applecross, not having pedalled a single rotation. We freewheeled the entire descent, looking across grassland to the sea below. The only energy I expended was in squeezing the brakes – which I had to do most of the way.

With its main route in across a 2,000ft pass, Applecross is one of the most isolated villages in Britain. It's actually a community of hamlets dotted around a remote peninsula, and was established in the 7th century by an Irish monk. It was busy. We pitched our tent at the campsite, found room at the inn for a hot meal, and wandered along the seafront to catch the last of the evening sun. It was a fine evening, and, as we gazed across the water to the Isle of Raasay, Edita told me she liked Scotland.

'If only they could find a way of getting rid of these damn midges,' she added.

The worst of the North Coast 500 was behind us. Or so we thought.

7 THE WEST COAST

Little did I know, as we strolled along the waterfront at Applecross, that by lunchtime the following day our sea-to-summit adventure would be on the verge of collapse. More specifically, one of its protagonists would be on the verge of collapse. And, in case you're wondering, it wasn't Edita.

I started the morning in a positive frame of mind as I read our guidebook in the tent.

'The beautiful and mainly flat coast road meanders into the Applecross peninsula, past scattered crofting villages that look out over gorgeous seascapes,' it prattled, with its fingers crossed discreetly behind its back.

The road was indeed beautiful, and it looked out over gorgeous seascapes. It even meandered around the Applecross peninsula. But this sentence had evidently been written by somebody who had passed that way in a motor car, because it pissing well wasn't 'mainly flat'.

We made a leisurely start, thinking that we had an easy 50km to Torridon. The first 25 were quite pleasant as the road weaved around the peninsula to the next village, Shieldaig. It was a single-track road again, but in the morning there wasn't much traffic, and we pedalled up and down gentle hills along a treeless shoreline, looking across a strait to the Isle of Raasay. The road turned inland briefly over rolling moorland dappled with lakes. Highland cattle grazed beside the verge.

It was when the road turned east to cross the northern part of the peninsula that the trouble started. An endless sequence of hills cavorted up and down, each more precipitous than the one before. Many were simply too steep to get up on a loaded touring bike. I stopped frequently to rest my legs, and four or five times I had to get off and push. Edita fared better. She stood up on the pedals and managed to stay on her bike, but often she was no quicker than I was as I wheeled my bike behind her.

The scenery was spectacular. One particular downhill section clung to the side of a cliff, with crash barriers to stop vehicles tumbling into Loch Torridon. At the bottom, the road circled around an arm of the loch, and we whizzed around it as the road plunged towards the shore. But the joy of freewheeling down a big hill is tempered when you know full well you'll round a corner and find the road surging back up again. And sure enough, it did, in endless sequence. I came to realise that 'mainly flat' has a different meaning when you're sitting happily behind the wheel of a car, touching the accelerator with a happy squeeze of the toe.

The hills weren't the only bothersome factor. There was a lot more traffic in the afternoon. We found this particularly annoying on the uphill sections, when it would take an age to reach the next passing place. Unless opposing drivers had the forbearance of Nelson Mandela waiting patiently to be released from prison, I had no alternative but to get off the road and let them pass. At one point a large truck approached from behind. I had no idea of its size, and when the driver beeped his air horn I jumped so high that I could have waved to him across the passenger seat of the cab. On another occasion a car tried to pass in a place that was far too narrow, barging me into the verge. I dearly wanted to respond, and even had a phrase in mind, but I was so tired that I couldn't even get as far as the 'F'.

Long before Shieldaig, I had exhausted all the profanities in the English language and even taught Edita some new words. It was the third day of what I'd hoped would be a nice easy training ride for our sea-to-summit adventure. But in Ecuador, we would be cycling up 4,000m, with none of the enjoyable downhill sections. I had to face up to reality.

I pulled up by the side of the road and slumped in my saddle. The day had been sheer hell, but at least I still had Edita to give me some sympathy. She rode alongside and waited for me to speak.

'I can't do this,' I said. 'If it's like this all the way round, it's going to kill me.'

She paused for a moment, then breathed an audible sigh. She looked annoyed.

'Perhaps you should turn back and abandon it.'

'Perhaps I should. And pull out of our Ecuador adventure too.'

I was unprepared for what came next. She sat up straight on the bike and looked away from me. There was a wistful expression on her face and an air of resolution in her bearing as she gazed across the churning waters of Loch Torridon.

'In that case I will go on alone.'

My heart had been pumping furiously all morning, but now it shattered like glass. Suddenly I felt very sad. She would go on alone, without me? My confidence was at its lowest ebb. I couldn't even pedal up a 20m hill without getting off to push, yet we had 4,000m of climbing ahead of us in an unfamiliar country. It seemed inconceivable that I could make it to the foothills of Chimborazo in this manner. But Edita said she would go on alone, and I believed she really would. What would happen to our relationship then? She was stronger in mind, body and heart – I doubted I could ever match her in any of those facets, but I had to try. There was no question that I would just have to keep going and put my faith in the cycling gods.

'Then I will continue for your sake,' I said.

This was the wrong answer. I rarely saw her angry, and she wasn't now. Perhaps it would have been easier for me if she were. Instead, there was a fierce expression in her eyes that I believed was masking a trace of contempt.

'I don't want you to do it for my sake. If you're not enjoying it, then go home.'

She looked away from me and resumed pedalling. I watched her for a few metres, then felt between my legs to confirm whether my balls were still intact. They certainly felt much smaller. I picked up the pieces of my shattered ego and tried to put them back together. I lacked the strength to pedal up the next hill, so I kept pushing, but now I did it silently.

I felt this was a key moment in our journey. I could feel the anger welling up inside. I wasn't angry with Edita; for her I had only admiration. It was the sodding cycle ride that was causing my blood to boil.

'Bollocks to this. I'm going to do this thing if it kills me.'

Edita was too far away to hear me, but I wasn't saying it to her.

I was determined to get to the end of the damn North Coast 500, even if I had to walk all the way around, ripping up the offending pages of the guidebook as I went, ready to shove them up the writer's arse (yes, I know – it was an e-book, but that's not the point).

We reached Shieldaig at three o'clock. It was another pleasant lochside village with a pub, a general store, and a number of B&Bs. The buzz of holidaymakers at picnic tables outside Nanny's Coffee Shop brought me back to life. The café was still open for sandwiches, coffee and – more importantly – carrot cake. I guzzled it all down like a hungry dog.

The last six miles to Torridon were much more enjoyable: after a short climb to get out of Shieldaig, we were back on two-lane roads. We no longer had to stop and wait for vehicles, and the gradients were manageable. I was much happier as I pelted along in the higher gears.

But I was forced to make another resolution as the road looked down upon the loch. A bank of dark clouds masked the forbidding hills of Torridon across the water. I knew that one of these hills was Liathach, an 8km knife-edge ridge with multiple summits perched atop tiers of sandstone cliffs. If the weather was fine then I had intended for us to climb this most exalted of Scottish hills the following day. The forecast wasn't good, and I knew there was no point going up if we were to spend the whole time in a thicket of dense, watery cloud.

I also had a bigger picture to confront. The endless pedalling was turning my legs into blancmange by the end of each day. Priority number one was to keep cycling and build up those cyclist's legs. Priority number two was to complete this hellish bike ride so that I could give myself a pat on the back. Alongside these priorities, walking up mountains was a nice-to-have. Priority number three was to keep Edita happy. Bugger, no: priority number one was to keep Edita happy. What if Edita was only happy if we climbed some mountains? But surely she would be most happy if we completed the sea-to-summit adventure – and, to do that, it was the cycling we had to train for, not the climbing.

I realised there was a solution to this dilemma. The one thing we did have on our side was time. We could complete the cycle ride, and then climb some mountains afterwards. I just needed to square it with Edita and make sure she was happy.

We could see Torridon village from some distance away, nestling in a flat area at the top end of the loch, and we had an enjoyable descent downhill through forest. With bigger wheels on my bike I always freewheeled quicker than Edita. This gave me a chance to rest and admire the scenery as I waited at the bottom. The campsite in Torridon was unmanned and for tents only – nice and peaceful. Though the only pub was a mile away, we were able to buy a couple of craft beers from the youth hostel next door. We drank them in the comfort of our tent as Edita cooked noodles over the stove.

An ascent of Liathach was out of the question the following day. I couldn't let Edita climb it alone; but, more importantly, I couldn't take the risk of her reaction if I chickened out. Sore buttocks was one thing (well, two things actually), but this other side effect of cycle touring had serious consequences for our relationship.

I needed to do this carefully

'Er… I've been thinking about climbing Liathach tomorrow.'

'Are you crazy?' Edita said. 'The weather's atrocious. Let's keep cycling.'

'Are you sure? I think the weather's going to be even worse tomorrow. It's going to piss down. And the wind will be howling like a wolf on the summit ridge. Our flimsy ponchos aren't great for these conditions and are likely to flap around like parachutes, but we can still give it a go if you want to.' I said, not entirely truthfully.

'No, I don't want to. I think it's a stupid idea, and I can't believe you're even thinking about it after your performance earlier.'

The last comment was perhaps a little unnecessary, but I felt I'd managed to steer through the conversation with a shred of dignity intact.

It rained all night, and the following morning the midges were out in force. A short distance away from us, two men wore full mosquito head nets as they dismantled their tent.

'Edmund Hillary was a beekeeper, you know,' Edita said as she wafted the damp morning air with her arms. 'He would have brought the right protective clothing for Scotland.'

We set off in light rain. To our left, the Torridon hills disappeared into a sheet of cloud only 50m above the road. It must have been bleak as a pathologist's birthday party on top of the mountain, and if I had any doubts about climbing Liathach, they were gone.

Down on the road, things were more positive. We powered along the single-track road to Kinlochewe, enjoying the freedom from traffic at that time in the morning. The road undulated gently, which meant we had no difficulty on the uphill sections, and could race back down them with plenty of freewheeling. We covered 16km in less than an hour – a rate of progress that would doubtless be laughable to experienced cyclists, the sort of thing Chris Froome could do without even putting his feet on the pedals. But it was our quickest yet, and we felt pleased with ourselves as we draped our sodden ponchos over the chairs and stopped for a big breakfast at a café in Kinlochewe.

The rain became heavier as we continued alongside Loch Maree, and a grey mist drifted over the lake; we could barely see its shores. Somewhere across the other side rose Slioch, my first ever Munro. I couldn't see much of it at the time, and I could see even less of it now. It was a sobering thought that I had climbed it nearly a quarter of a century earlier. I would like to think that I'd grown up in that time, yet here I was, doing this.

The road was flat and the cycling monotonous. My poncho billowed like a sail as I pedalled into a damp headwind. After several miles the road turned away from the loch to cross a peninsula. A long, straight hill beckoned – though perhaps 'beckoned' is the wrong word. Beckoning implies a wish to approach, but 'shoved me up it with a firm kick up the backside' would be a more appropriate expression. I felt the pressure from that kick as I gritted my teeth and squeezed the pedals. I was determined to get all the way to the top without stopping for a butt rest, but nature had other plans. Scotland's weather pounded me with a 'take that, you wee English bastard' and for 10 minutes I leaned forward and thought of England. Just before I reached the top, a powerful gust literally stopped me in my tracks, and I was forced to put my feet down to avoid falling into the verge.

'You arsehole!' I roared into the wind.

I don't know if the wind heard me, but it needed to be said. I was so disappointed.

I glanced around and saw that Edita was right behind me. I had no idea she had been so close, but there was a remorseful expression on her face.

'It's my fault,' she said. 'I've been letting you break wind for me.'

I felt a glow of pride; perhaps my battle with the wind had restored some of her faith in me. She took over the lead and brought us to the top of the hill. The wind was right in our faces, and we couldn't freewheel for several minutes as we passed over bleak moorland on the other side. But then the road turned north again and we entered forest. Sheltered from the wind, we had a bit more fun zooming down hills again.

Later in the afternoon, my confidence received another boost as I waited outside a supermarket in Gairloch for Edita to buy supplies for the evening. A man passing by stopped to admire our bikes.

'Are these yours? I have a Specialized bike at home. I'm very happy with it. How many speed are these?'

'Oh, very speedy. But the panniers slow you down a bit.'

'I bet. Fair play to you for carrying so much gear. Are you cycling a long way?'

'We're doing the North Coast 500.'

'Bloody hell. Fair play. I guess you must do a lot of cycle touring then.'

'Er… it depends what you call a lot. Actually, this is my first time. I used to ride a bike to work, but I've never done anything like this.'

'Bloody hell. Your first cycle tour and you're doing the North Coast 500? Fair play to you.'

My head swelled, and I felt like Superman as we left Gairloch. Unhappily, there was another steep hill right out of the village. I wasn't even halfway up it when I felt like there was something tugging on my cape. Superman never has this problem, or at least they never show these things in the movies. I made it to the top, but then I had to stop and gasp.

The afternoon was a bit of a blur. I remember a picturesque moorland plateau alongside a loch, and a hair-raising section on a wet road as I hurtled down the hill into Poolewe. I felt a car on my shoulder as I squeezed on the brakes to get around a tight corner. Terror gripped me. Perhaps if I'd actually shat myself then it would have slowed me down more safely, but my only thought was that if I fell off here then I was dead, no question.

A stiff downpour lashed us as we cycled along the secluded sea loch at Poolewe and up another huge hill the other side of the village. It wasn't that steep, but it went on for so long that my buttocks were exploding in pain. To compound my misery, a powerful wind hurled rain into my clothes like a school bully whipping me with a wet towel in the showers after a muddy PE lesson. I looked forward to freewheeling back down the other side, but once again fate had written a different script. My poncho tried to tack across the prevailing wind and turn my course back up the hill. If there's one thing worse than gritting your teeth to pedal up a steep hill, it's working just as hard to pedal down again.

There were some positives. The village of Aultbea looked idyllic on the shoreline below us as we descended. Just offshore we spotted the quaintly named Isle of Ewe, which is pronounced the same way as an amorous phrase (if you don't believe me, say it out loud to a Scotsman in a kilt and observe their reaction).

There was just one more hill and one more peninsula to cross. We had another publess evening ahead of us at the campsite in Laide, but Edita suggested we stop at the nearby post office and get some wine for the evening.

'Where in the world can you find a post office where they serve wine?' I said.

The answer was Scotland.

I opened the door and faced a towering wall of bottles and cans that could have kept out an army with siege weapons. Every square inch of shelving was packed with every conceivable alcoholic beverage. It was the only post office I'd been to where there was barely enough room for the stamps. We found a bottle of Abruzzo Montepulciano to remind ourselves of Italy as we rested in our tent that evening.

If I'm giving you the impression that I was a miserable, cantankerous old fart, who hated cycling and could do nothing but contemplate the ordeal ahead when he woke each morning, then I'm only telling you part of the story. It was tough, and there were moments when I would have preferred to have my legs flayed with stinging nettles, but this was because I'm no endurance athlete. In fact, I feel alive outdoors and I enjoy physical activity in moderation. As we cycled among the sea lochs, through ever-changing scenery of islands and mountains, I always felt that happiness wasn't far away.

On the day we cycled around the coast of Gruinard Bay from Laide, and over the Dundonnell plateau to Ullapool, I actually started to enjoy myself. It was a fine morning, pleasantly sunny with few clouds – something that always helps with the mood. The sun gave a silver sheen to the water. Beds of purple heather by the roadside glistened in the breeze. The coastline was pleasing rather than breathtaking, and we enjoyed the early morning with very little traffic as we pedalled along in leisurely fashion.

We turned inland to cross another peninsula, which meant another climb. This time I put my head down, got a rhythm going with my legs, and managed to reach the top without stopping. I was pleased with myself. I decided it was because my muscles and technique had improved since the previous day, but the absence of a belligerent headwind may have helped.

At the top was an airy car park looking across Little Loch Broom to the hills of Assynt. These were the Sutherland mountains I had visited 20 years earlier, whose landscape Ecuador's isolated volcanoes had reminded me of. There was a massive hill parallel to the coast and down to the shoreline. Over to the east, grey clouds gathered over bare hilltops. It looked like rain was on the way, but we didn't need to think about that just yet. We whizzed down the road, covering 7km in less than the time it takes to say His Royal Highness Prince Charles, Duke of Rothesay, Lord of the Isles and Great Steward of Scotland.

We took lunch at a little café on the shores of the loch. Somewhere up above us was An Teallach: a giant horseshoe of a mountain with many ridges and summits, and a fearsome reputation. I very much wanted to climb it, but at that moment, like most of the mountains so far, it was nowhere to be seen.

In the afternoon we took turns to break wind as the road climbed up through forest to grassy moorland. There was a long, straight section of road where the occasional car hurtled past at speeds that would make Lewis Hamilton blush. But I was finding things easy by then, and I even had the confidence to cycle one-handed, videoing Edita in front of me as I pedalled along.

A trio of mountains rose in front of us at the top of the climb. At last we could see some summits. They were the Fannich Munros – gentle, green and inviting. I would have loved to camp here and climb them the following day, but I knew it wasn't to be. We had abandoned our idea of combining hill walking with cycle touring. It had sounded like a nice idea as we planned our trip, but we had fallen for the old adventurer's pitfall of making elaborate plans, then abandoning them when the realities of the task we had set ourselves became apparent. When Ernest Shackleton set out for Antarctica on his ship the *Endurance*, he had intended to make the first ever crossing of the Antarctic continent. When the *Endurance* was crushed by sea ice, his only aim was to return home alive. It became one of the great survival stories of polar exploration. Likewise, when I was a 17-year-old schoolboy, my friends and I had set out one Friday night intending to have a pint in all seven pubs in our village. Half an hour later, having been asked for photo ID in the first two, our only ambition was to get an alcoholic drink in at least one of them. Our cycle tour of Scotland fell somewhere between these two.

We stopped for a butt rest in a lay-by, and looked behind us. What I saw had my feet twitching in my pedals. Three ridges converged around two precipitous corries like the arms of a letter 'M'. I could see six or seven distinct summits. The highest rose gently above a silver-topped spur that divided the two corries, but the more dramatic peaks lay further along the ridge to its left. A jagged line of pinnacles, like a row of black teeth, drew my eye upwards to a steep pyramid. An Teallach is a feast of summits, cols and ridges – a whole massif, far more than one mountain. Like the famous Snowdon in North Wales, it has many interesting routes; but, unlike Snowdon, which is encircled by roads, An Teallach's routes are far less accessible. The only road here was the one we had just pedalled up. Now wasn't the time, but we knew we had to climb this mountain.

'How would you like to make this one your first Munro?' I said.

'You keep talking about Munros,' Edita replied. 'I don't know what they are, but I'd like to climb this one.'

Soon after the Scottish Mountaineering Club was formed in 1889, some of its members decided to make a list of all the highest hills in Scotland. The task fell to the 4th Baronet, Sir Hugh Thomas Munro, a member who I'm guessing had time on his hands on account of not having a real job.

Sir Hugh cobbled together his first list in rapid time using Ordnance Survey maps. He surprised many people (including himself) when he published it in 1891. He discovered there were nearly 300 distinct peaks in Scotland over 3,000ft, instead of the 30 or so that people thought. The first Munro's Tables listed 538 summits crossing the magic mark, but he only classified 282 of them as separate mountains. These 282 peaks came to be known as 'Munros', while the other 256 acquired the rather more mundane name 'Tops'. The tables gave birth to the sport of Munro bagging.

I use the phrase 'distinct peak', but – somewhat annoyingly for would-be Munro baggers – Sir Hugh never defined precisely what a mountain had to do to get on his list. This means that every few years some clever dick from the Scottish Mountaineering Club goes through the list, adding new ones just to annoy people who think they've done them all. It must be a real pisser if you've spent the best part of your life ticking them off, and were looking forward to spending your autumn years playing tiddlywinks instead of wading across another peat bog.

On Sir Hugh's original 1891 list, only the highest peak of An Teallach, Bidein a' Ghlas Thuill, was classified as a Munro, while there were no fewer than seven further tops. But in 1981 its second summit, the steep pyramid of Sgùrr Fiona, was honoured with Munro status. A Highland regiment marched up with bagpipes, broke a bottle of Scotch against the summit cairn and consecrated it with a sword (actually I made that last bit up, but I'd like to think the Scottish Mountaineering Club does something special to mark these occasions).

On previous days the sight of An Teallach towering invitingly above the moorland would have had me yearning to throw my bike in a ditch and put on my hiking boots, but I had quite enjoyed the cycling that day. I turned my back on An Teallach, promising myself we would come back after the bike ride.

Later that afternoon we breezed into Ullapool. I was happy to return to this bustling fishing port and ferry terminal on the shores of Loch Broom. With only 1,500 inhabitants, it would be little more than a modest village elsewhere in Britain, but here in the north-west Highlands it was a metropolis – the largest community we would pass through before we reached the far north-east.

I was returning to old territory. A quarter of a century earlier I had come here with my father and brother. We journeyed north to the mountains of Assynt, a wild expanse of open moorland and isolated peaks. I was young then. I felt like I had never been in such a remote place, and it left a deep impression. We climbed two of the peaks, Stac Pollaidh and Suilven, and had the summits to ourselves. We gazed across moorland and lochs to the ocean and islands beyond, but what struck me most was the silence. We must have been the only people for miles around, and could hear our voices across great distances.

But memory fades and mutates across so many years; I wasn't so much returning to a familiar place as remembering a dream. We cycled along the seafront between whitewashed terraced houses and a pebble beach. Fishing boats with high masts floated in the secluded harbour, a sea loch surrounded by rolling hills. Ullapool wasn't as busy as the guidebooks had warned us. The campsite was big and spacious, with its own beach and a view across the loch.

We hastily erected our tent before the midges emerged for their evening feast. It was a sunny evening, and we wandered beside the pubs, restaurants and souvenir shops on the loch shore. Wooden booths offered sea kayaking and wildlife boat trips, but the harbour was dominated by the ferry terminal. From Ullapool it's three hours by boat to Stornoway in the Outer Hebrides. I couldn't imagine many people stampeding to visit such a remote outpost of the British Isles. I must confess that I half-expected a little fishing boat to be chugging back and forth between the two places. I was therefore amazed when the 8,680-ton *Loch Seaforth* steamed into port. This monstrous 118m vessel is capable of carrying 700 passengers and 143 cars. Docked up against the ferry terminal it was as if a floating football stadium had suddenly appeared on the seafront.

We had a three-course meal in the bustling Ferry Boat Inn, amusingly known as the FBI. It felt as cosmopolitan as any pub in London. The bar staff were from Poland and the Czech Republic, and tourists like us were from all over the world. I couldn't hear a single Scottish accent until the tables were cleared and a man with a giant beard the size and shape of a bird's nest appeared with a guitar.

In the climbing community, Ullapool is known as the place where Tom Patey was the local doctor for 10 years. This larger-than-life figure was one of Britain's most colourful and successful mountaineers of the 1950s and 60s. He made the first ascents of Muztagh Tower (7,276m) and Rakaposhi (7,788m) in the Pakistan Karakoram, but was more comfortable on Scottish rock. He was involved in Chris Bonington's famous televised ascent of the Old Man of Hoy in 1967, a sea stack off the coast of the Orkney Islands.

One of Tom Patey's more unusual legacies is a body of comic climbing poetry. As well as being a talented climber and a doctor, he played the accordion and was known for performing some of his comic masterpieces in pubs. History doesn't recall whether he was also good with the ladies, but if you're thinking some people have all the luck, this is rarely true of elite climbers. He died in 1970 abseiling off another sea stack, the Maiden, at the tragically young age of 38.

It seemed that we had encountered Tom Patey's musical legacy here in the Ferry Boat Inn. Conversations fell silent as the voice of a true Caledonian reverberated across the room. But if I was expecting folk tunes about routing the English at Bannockburn, I was in for a surprise when he launched into a Johnny Cash number. For the next hour and a half we were treated to a cascade of American country classics fused with Highland banter. Our trip was full of surprises.

It was the first time I'd ever woken up in a tent with 'Ring of Fire' echoing in my ears. We had a huge and delicious breakfast at the Seaforth Bar opposite the ferry terminal – the first bar I'd visited where they were playing bagpipe dirges. The novelty soon wore off. By the third tune I was wishing they would hurry up and strangle that cat so that we could finish our breakfast in silence.

We faced a long ride up a hill out of Ullapool, climbing above Loch Broom. I didn't mind, because the sun was shining brightly, and I knew that morning I would be entering the landscape of my dreams. We crested a rise and dropped back down the other side to the beach at Ardmair. The long ridge of Ben More Coigach, the most southerly of the Assynt peaks, rose across the bay. The country had a wilder feel as we turned inland, passing Ben More Coigach on our left. Then the isolated peaks I'd been waiting for came into view: Cul Mor, Cul Beag and Stac Pollaidh. Canisp and Suilven hid somewhere behind them. All five were standalone mountains rising above the moors, like weird-shaped volcanoes. It was a wet version of Ecuador's Central Highlands.

A number of writers have used the word *stegosaurus* to describe Stac Pollaidh and Suilven, with their solitary outlines and jagged, saw-like crests. Why, out of all the dinosaurs, they have chosen the one that looks like it has a jungle growing on its back is a little puzzling. Both peaks have astonishing rocky outlines. Side-on they look like rough-backed sleeping monsters, for sure; end-on, looking along their crests, they are even more striking. One 19th-century writer, Henry Cadell, likened Stac Pollaidh's form to the west side of the Matterhorn, albeit a smaller version. Pocket-sized might be a better description. It was the first mountain I ever climbed in Scotland – though to be clear, at 612m or 2,008ft it only just squeaks into the official British definition of a mountain.

The road beyond Ullapool was a busy highway north. Cars hared past, and we were glad to turn off to the west on the peaceful Inverpolly road beneath Cul Beag and Stac Pollaidh. The gently undulating single track with few cars made for enjoyable, undemanding cycling, with plenty of freewheeling (and not too much effort needed on the climbs). We reached the tranquil waters of Loch Lurgainn and pedalled above its shores. Stac Pollaidh rose abruptly from the grassy moors like a red sandstone fortress.

Times had changed, and the Assynt hills were no longer the peaceful backwater I remembered, or at least Stac Pollaidh wasn't. The car park at its base was jam packed, and people had parked in the passing places. One idiot overtook me on a single-track section without waiting for me to reach a wider part or move to the side. Their vehicle was inches from my leg; Edita was barged off the road.

Beyond the car park we found it much quieter, and without the hills it would have been the most serene cycle ride. We rode through peaceful woodland glades, beside bubbling rivers in mini valleys, and passed many beautiful wild-camping spots. The road touched the sea briefly in a couple of places, and the views out to the islands were breathtaking.

It would be lovely in a car, I was sure, but I was gorged on hills, and the day had a gratuitous ending – the cycling gods peppered the final section to the campsite at Clachtoll with some of the steepest hills yet. It was a spacious seaside campsite surrounded by grassy knolls and rocky outcrops. I felt we deserved a nice gentle day, but in the tent that evening my Ordnance Survey map provided no comfort. It lined the next section to Kylesku with an ominous sequence of double chevrons, indicating Britain's steepest hills. With dismay I noted the section between Lochinver and Clachtoll merited only a single chevron. It felt like I was going to need a new pair of thighs.

Mark on the North Coast 500 with Stac Pollaidh behind

The following day had the worst possible start before we even got on our bikes. I discovered a flat rear tyre. We pumped it up, and it seemed firm enough, but my mind went back to my father's cutlery set and the bathtub. I knew that if I had a serious puncture then it would be a bigger pain in the arse than sitting on a narrow bike saddle, sandpapering my buttocks with every turn of the pedals.

'How the hell do you remove a back wheel with all those damn gears?' I said aloud to myself.

Luckily Edita is a lot more practical than I am.

'Don't worry, I will help you,' she said.

By which I hoped she meant that she would do it for me. I counted my lucky stars.

The morning followed a familiar, unsettling routine. The hills were relentless – hard work, sure, but they remained doable for the first hour and a half to Drumbeg. I could get up them without getting off the bike, and there were some pleasant coastal sections. We stopped at a viewpoint above Drumbeg, looking out across the crowded waters of Eddrachillis Bay, cluttered with tiny islands.

I felt a sense of achievement. Were my legs getting stronger? Was I at last getting used to the ups and downs?

Like hell I was. After Drumbeg, things got silly: hill after hill, stupidly steep, and way too much for a loaded touring bike. I really wanted to stay on the bike, but my legs just didn't have the strength. Some hills I managed without walking, but I had to stop and rest in every passing place. Edita became impatient with me.

'Stand up on the pedals,' she said. 'It's much easier that way.'

This technique worked in short bursts, but it wasn't sustainable up long hills. We must have looked a funny pair to passing motorists – Edita standing up and cycling, but moving so slowly that I could keep up with her as I wheeled my bike behind.

On one particularly bleak spot, sweeping over rugged moorland high above the sea, the wind picked up and lashed rain into our faces. When the road dipped down into a sheltered spot between trees, I asked Edita if we could stop for a snack. I needed warmth and energy quickly.

'This is amazing. It's so beautiful here,' she said.

'I'm cold, wet and knackered,' I replied.

We continued down the hill and I squeezed hard on the back brake to slow my descent, but I soon realised there was no more friction. The back wheel scraped along the ground. I had visions of the tyre igniting and setting fire to the seat of my trousers a split second before I had to hurl myself into a ditch. Which would of course have been the moment when I discovered that butt cream is highly flammable. Luckily the road was quiet and I was still on the bike when I reached the bottom.

'Blimey, I'm glad we didn't have to cycle *up* that one,' I said to Edita when she caught up with me.

This was premature. The road up the other side was so vertiginous that Alfred Hitchcock could have made a movie about it. It was almost too steep to push the bikes up. An old Volkswagen camper van spluttered past us, inching its way down the hill. The driver looked terrified, and I knew why. I had driven around France in one of those things when I was a student; the brakes might just as well have been hand-operated with a pair of pliers. I was pretty sure that the VW had no chance of stopping. I could see the driver muttering every prayer he could think of to prevent anything coming the other way. It took another five minutes for the vehicle to make it up the other side, wheezing like a chain smoker as it slowed to a crawl. We watched, enthralled. The snails were probably overtaking it, and we expected it to start rolling backwards at any moment.

But every tough ride has its rewards, and ours came in the form of Quinag, a sprawling mountain shaped like a three-pronged grappling hook, with three summits on three long ridges converging together. Its western face stood proudly above the moorland and it dominated our view for the later part of the morning.

It was with some relief that I saw Kylesku Bridge spanning the water below us. When we reached the main road, I knew our lunchtime stop wasn't far away. I hurtled along the blessedly smooth surface and almost missed the turning for the pub as I tonned it down a hill. A sign read 50m on the right, and I slammed on the brakes. Kylesku village was just off the main road on the southern side of the narrow inlet to a remarkable inland harbour nestled among mountains.

We arrived at one o'clock after one of our hardest mornings. The Kylesku Hotel was a haven, a pub that took its food seriously. We could tell this when the first thing the waiter asked was whether we wanted water.

'I think he'd like some brown water,' Edita said.

'There's nae brown water here,' the waiter replied. 'All our water's as clear as crystal.'

'You're joking,' I said. 'But what about all those handpumps on the bar?'

'Oh, you mean beer!'

'Of course I mean beer. What on earth did you think we meant by "brown water"?'

'Ah well, you're an outsider I can see. You're welcome here. But when you've been in the Highlands long enough, you'll notice that sometimes the water can be a little peaty.'

Edita ordered langoustines, which I believe is a posh word for scampi. Her eyes bulged like cannonballs when the waiter returned with our food. Mine was a standard no-nonsense burger, served on a plate, just like any normal food should be. I don't know where to begin with Edita's. We had to clear most of the table to accommodate what I can only describe as some sort of portable gallows. It was made from cast iron in the shape of an inverted letter 'L'. The horizontal section had a hook for hanging the victims over a plate, and from this hook dangled six plump shellfish impaled on a skewer. Edita looked bewildered. I roared with laughter. She was given four implements to eat them with: a knife, a fork, a nutcracker and a knitting needle. The first two didn't look like they'd be much use.

I munched my burger, keeping one eye on Edita as she figured out her strategy. She slid the lower shellfish off its hanger and put it on the plate, but its hard shell thwarted her initial attempt to eat in the normal way with a knife and fork. She sat back, a quizzical expression crossing her face.

'Try prodding it with the knitting needle,' I suggested.

'I think I'm supposed to use these,' she said, picking up the nutcracker. 'But I don't know which bit I'm supposed to crack.'

She called the waiter over and explained her predicament.

'No problem. I can give ye a wee demonstration,' he said.

I roared again when he returned with a pair of surgical gloves.

'I think I'm going to wet myself.'

'Ach, what's so funny?' he said.

'Do you need to be a surgeon to eat them?'

'No, it's very straightforward. Watch…'

Diners on adjacent tables stopped eating, and we all watched eagerly. He demonstrated how to use the nutcracker to snap the claws off, and the knitting needle to prod around inside the shell and pull out the meaty bits. Some meals are instantly forgettable, but I'm pretty sure this one will stay in the memory for many years to come.

We had just 15 short kilometres to the campsite at Scourie – a doddle after the morning's exertions. Despite a couple of long climbs, we were on the main road now, which meant the hills were not as steep. We raced along, and the scenery never failed to impress: rugged green hills, rocky outcrops, pine woods and lochans, with the sea never far away.

At Scourie we were blessed with another beautiful seaside campsite perched above a rocky bay, our third in as many days. With 7 days of 13 done, we were past the halfway point, and it was time to reflect. You only need to glance at a map of Scotland to see that the mountains are concentrated in the west, and the coastline looks like it's been drawn by a man with hiccups. For five days we had been crossing a series of peninsulas, climbing into the hills and dropping back down again to the coast. Hill after hill had been relentlessly steep and I had aches and pains in muscles that I didn't know I had. But I looked with satisfaction at our map to see that the north and east coasts were comparatively smooth – no fjords and peninsulas, and only gentle rolling hills.

We had completed the worst that the North Coast 500 had to offer, and from now on it should be a piece of piss.

8 THE NORTH COAST

When I was a child, I loved gazing at maps and imagining what a place might be like. I spent a lot of time looking at the Scottish Highlands, a region so impossibly far away that it might as well have been the surface of the moon. The north coast of Scotland held a particular mystique. The map showed very few roads; villages appeared to have only a handful of houses. I imagined giant waves crashing against towering windswept cliffs, and battalions of seabirds covering the countryside with dribbles of white excrement. There wasn't much traffic on the roads of my imagination, but I did wonder if cars were ever held up by a walrus in the middle of the road. I was pretty sure everyone knew each other; no doubt a group could quickly be rustled up to usher the walrus towards the verge with pointed sticks.

Pride of place in the top left of the map was Cape Wrath, an area of headland that was clearly shouting *bugger off, don't come anywhere near me,* and presumably hardly anyone ever did. Just a short distance east of Cape Wrath there was actually a village called Durness, a place so dour and gloomy they'd given it a name that was a noun made from an adjective. I had wondered why on earth anyone would live there. Presumably it was just one lonely farmer with acres of sheep who didn't realise there was any other life.

As you grow older and wiser, life's perspective changes, but I hadn't given Durness a thought since I was a small child gazing at a map. Consequently I still carried that child's impression of sheep and walruses. Had I thought about this in more depth, I might have been quite excited about the day's cycle ride. At the end of it I would get to see a walrus. But my mind was on more mundane matters.

'It might be an idea to stock up on food here in Scourie,' I said to Edita as we packed away the tent. 'I can't imagine there will be much in Durness.'

'I'm sure there will be everything in Durness,' Edita replied. 'It's a tourist centre with a campsite. I'm sure there will be shops, pubs and restaurants.'

Then it occurred to me that, despite never having been to Scotland before, she had a better impression of Durness than I did. Now my mind was focused on it again, I was pretty sure there was more likely to be a shop than a walrus.

We left the sea behind and turned inland, touching it briefly again at Laxford Bay, another island-strewn sea loch reaching its intricate arms into Scotland's interior like a Norwegian fjord. We had a short day of only 40km. For the early part we were able to speed along a broad road across a bleak landscape of rugged bogland and lochs. Stark mountains rose up into a shallow ceiling of grey clouds.

The only breath of civilisation streaked past at Rhiconich, where another narrow sliver of water broke through the moors and a small hotel stood on a junction. The road swooped down into a trough, then climbed back up the other side before narrowing to single track. The long ascent that followed was sufficiently gentle for us to breeze up without putting too much strain on the legs. Drivers seemed to be more aggressive here, believing the road to be wide enough for a vehicle and a bike. I cycled in the middle of the road, forcing them to stop and give me room.

At the top we found ourselves on a high moorland plateau stretching for miles. There was a roof-of-the-world feel, with a sense of space at the far end, a feeling that the land dropped away. This may have been my imagination, for I knew the Atlantic Ocean and the far north coast of mainland Britain were just over the horizon. It was an uplifting thought.

We passed a deep blue lake in the middle of the plateau, and opposite, on our right, towered the mountains of Foinaven and Cranstackie. The latter sounded like a Caledonian insult. I scanned the map, half-expecting to see a nearby hill called Pishladdie. Cloud touched both summits. The space in between was a treeless expanse of thick grass. But for the dark clouds on the mountains and the brisk chill in the breeze, it could have been the plains of the Serengeti. This was deceptive, though. Any scenes of lions chasing wildebeest across this country would descend quickly into farce when both predator and prey sank gently into gelatinous peat bog. It wouldn't surprise me to learn that the deeper layers of sludge contained the preserved remains of native wolves, eradicated from Britain in the 17th century.

We pedalled joyfully across this tableland, stopping frequently to let traffic by. After about five miles the hills on either side began to part like the curtains opening on a stage, and we found ourselves at the top of a long descent to the ocean. We flew down the hill. I didn't have to move my legs for nearly two miles – but Edita shot ahead when we reached the lowlands again, and I found her waiting for me on the shores of the Kyle of Durness, the northernmost sea loch in Britain. It's across this stretch of water that a ferry takes sightseers hoping to visit the lighthouse at Cape

Wrath. We turned away from it, up and over another hill.

We reached Durness soon after midday. I was tired, but exhilarated. Sango Sands was our fourth seaside campsite in as many days, and the most scenic of them all. We erected our tent at the top of a cliff above a pristine sandy beach. All around were acres of rugged coastline. These flawless beaches must be among the most immaculate in Europe, but there wasn't a single person lying there. Why? For the same reason it took us ages to erect the tent: it was windy as hell, and goosebumps were certain to reach record proportions for any determined sunbathers. For us, this wind provided one huge advantage. We could be confident the campsite would be midge free.

The downmarket pub next door was as far removed in tone from the scenery as Eminem's lyrics are to a Shakespeare sonnet. The food was the sort of thing any fool can heat up in a microwave, but the pub did have Wi-Fi, and this meant I was able to get real-time travel advice from Angus as he tapped away in an office in Hong Kong.

We skipped his advice to try the nine-hole golf course where the sheep were very accommodating and the ninth hole featured a tee shot over the sea (we were fine with the sheep, but I would rather attend a knitting fair than play golf). More our thing was his suggestion to visit Smoo Cave: a vast cavern a mile down the coast, hewn into cliffs by the action of the sea.

It was a beautiful day, and as we walked above the silver sands of Sango Bay, the deep blue of the Atlantic Ocean lapping against rocky outcrops rising out of the surf, I found it impossible to believe that this sleepy tourist village was once the scene of violent rioting. The Highland clearances were a series of black episodes in Scottish history that are impossible to avoid hearing about if you travel through the northern region of Sutherland. The land seems wild and desolate, but it was once far more heavily populated. Peat cutters and crofters lived cheek by jowl on tiny plots of land that they leased from wealthy Highland lairds. Despite paying their rents and causing no trouble, they were forcibly evicted in their thousands over a period of 70 years from the 1780s to 1850s when landowners realised they could earn more renting the land to wealthy sheep farmers. Many people decided to emigrate to the United States, Canada and Australia, and those who remained were driven homeless to unusable land on the coast.

In Durness there was a brief flurry of resistance. The principal landowner was a man called James Anderson – not the England fast bowler, but a notorious fish-curer who rented the sea to his tenants, then bought the fish off them for meagre prices. These profits weren't enough for him. In 1841, he decided he could earn more from sheep farmers. He asked the local sheriff to issue his tenants with writs of eviction. The people decided to resist. Men armed with sticks, and women with stones in their aprons, they besieged a local inn where police officers were sheltering. Eventually the British Army was sent to restore order.

Despite the bleak setting, it's hard to imagine a mob of angry women trooping past with boulders held in their aprons. We soon learned that more peaceful people were also associated with this place. As we passed the village hall on a lonely section of road, we were astonished to see a signpost to the John Lennon Memorial. I couldn't believe Angus had suggested a sheep-infested golf course, and not mentioned a memorial to the most famous Beatle. A sign inside the memorial garden informed us that John had spent a number of childhood holidays in Durness between the ages of 9 and 16, and that he was certain to have been thinking of the village when he penned the lyrics to 'In My Life'. Sadly the memorial itself was instantly forgettable: just three crude vertical slabs of slate and a couple of rough logs. Luckily somebody with a sense of humour had left a small garden gnome there, to at least give us something to remember about it.

We continued on to Smoo Cave. As we approached I realised that I had no idea what a smoo was, and therefore what we could expect to find there. It sounded like a creature out of Lewis Carroll's *The Hunting of the Snark*, and I wondered if the cave would turn out to be the home of the frumious bandersnatch. That didn't help much, for nor did I have much idea what a bandersnatch looked like. I knew it had wings, a long neck, and a jaw that snapped, but that only conjured up the image of a goose. I took my phone out and googled *smoo*. I was embarrassed to read in the Urban Dictionary that it was a slang term for female genitalia. This would have been news to the nice lady in the information centre at Durness, who had given us a map and didn't blush when I asked her how to find it. Eventually I discovered the more likely explanation was that the word *smoo* was derived from an old Norse word *smuga*, which meant 'hiding place'.

After a short walk along the coastline and a scramble along a tongue of rocks jutting into the sea, we doubled back along the cliffs into a sheltered bay, where a giant limestone archway formed the roof of Smoo Cave. The main cave was quite homely, around 60m deep, 40m wide and 15m high. It must have felt warm and safe to any prehistoric settlers, as long as the sea didn't trespass in too far. A covered walkway led into two more side chambers, the first of which was home to Smoo Cave's most impressive feature: a hefty 20m waterfall crashing down from above. The inner caves were entirely waterlogged, and unlike the main cave, which had been carved by the sea, the action of freshwater had created both these caves. We could go no further on foot. A local company was running boat trips, which seemed to involve paddling out 6m to the foot of the waterfall, then paddling back again.

Edita wasn't impressed. 'The cave is OK', she said, 'but they make such a big deal of these things.'

I guess when you've been to the Himalayas and seen Tolkienesque cascades roaring down gargantuan cliffs in every valley, then most caves and waterfalls are a bit dull.

We were intrigued to know where the waterfall came from, so, after climbing back up to the car park, we crossed the road and found the burn that fed it. It was as impressive as the cave (which by Edita's reckoning wasn't very). A seemingly minor stream disappeared into the ground in a powerful cascade. But apart from us and a rotund lady – who I couldn't help observing could have become wedged had she fallen down the hole, stopping the water flowing altogether – none of the hundreds of people we saw in the cave were coming to look.

I woke up the next morning in a positive frame of mind, knowing that we only had the easy north and east coasts ahead of us. Had I known what was coming that day, I may well have turned around and cycled back the way we had come.

We found the stretch of coastline immediately east of Durness pleasant, with rugged cliffs and sandy bays. After four miles, the road took a giant loop inland to skirt around a sea loch, Loch Eriboll. From the western shore we had a fine view of Ben Hope, the most northerly Munro, rising across the water. Desolate and isolated like a volcano, it wouldn't have looked out of place in Ecuador's Central Highlands.

My principal impression of this peak was of the Welsh

comedian Griff Rhys Jones, climbing it in a blizzard with outdoor writer Cameron McNeish in the BBC documentary series *Mountain*.

There is a well-known story of the Reverend Archibald Robertson, the first man to complete the Munros in 1901. His final Munro was Meall Dearg on the Aonach Eagach ridge in Glen Coe, which he climbed with his wife Kate and good friend Sandy Moncrieff. As every sensible mountaineer should, they carried a bottle of champagne up with them to toast their success on the summit. With this important ritual completed, Robertson shyly admitted in his diary that 'Sandy made me first kiss the cairn and then my wife'.[26]

As they arrived on the summit of Ben Hope in the BBC documentary, Cameron recounted the story to Griff, and invited him to kiss the summit cairn, which in this case was an Ordnance Survey pillar composed of concrete and metal.

'What happens if you kiss in these conditions is that you end up with your tongue stuck,' Griff said as the snow swirled around them.

'You don't have to use your tongue,' Cameron politely explained.

It may have seemed an epic ascent to Griff, but when Sir Hugh Munro himself climbed the peak in 1898, he reached the summit from Kinloch on its east side in just 2 hours and 40 minutes. He said that he didn't know 'any mountain of the height (3,040ft) which can be climbed with less exertion'.[27] This was a full 18 years after Whymper and the Carrels had explored Ecuador, but they could have told him that over there 3,040ft wasn't even a mountain.

Our road passed through bleak, treeless moorland, broken only by an oasis of pine trees that sheltered the rambling village of Laid, with its dozen or so properties spread along the lochside. The landscape had an air of loneliness about it, as if we were passing through Arctic tundra. Nevertheless, the amount of traffic surprised us.

On the eastern side of the loch we were overtaken by a rainstorm and had to put on our ponchos. The lochside section ended with a steep climb before turning inland. We whizzed downhill, but the respite was short-lived as we began to climb one of the most soul-destroying hills of the entire circuit, up over a featureless grassy plateau. The first part was too steep to cycle up. I got off to push. The gradient lessened, and I was able to get back on the bike, but the hill ground ceaselessly over a series of bends and false summits. Exhaustion set in. Several times I had to stop for snacks, but the hill just kept on going. I kept pedalling, painfully slowly in bottom gear, with a horizon just 50m in front of me – but which moved further away with every turn of the pedals.

Cycling around Loch Eriboll with Ben Hope across the water

Eventually the boredom became intolerable, and I lost my temper with the mobile horizon.

'Fuck off, you stupid road. For fuck's sake, get me over

this sodding hill.'

It's not easy to be eloquent in the throes of exhaustion.

I put on a burst of speed, thinking I was near the top, but this only made the horizon move more quickly. Edita cycled behind me, trying not to laugh.

There was worse to come. The summit passed with a wave of relief, but I discovered to my horror that there was a furious headwind on the other side, and a slope so gentle that we had no reward for our toil. In a nutshell, it was another one of those fiendish hills, hellspawn of the devil, that you have to pedal *down* again. Far to the right, Ben Hope and Ben Loyal rose up like beacons across the featureless grassland, but I couldn't care less if they started kicking their legs in the air and dancing the can-can. I was in no position to appreciate the scenery.

The road dropped to a long causeway across the shallow estuary of the Kyle of Tongue. I looked at my watch. It was ten to two. On the other side of the estuary was the village of Tongue, which a perkier me might have associated with Griff Rhys Jones licking a cairn at the top of Ben Hope. At that moment, my only thought was that the village contained a pub that would be certain to stop serving lunch at two. It was so close, but I knew I wasn't going to get there in 10 minutes. My legs were gone. Even here on the flat, in the lowest gear, I had to pedal hard to make any progress. I pleaded with Edita to go on ahead and order food.

'But why would they stop serving food at two?'

'I don't know,' I replied. 'It's a pub. They just do.'

I watched her disappear ahead of me with impossible speed. I nearly cried when I reached the first hotel and saw that she had cycled right past it and was miles down the road.

I struggled on towards the village, the four granite buttresses of Ben Loyal rising before me. This was another peak I had identified as one we might climb on one of our rest days. Fat chance now. Those four fingers of rock were like a double dose of V-signs giving me the two-fingered salute.

'Up yours, Horrell,' they were saying.

A few minutes later I pedalled up another short hill, and saw Edita's bike parked outside the Ben Loyal Hotel.

Walking inside was like walking into heaven. There was a warm fire, comfy chairs, and – best of all – Edita had bought me a bottle of Punk IPA. For over an hour the morning toil was forgotten as I rehydrated, warmed myself, and filled my body with hot food. I could feel the energy seeping back into me, and my mood lightened.

We left at 3.45 for the last 20km to Bettyhill. But my resolve was about to be punctured like a tyre going pop – appropriately enough, for as I unlocked my bike and wheeled it onto the road, just as I was lifting my leg over the saddle, I glanced down at the back wheel.

The tyre was completely flat.

Not just soft; not somewhat deflated. It was as airless as a vacuum bag. Suddenly my morning toils were put into context. How far had I cycled with my 56-litre saddlebags pushing down on this thin layer of rubber? No wonder every turn of the pedals had been a struggle.

I had pumped up the tyre every morning since discovering the slow puncture at Clachtoll Beach three days earlier. I had prayed it would last till Inverness, but now I had to accept the inevitable. Edita had seen a garage on the way into the village. We pedalled back down the road to see if they knew anything about bikes. Edita lifted the wheel off easily without troubling the gears. Three mechanics took 20 minutes to remove the tyre and change the inner tube. It was clear they'd never been asked to change a bicycle tyre before, but it was a quiet afternoon for them, and they were cheerful about it. They weren't even going to charge us until I asked the price.

'Oh… ah, call it a fiver,' the oldest one said.

I gave him a tenner as Edita replaced the wheel on the bike and packed away the cycle repair kit beneath the saddle.

It was 4.30 when we continued. I felt satisfied, but it was late in the afternoon, and I had no inkling that we were about to face the road to hell.

My memory of what followed is indistinct. There was one upbeat moment, when a driver coming the other way wound down his window and offered us biscuits, but otherwise it was hill after hill across bleak, windswept moorland.

For one terrifying moment a side wind buffeted me as I was tearing down a hill. A sheen of water glistened the road, and I could feel a car on my right shoulder, like the Grim Reaper breathing down my neck. We were going so fast there was no way the car could stop if I came off the bike. I was a whisker from death. I dared not squeeze the brakes for fear of losing control. For a few brief seconds I battled the wind, knowing that my life depended on keeping the bike in a straight line. I felt like a cowboy trying to break a wild horse. We reached a dip, and the car overtook me as I allowed my bike to slow to a halt. Edita shot past, oblivious of the danger I'd been in.

I pulled in to the side of the road and closed my eyes as I waited for my panicked breaths to subside. I was still alive, but I knew it was only by luck. I had been in many dangerous situations on mountains but never had I felt so helpless before.

Some of the hills that followed were too steep to cycle up. I have no recollection of reaching the top of the last one. All I remember is steaming down the other side, the side wind buffeting me as traffic roared past. I was physically and mentally exhausted. My brain was somewhere outside my body, watching me with only half an eye – just enough for me to realise that my situation was beyond dangerous. I could see that the hill was too long, and there was no way I could allow the bike to accelerate to a suicidal velocity. I pinched the brakes just enough to slow down without coming off. When I reached the bottom I skidded to a halt on a grassy verge, heart beating like a drum. I parked my bike and fell down on my back, unable to do anything more.

I don't know how long I lay there, or whether I fell asleep. After a span of time – which could have been for ever – I heard Edita's voice behind me. She offered me water and food, and said she would pitch the tent when we got to Bettyhill. It was soothing, and I was grateful. She started asking me questions. I kept my eyes closed as I mumbled back my answers.

'What are you saying?' she asked.

'Walking is a lot safer than cycling.'

'What are your last words?'

'They're not my last words, my love. Don't worry, I'm not dead yet.'

Then she said something that brought my brain back into my body with a jolt:

'I'm trying to record this for memory.'

My eyes opened and my head popped up like bread from a toaster.

'What – you're not videoing me are you? You're not videoing me? That's cruel. That's heartless.'

But Edita was laughing, and suddenly life didn't seem so bad. Apart from a pair of sore legs and a dented ego, there was no harm done. I stood up and had a snack. I hoped it would provide enough energy for the last wee push. It was 6.15, and there were two more miles to Bettyhill. I took them slowly, but comfortably.

The village sprawled along the mouth of the River Naver. Despite the peaceful setting, the campsite was a disappointment, just a few temporary homes pitched above a farmer's field. After the busy sites on the west coast, this one was almost deserted – we saw just two other tents pitched there. The toilets were filthy, but the shower worked. There appeared to be no reception area, and I paid our money to a farmer standing near a gate at the top, who told me that the campsite belonged to his mother.

It had been a beast of a day. Some people might call it a fiasco. I'd had enough of this damn bike ride; but we still had four more days.

As I lay in my sleeping bag, I pondered how poorly equipped I must be for cycling from sea to summit on Chimborazo if I couldn't even pedal around the coast of Scotland. This was brought home to me by one of the many messages of 'encouragement' that Edita received in response to the photo updates she was posting to Facebook. One of these was from Lloyd, whom I'd climbed Aconcagua with 12 years earlier. He had a connection with the North Coast 500 and decided to post a message of support.

'Happy memories – this time last year we spent a wonderful week cycling the NC500.'

This well-meaning message had arrived during our afternoon of rest and relaxation in Durness, and probably didn't elicit the response that Lloyd expected.

'A week? We've been at it more than a week already, and we're only as far as Durness,' I wrote back.

'Oops!' Lloyd replied. 'Yes, it took us 5 whole days plus two half days at either end. Wonderful!! The only really long day we had was from Bettyhill to Helmsdale. I trust you stopped at the hot chocolate place in Durness? Mmm…'

Oops indeed. In my consternation I didn't even register that there was a hot chocolate place in Durness, which was now a hard day's cycle ride behind us. As I pondered in a tent over 60km away, I had visions of lying in a hot spring on a grassy hillside, relaxing in a steaming bath of dark Belgian chocolate. The John Lennon Memorial could peace off.

But that wasn't my main concern. When we started planning the North Coast 500, we had allowed ourselves two full weeks, believing that it would give us so many contingency days that we'd even be able to pop up a couple of peaks on the way round. It was now becoming abundantly clear that not only were our legs too tired from pedalling to get us any great distance on our feet, but that we'd pretty much need all of those two weeks just to complete the circuit.

On current estimates, we – a pair of Everest summiteers – were due to pedal into Inverness on day 13, yet here was an old friend telling me that he and his wife had breezed their way round in less than half the time. It didn't seem possible. What did the Lloyds have that we didn't? Perhaps they didn't have huge great panniers of hiking and camping equipment? Maybe they had better bikes, and cycled for hours longer every evening? Or perhaps they were just regular cyclists, with proper cyclist's leg muscles? I decided to put all these things to Lloyd and wait for his answers.

There was a look of resignation on my face when I woke up in the tent at Bettyhill. My legs were weary and my buttocks sore, but more than anything my heart was deflated after yesterday's breakdown – I'd left any remaining enthusiasm for this trip beside that patch of gorse on the side of the road. The thought of getting back on the bike and pedalling for another full day left me feeling despondent. Edita noticed that look.

'You don't want to be here, do you?' she said. Her gentle tone expressed compassion rather than anger.

'Just four days left. Don't worry, I'm not about to give up.'

'Maybe we could even do it in three?' Edita said.

'If we could reach John O'Groats tonight, then maybe we can do it in three. It would be great to spend the night in John O'Groats, but judging by yesterday's performance, there's no chance of that.'

'What's special about John O'Groats?'

'It's the furthest point in Britain.'

'Furthest from what?'

'Er… that's a good question. I guess it's the furthest point from Land's End,' I replied, knowing perfectly well what question was going to come next.

'What's Land's End?'

'It's a place in Cornwall.'

Edita knew where Cornwall was, because it's where my father is from, and she'd been there, but I knew this answer on its own wasn't going to do.

'Land's End is in the far south-west, and John O'Groats is in the far north-east. They're the two places in mainland Britain the furthest away from each other. They are both famous pilgrimage sites for walkers and cyclists. One of life's great challenges for British people is to walk or bike all the way from Land's End to John O'Groats in one go.'

'Cool,' Edita said.

She looked genuinely excited, and it wouldn't have surprised me had she suggested there and then to do it ourselves, but happily she realised that now wasn't a good time.

'Well, if we can't reach John O'Groats today, we can stop

for a photo on our way through tomorrow.'

'Yes, let's do that. There's one of those signposts that says "Land's End 874 miles, New York 3000, the North Pole 1500".' Then I added, for good measure, 'Vilnius 1000.'

'They have Vilnius on the signpost? Then we have to stop there.'

If not John O'Groats, then I hoped we could reach Dunnet that day – at 65km, a similar distance to yesterday. I didn't expect to be cycling any long hills with a flat tyre, but if comparable in physical difficulty then it was going to be another long and tedious day. To cope with the ordeal, I resolved to stop looking upon this trip as a holiday, and instead regard it as a training exercise. Only then, I believed, would I be able to tolerate what was to come.

Relentless hills confronted us on the first part of the morning's ride. We biked up, then freewheeled down. I was beyond feeling sorry for myself, and just got on with it, but I knew that if it remained like that all day then, once again, it would slowly grind me down until I could pedal no more. On the positive side, we had the best weather of the trip that day, with clear skies and not much wind.

The scenery was becoming gradually less dramatic. We passed across heather-clad moorland, but the high mountains were gone. I stopped for another lie down by the side of the road at the top of a hill above Strathy Point. Rugged coastline stretched out before us. A bleak wind blew from the Arctic over cliffs as waves crashed against the shore. I was tired already, but otherwise enjoying the clear skies, and we had our first sighting of the coast of the Orkney Islands, 50km away.

After this, the landscape became decidedly dreary. Highlights of the next section included Dounreay nuclear power plant, and miles of straight and featureless road looking across ploughed fields. The smell of manure was overpowering. I was reminded of Cornwall as we rolled down the hill into Thurso, a gloomy fishing port of 8,000 people that is north-west Scotland's equivalent of Barcelona (I expect they say in their tourist brochures). More truthfully, it lies as far north as Juneau, the capital of Alaska. In 2018, its ferry port of Scrabster hit the headlines when a woman was reported to have been taped to a chair and gagged by male colleagues for complaining about office bullying. It wasn't a town to inspire the imagination. Disappointingly, given its privileged coastal location, there was no seafront promenade of pubs, restaurants and coffee shops. With the help of our guidebook, Edita brought us to the Café Tempest, seemingly Thurso's only sea-view eating house, set among grey concrete buildings beside a harbour-front car park.

On our way out of Thurso, our plans changed when we saw a sign reading 20 miles (or about 32km) to John O'Groat's. As was my custom, I stopped for a butt rest in a gateway a mile or two further out of town to give my sore cheeks a bit of a break.

'You know what I'm thinking?' Edita said when she pulled alongside me. 'We should push on to John O'Groats this afternoon. We still have plenty of time.'

It was true. It was still early afternoon. I believed the road ahead to be relatively flat. Even so, it's best not to commit to these things too early.

'Let's see what we're feeling like when we reach Dunnet Bay,' I said.

But Edita was right. Already we could see the coastline of Dunnet Bay ahead of us, where the land curved north to Dunnet Head, the most northerly point on mainland Britain. The road was smooth and we were racing. I was up to my highest gear, and my legs pressed easily against the force of the pedals. Never on the entire cycle ride had I felt so much energy pulsing through me – an extravagant contrast to the previous day.

At 4.15 we raced past the campsite in Dunnet Bay, in a tranquil setting beside a pristine beach with grassy dunes. The rest of the afternoon passed quickly. Things are so much easier when the roads are flat. Regular signposts informed us of our progress as we counted down the distance to John O'Groats. Then we saw the last corner of Britain's coastline swing round to our left. The land sloped gently down towards the Pentland Firth, the stretch of water dividing the Orkneys from the mainland. We could see villages on the hillside, and I guessed the last one must be John O'Groats. It spurred me on.

We passed through the penultimate village, Huna, which is named after the Gaelic word for throwing up on a roadside. It was here that two brothers, Robert and John Naylor, came in 1871, believing themselves to be the first people to walk from one corner of Britain to the other. They stopped for a night at the Huna Inn, and were handed a visitor book, where they read the following nonsense rhyme:

I went in a boat
To see John o' Groat,
The place where his home doth lie;
But when I got there,
The hill was all bare,
And the devil a stone saw I.[28]

John O'Groats has a legendary status among long-distance hikers and cyclists, being the northernmost point of the 'End to End', as the Land's End to John O'Groats challenge is sometimes known. Even in 1871 John O'Groats' fame spread far and wide, and received travellers from all over the world. Many expressed consternation that, having come all this way, there was bugger all to see.

It's a feeling that persists to this day. Having built John O'Groats up myself, I was certainly conscious that there would be nothing much to see apart from a signpost that didn't even have Vilnius on it. I wished we hadn't had that conversation in the tent earlier in the morning.

A couple of kilometres beyond Huna, we left the main road on a corner and descended a short hill down to the waterside. However innocuous John O'Groats might prove to be, it felt like a defining moment, with the coastline ahead of us and the Orkney Islands across the firth. We saw two men coming up the other way on touring bikes.

'Not long to go now,' I said to them.

'Idiot,' I expect they said to themselves after I cycled past.

I did wonder why they were starting their End to End this late in the afternoon. With John O'Groats renowned for being situated in the arse end of nowhere (as the saying goes), it was likely to be a while before they reached the next place.

Thankfully John O'Groats had a little more to offer than the author of the nonsense rhyme in Huna's visitor book had promised. There were some tourist chalets, a hotel with a spire, a campsite, a few shops, and a ferry terminal over to Orkney. There was no residential property, but that didn't matter. We were pleasantly surprised to find the campsite quiet. We camped at the top of a cliff looking out over the sea, with South Ronaldsay, the southernmost of the Orkneys, just a stone's throw away across the water. It was a beautiful evening. The soft blues of the Pentland Firth matched the colour of the sky, and light bands of cloud provided some contrast. A gentle sea breeze deterred many of the midges, though a few persistent blighters pestered us as we erected the tent.

'This is a famous pilgrimage site for the Brits,' I said to Edita as we took our obligatory selfie beneath the signpost.

'Many of us never come here, and here you are on your first visit to Scotland.'

'I'm happy to be here,' she replied.

And she was. She hadn't even complained that Vilnius wasn't listed. New York was the only overseas destination that made the cut.

The village seemed strangely quiet for a warm evening in August, but for us that was a good thing. Perhaps End-to-Ending was no longer as popular as I'd thought. Apart from the ferry to Orkney, there weren't too many reasons for coming here. Even the shops and restaurants were hiding away, and we explored most of the site before we found John O'Groats' only bar, Slacks, tucked away among the chalets. It had a good vibe; we stuffed ourselves with pork belly and some fine local beers in a relaxing atmosphere.

I thanked Edita for encouraging us to push further today. We had covered 80km, by far our longest day, and we'd completed the afternoon's ride from Thurso at a pace I never believed possible. Now I was feeling positive about the ride again. There was one simple reason for this turnaround: hills. There hadn't been any, and I prayed for more of the same in the days ahead.

As we sat at the table, I checked my phone and discovered a reply from Lloyd, explaining how he had managed to complete his circuit of the North Coast 500 so quickly. I read it out to Edita as we munched on our pork crackling.

'Hi Mark. We used our road bikes, with panniers fitted – so we did it unsupported, carrying all our own kit. However, our big advantage was that we were staying in B&Bs, so we didn't have to carry tents.'

'I knew it. Our saddlebags make such a big difference,' Edita said. 'It's not just the tent. We've got sleeping bags, mats, pots and stove. I've got my trek towel and toiletries as well.'

'Yeah, and our walking gear. I'm carrying a thirty-five litre rucksack folded up and Gore-Tex that I've never used. But even so, I'm impressed by their stamina. Listen to this: "We were usually cycling before nine and a typical day saw us cover eighty miles, which is probably about six hours cycling. So with loads of coffee and food stops we usually finished by five. Our one long day from Bettyhill to south of Helmsdale was over a hundred and ten miles – got there after seven!" Bloody hell,' I said.

It took me a few seconds to absorb the full import of this. Lloyd's days were essentially the same length as ours. He wasn't cycling for more hours. He just cycled more quickly than we did. More precisely, by completing it in 6 days to our likely 12 or 13, they were cycling twice as quickly; 80 miles a day was nearly 130km. We were delighted with the 80km we'd done today, but Lloyd's biggest day had been 110 miles, or nearly 180km. It made my head swim.

'Wow, they cycled a long way every day,' Edita said. 'They must be fit. Are they young?'

'Are they bollocks. Lloyd's older than I am. And he's got a bald head like I have. But they do a lot of cycling. Here: "And yes, we both enjoy cycling and often go out for twenty or thirty miles in the evening, or cycle forty miles on Sunday morning to find somewhere for lunch, then forty miles home again. Hope you are enjoying it – the north-west corner above Lochinver is simply wonderful."'

'That last bit was nice,' Edita said.

'Yes, he needed to say how nice the scenery was, to show that he has a life, and isn't just a cycling machine.'

This confirmed to me what I suspected: that I was rubbish at cycling because I didn't do enough of it. While Lloyd's reply underlined just how rubbish I was, in one respect it was also encouraging. It suggested that our two-week bike ride around north-west Scotland was having an effect, and that by the time we reached Ecuador we would be stronger cyclists.

I could hit the east coast in good heart.

9 THE EAST COAST AND BEYOND

The day started full of promise. The forecast was for heavy rain, but the sun was shining and we gazed across to the Orkneys as we devoured a bacon, sausage and egg sandwich from a van beside the pier. After the previous day's 80km, including the 30 or so we'd raced in the afternoon, we were bullish about the distances we could manage now that the big hills were behind us. We aimed to cycle 100km all the way down the east coast to Brora, close to the Dornoch Firth. It was an ambitious plan, but if we pushed ourselves then we believed we could reach Inverness in two days, instead of three.

End-to-Enders leaving John O'Groats bound for Land's End, 874 miles away, must be discouraged by the start of their cycle ride. There was a gentle hill out of John O'Groats that continued for several miles. The land was completely featureless: not a single tree, and hardly a hedgerow, broke the monotony of bleak moorland that soon became ploughed fields. We passed through landscape and villages that made the scenery in a gym seem inspiring. Had I not had a bike saddle wedged up my crack then I might have fallen asleep. I pushed along in the higher gears and counted down the miles, but I didn't realise that, little by little, I was grinding away my energy.

The town of Wick passed by in a blur – not because we were pedalling so fast, but because my mind was dazed – and the town seemed like a giant smudge on a shadowy canvas of despair. It was 11.30 when we stopped for a snack at a grassy verge on the other side of town. A few metres away a road sign read 'Brora 46', and it was then that reality struck. The 46 was miles, not kilometres. We had come just 17. Most of the morning had vanished in a haze and we were less than a third of the distance.

More to the point, I was knackered.

Not long after this I experienced what I believe Americans call *bonking*. This is not the same as what Brits call bonking which, let's be honest, I wouldn't have had the energy for. My speed had dropped dramatically. I could only cycle short distances before stopping for a butt rest and some snacks. Edita (who was absolutely fine) waited patiently at every stop; she even tried breaking wind for me, but I couldn't remotely keep up with her.

My difficulties weren't just physical. Part of the problem was that my heart was no longer in it. I'd been struggling with the cycling all along. It hadn't mattered in the first part of the trip, passing heather-clad mountains painted pink, cycling alongside intricate coastline rocked by the ocean waves. However much I suffered, I could look around at the sweeping moorland, peaceful lochs, or emerald islands rising above the swell, and my spirit would be lifted.

Now we seemed to be passing through one of the dullest parts of Britain. If the North Coast 500 were a roomful of snooker players, we had reached Steve Davis, and were now quite unable to get away as he spent the morning telling us how to play safety shots. The land was featureless, but not so featureless that we didn't have to pedal up hills. And the land was the exciting bit – the villages were so dreary that if I'd bothered to take any photographs I would still have forgotten what they looked like. Grey concrete bungalow followed grey concrete bungalow. I pictured people sitting inside them watching the Highland version of *EastEnders*, wearing grey kilts and listening to drilling noises on the radio. There were no facilities anywhere. We cycled for 20km without seeing a single shop, café, pub, or any sort of commercial premises. There was no feeling of community. If I lived in such a place then I would have to repeatedly paint the walls of my bedroom and watch them dry again to keep myself entertained.

Only the names of some of the villages kept me sane: Humster, Thrumster, Ulbster, Occumster. I passed the time by dreaming up more: Hamster, Hipster, Lobster, Gangster... Prankster, Polyester, Sandblaster, Stationmaster. But the game stopped being fun when I got to Sinister, Twister, Disaster, Weatherforecaster and finally Sou'wester.

The forecast rain had not materialised, but the sky was darkening. We looked for shelter and a place to stop for lunch. For mile after mile there was nothing. Eventually, with relief, we reached the village of Lybster – a place that looked large enough for a pub. At the edge of the village a sign read 'tourist facilities'.

Briefly my spirits lifted, but they soon sank beyond despair. A big grey hotel loomed up on the corner ahead of us. It was boarded up. We turned into the village and cycled down the main street of dull stone buildings. Two more pubs and a B&B had also closed down. The streets were deserted. I expected any minute to see tumbleweed drifting across the road.

'This is a strange place,' Edita said. 'Perhaps we should ask someone to recommend somewhere.'

But it didn't seem strange to me. It just looked poor: one of the forgotten places that had been left behind, with no jobs, nothing to do, and little hope. We were just a short drive from Ullapool on the west coast, but could have been in a different world. I remembered the Czech and Polish bar staff in the Ferry Boat Inn, who had travelled the length of Europe for jobs, and believed they had arrived in paradise. In some ways they had. But here, just a couple of hours' drive away, the economy had collapsed, and the few businesses had closed down. I wondered if anyone thought of moving to the west coast in search of jobs. The tourist industry seemed to be thriving there.

At the end of the village a bus stopped as I cycled past, and half a dozen people stepped into the road without bothering to check for traffic. I slammed on my brakes to avoid riding into them. They walked in front of me. There was no apology, not even an acknowledgement. All I saw were faces devoid of awareness. They probably didn't even notice I was there.

Back at the top end of the village, we did find one tourist service that was open: a public convenience where we could fill our water bottles. The sky was darkening, and Edita suggested we put on ponchos.

'Or we could shelter in the toilets until the storm passes,' she said.

'But it's not raining yet. Let's press on and see how far we can get before it does.'

The last place I wanted to spend my afternoon was inside a public toilet in Lybster, and our diversion into the village had left us even less likely to reach Brora that day. But we soon regretted our decision to cycle on.

We had barely made it out of the village when the storm finally caught us. It was sudden, like the woman throwing slops over the minstrel in Whymper's engraving. We swerved into a side road and put on our ponchos – the work of a minute, perhaps a minute and a half, but before we even started on the road again the rain was bouncing off puddles and had turned the air into a wall of water. Cars sheeted past and sliced buckets of the stuff onto our legs. Had we ridden into a sea loch we could not be wetter.

'This is crazy. It's dangerous to go on. The cars cannot see us,' Edita said.

'What can we do? We can't stay here and drown. We'll be freezing. If you like I will cycle at the back so that they see me first.'

We got back on the bikes and pedalled through puddle after puddle as traffic hared past, slarting more water over us. Soon there were no longer puddles and the road was just one continuous sheet of rain. My poncho carried a pond of its own within its folds.

About 3km beyond Lybster I glanced to the right and saw a sign at the end of a driveway.

'Forse of Nature, Craft Shop and Café.'

Having cycled for over 20km without even a sniff of commercial premises, I couldn't quite believe my eyes. Was this some sort of reverse oasis: an imaginary dry place to taunt the sodden traveller when all around was rain?

Another sign on the opposite gatepost was even more alluring.

'Open Today, 10am to 6pm.'

I screamed at Edita, who had by now cycled far beyond. She turned around, and I gestured frantically for her to come back.

'There's nothing up there. There can't be,' she said when she arrived back at the gatepost.

We were looking up a long, dark driveway, lined with trees on either side. It stretched into the distance, and there appeared to be no end to it.

'Maybe you're right, but what have we got to lose?' I said with the air of a man passing a door marked 'Eunuchs only'.

Edita needed some convincing to cycle up it. Twice she

stopped as the rain pounded around us, but I insisted we keep pedalling. After 1km, the driveway turned a corner to the right, and we found ourselves at the door of a whitewashed, four-storey stately home. There was no sign that it might harbour a café.

'It's a private house,' Edita said. 'A posh one. They're not going to let tramps like us inside.'

I cycled across a sizeable forecourt and around the side of the house. There, like a beacon of hope, I found a small one-storey extension and the sign I had been dreaming of for the last kilometre.

'Forse of Nature, Craft Shop and Café.'

There was even a cycle rack. I was too relieved to congratulate myself.

As we parked our bikes in the driving rain, a genial lady opened the door and greeted us.

'Are you OK? Come in, we're open.'

I couldn't imagine they were expecting anyone today – least of all a pair of idiots on bikes – but here we were, and they welcomed us. She brought us towels, and allowed us to bring our panniers inside to keep them out of the rain. We were ushered into the warm and cosy craft-shop-cum-café where we hung our coats by a radiator.

Truly we had entered a sanctuary from the storm. The place appeared to belong to a family: husband, wife, son and daughter. The son made us coffee and toasted sandwiches while the lady who had greeted us described the house. It had existed since the 18th century, and until the early 20th century had been owned by the Sutherland family. Since then it had been a poorhouse, a care home and a hotel. As well as the craft shop and café, it was now a wedding venue, offering bespoke accommodation for any size of party in the various wings of the house. She told us that most of this part of Scotland had been hit by the tail of Hurricane Pisspot (I forget its real name, but it was something along those lines), and that the rain was likely to last all afternoon.

Although it wasn't yet two o'clock, cycling the remaining 50km to Brora in this waterfall seemed like lunacy. I was sure we would be swept to sea.

'You know there's a long hill into Brora,' she said when I told her our plans.

I didn't, but I might have guessed.

From our haven of tranquillity, I peered through the glass into the storm outside. The rain was now falling with such force it bounced off the tarmac like ping-pong balls. If it continued like that all afternoon, then we'd need oars to make any progress.

Yet it didn't occur to us to abort the day's cycle ride and treat ourselves to a night in that lovely place. Having camped every night so far, that would have felt like failure with only a couple more nights to go. It seemed that our only option was to wait for a lull in the storm and cycle the remaining 8km to Dunbeath, where there was another campsite that we had dismissed as too close when we discussed our options that morning.

We ordered more coffee, as well as scones with jam and cream, and settled in for the afternoon. The lull eventually came around three o'clock. By then the ping-pong balls had stopped bouncing; the rain seemed to be falling more like confetti in a churchyard. We thanked our hosts for their kindness, and left what had truly been an oasis of calm, and a shaft of sunlight in the drab world around it.

But the lull only seemed like a lull from indoors. During the short time that we had been sheltering inside, the long driveway had turned into something resembling a river. Our bike wheels sliced through an inch of water, but the trees on either side kept us sheltered from the worst of the storm that still raged. As soon as we turned back onto the main road, a headwind struck us with full force, tossing buckets of rain back into our faces.

I pedalled onwards with my head down, forcing a passage through the wind, and carrying a puddle of water in my lap as I held the poncho over my knees. Behind me, Edita was cackling manically.

'I love it,' she cried. 'I'm loving this.'

I believed she was telling the truth. Hardship is her thing. Despite her enthusiasm, I remained steadfastly grumpy. I didn't have to try very hard.

At last the campsite at Dunbeath appeared on the right as the road descended to a bay. There was a yellow-washed private house; it looked like we would be camping on somebody's neatly manicured lawn. I knocked on the door labelled 'Reception'. A man led me into his kitchen to complete the paperwork, but he didn't seem to mind that I was dripping the remains of Hurricane Pisspot onto his carpet. The camp facilities were as good as, if not better than, many of the commercial campsites we had stayed at. The shower was a private bathroom, with super power shower. This was especially welcome in our drowned and dishevelled state.

We wrestled to put the tent up in the driving wind, but once inside we were cosy and warm again. I have been in many worse storms than that one, and it never ceases to surprise me how tents can be such places of sanctuary and security amid the worst of them. Edita had been carrying a feast since passing a supermarket in Thurso. As the storm gently abated we tucked in to lasagne and a precious bottle of Abruzzo Montepulciano inside the tent.

The demons crept back in as I slept. Once again I awoke

with that same feeling of resignation I had felt in Bettyhill. The road beyond the campsite plunged steeply as it curved around Dunbeath Bay and across a river. From the door of our tent we could see another long hill climbing up the other side, and the map showed me that between Dunbeath and Brora another range of mountains came down to the coast. The lady in the craft shop had told us there was a long hill into Brora, but it looked like there could be many. I yearned for the end in Inverness.

I pedalled slowly up the hill out of Dunbeath, trying not to tire myself so early in the day. For a short while beyond it we cycled high on a hillside overlooking the sea. The horizon to our left was littered with oil platforms, and the sun provided a silver sheen beneath them – a reminder that we had cycled from west to east and were no longer looking across the Atlantic, but the North Sea.

At Berriedale the road dropped steeply in a series of zigzags. It was much too steep to freewheel down, and another side wind petrified me. Once again the bike felt out of control. I squeezed the brakes hard, crawling down like a snail on skates. It seemed a waste of a good hill. To compound matters, immediately – without even having the decency to provide a 10m break – the road went straight up the other side on a 13 per cent incline. For a short while I tried to tackle it, but with each rotation of the pedals I could feel myself slowing down. I knew it was going to be a long day and I needed to conserve my energy, so I got off and pushed my bike uphill for half a mile as the traffic roared past.

More hills followed, but the road was wider and faster. We reached Helmsdale, nestling in a dip between hillsides where a river spills into the North Sea. It was planned as a resettlement community in the early 19th century for crofters who had been displaced during the Highland clearances.

Highland games were being staged as we cycled through. I zoomed past some bagpipers who were parading in a square (I don't often get to say that) and out the other side of the village.

As I hurtled across the A9 road bridge, I recalled that Helmsdale was the village where Lloyd and his wife had stayed after their epic 110-mile ride from Bettyhill. They'd got here after seven, Lloyd had said, which wasn't very late at all. We had taken two and a half days. The morning's ride from Dunbeath had been almost as mountainous as any section of the trip. I was tired already, but they had completed this part at the end of a 110-mile day. If I didn't know it already, this was my clearest indication yet that I was a shit cyclist.

We were down at sea level again and the road was flat. We passed a sign that read 'Brora 10'.

'It will be great if it's like this all the way to Brora,' Edita said.

'It would, but the lady at the craft shop said there was another big hill before Brora.'

'Perhaps it's the one we've passed.'

We had already passed several. A few seconds after finishing this conversation, we came to another. Then there were several more. On one of them, the wind lashed rain into our faces and I pedalled faster. This only made the rain beat against us harder. I slowed down again, then slumped in the saddle, exhausted.

We could see the village of Brora on a flat peninsula ahead of us. Our plan was to have lunch there, but once again I started bonking. I slowed to a crawl and stopped frequently for rests. The road was narrow and traffic sped past, pulling off some risky overtaking manoeuvres on the road ahead of me. One car only managed to get back in lane a few metres before reaching me. I was gritting my teeth and staring at the ground rather than the road ahead, and I didn't see it coming in my direction. This was probably a good thing – it would have scared the living daylights out of me. I was dimly aware that I was losing control of the bike, like I had on the road down to Bettyhill, and reaching dangerous levels of exhaustion.

I was desperate to reach Brora, but I knew it was too much.

'To hell with this,' I said as my pedals ground to a halt.

I mounted a grassy kerb and threw my bike down in disgust, without bothering to prop it up with its kickstand. I hurled myself on my back and lay there. My head was only inches from the road as traffic hurtled past, but I didn't care.

I rested for five minutes. Perhaps I fell asleep – I don't know – but once again I became aware of Edita's voice a few metres away. This time she was less sympathetic.

'Come on, get up. This is embarrassing.'

I ignored her, so she tried again.

'It's embarrassing. People will think you've had an accident, or you're dead or something. Please get up before you stop the traffic.'

I opened my eyes and sat up. She had parked her bike and was sitting next to me.

'Why do you keep doing this? It's embarrassing for me.'

'Because I'm exhausted. It's dangerous. I thought I was going to fall into the traffic. I had to stop. I don't care if it's embarrassing. It's better to be embarrassed than dead.'

This seemed to calm her. She offered me some snacks.

'Here, have some chocolate. Get some energy back. It's not far to Brora now. We can stop for some lunch, and you can rest.'

A few minutes later I had recovered enough to cycle slowly along the road into Brora. It was a sprawling village, and we cycled a long way through it before we found anywhere we could stop to eat. It was a relief to find the Sutherland Inn, which even had bike racks outside. I eyed the outdoor tables, but the sky threatened rain; I wondered if it was safe to leave the panniers outside.

I went in, and saw that the barman had a grand view of the bikes through a window in the bar.

'Aye, you can leave the bikes there,' he said. 'They'll be safe, and I'll keep a wee eye on them.'

We spent two hours recovering from our morning exertions with pints, coffee, and massive blue-cheese-and-bacon burgers. The barman was a machine. He appeared to be the only member of staff. He served at the bar, waited at tables, and kept an eye on our bikes. It wouldn't have surprised me to learn that he was popping into the kitchen to cook the food as well. Despite the busy pub, the service was still quick. He was some kind of super-barman.

As we waited for our burgers, we did some planning. We had been following the busy main road, the A9, since Wick, and it was beginning to grind us down. The sound of traffic rang in my ears like church bells (yes, as annoying as that). Cars roared past at speeds in excess of 100km/h, and with no decent cycle lanes they were often only inches from my right leg. This was dangerous and alarming, but we'd had no choice since John O'Groats. Now we were approaching more populated areas, alternative routes presented themselves.

We could avoid the A9 for most of tomorrow by taking a ferry across the Cromarty Firth and cycling across the Black Isle. But it looked like we could get off the A9 that afternoon if we took a short diversion off route and stayed the night in Dornoch, a small town at the mouth of the Dornoch Firth. Our guidebook described Dornoch as an upmarket resort with gourmet restaurants, a world-class golf course, and the odd celebrity sighting. By 'odd celebrity' I assumed they meant famous Highland fiddle players and champion cabertossers, so I was surprised to discover this included Madonna, who married the film director Guy Ritchie in nearby Skibo Castle. While the world-class golf course could happily sod off, the thought of gourmet restaurants had our appetite whetted after last night's dinner under tent nylon.

I don't know what our friend the super-barman put in his burgers, but when we got back on the bikes at 2.45 we raced the next six miles to Golspie, a posh village that was home to Dunrobin Castle. The castle's 19th-century owners were certainly not done with their robbing when they lived there. It was the place from which George Leveson-Gower, the 1st Duke of Sutherland, and his successors masterminded the Highland clearances. A 30m statue of the Duke of Sutherland stands on top of 397m Ben Bhraggie, a hill rising directly above the village. Not surprisingly, the statue is frequently vandalised. So would a sculpture of a giant hand raising an enormous 30m middle finger to the people down below.

We shot through the village and out the other side. Four miles later we turned off the A9 and onto the scenic coastal road around the tidal estuary of Loch Fleet. It was such a relief to be back on a single-track road again. For most of the last two days we had become accustomed to the sound of traffic hurtling past. Now, as we looked across the water to Ben Bhraggie and the other mountains we had cycled past, all was peaceful. There was no traffic; we could pedal along slowly, perfectly relaxed. If cycle touring could be like this all the time, instead of the grinding endurance test it had proved to be, then I could easily become a fan.

A short while later, we passed a car park by the side of the road where a handful of people were standing with binoculars, peering at some black smudges across the water.

'Wow, seals!' I cried.

Around thirty common seals were basking on a sand

bank a few metres offshore. I don't often like to spend my precious time watching something sleep, but for the next 10 minutes we did just that as the waves lapped the shore and a gentle breeze brushed our hair (at least it might have done if I'd taken my trousers off).

The seven miles to Dornoch were some of the most pleasant for days. We left the lochside to cycle up an easy hill, then zoomed down the other side into the town. Dornoch was a sleepy place of handsome stone houses. The campsite nestled among the sand dunes of the Dornoch Firth, and we found a private section hidden from the rest of camp by tall grasses. A stiff breeze meant the camp was midge free.

We had dinner in a curious stone folly on the main street called the Dornoch Castle Hotel. It didn't look like a real castle, and it certainly wouldn't have withstood much of an attack. I learned later that it was once a bishop's palace. We were just sitting down for a drink when a band of kilted bagpipers passed by along the street outside, and everyone rushed out for photos. A light rain was falling; the pipers stopped outside the entrance and marched on the spot.

'Wow, they must be cold,' Edita said. 'I guess this happens all the time in Scotland.'

It was the first time I'd seen it, but I was unable to convince her that this was no more normal than Morris dancers prancing around English villages waving handkerchiefs. We were told that the Dornoch Pipe Band parades through the town every Saturday throughout the summer.

We wandered back to the campsite at ten o'clock as darkness was falling. We were pleased with our diversion to Dornoch, and a lightness overcame me. I'd found our trip an ordeal, but we had nearly finished now – just one more day, one more sodding day, and this endurance hell would be over.

We left our campsite among the dunes at nine o'clock the following morning. The day began with a relaxing ride along a quiet back road. Back on the main road, we cycled across the wide coastal estuary of the Dornoch Firth on a long, flat bridge that resembled a causeway. We had joined National Cycle Route 1, which meant that finally, after nearly 500 miles of pedalling, we had a cycle lane. One metre of tarmac with a white line to divide us from traffic might not sound like much, but after two days of the busy A9, with traffic roaring past a fan's waft from my right thigh, it felt like having a police escort.

We reached a roundabout, and turned off onto quiet back roads again. A sign read 'Nigg Ferry 7'. We were making good time, but for the next seven miles I had a sinking feeling in the pit of my stomach. Despite the wide, flat and pleasant road, the land had a back-of-beyond feel – the sort of place where sheep have five legs and strange rituals take place in the woods. We passed no villages. I counted only three vehicles as we ambled along those country lanes for 11km. I'm sure I heard church bells tolling in their wake. We were heading to the southern tip of the Fearn Peninsula, from where we hoped to catch a ferry to Cromarty. During our trip-planning stage, I had checked the website of the Nigg to Cromarty ferry to confirm that it existed, but now I had the awful sense that we were heading for a dead end on a Sunday. There would be no ferry, and we'd have to pedal those 11km back again to rejoin the busy A9.

My feeling of gloom intensified when Nigg proved to be an industrial complex rather than a proper village with real homes and ordinary people. There was an oil-processing depot and a fabrication yard with giant cranes and warehouses. I expect on a weekday the site is bustling with oil workers, but on a Sunday it was desolate.

'I feel like we're about to cross the River Styx,' I said as we approached the end of the road. 'If this ferry's open then some boatman in a hooded robe is going to punt us across with a pole.'

'Let's just keep going,' Edita said. 'What else can we do?'

Then, an encouraging sign: a battered green VW camper van chugged past us.

'At least some other fool is going to share our journey to the underworld.'

'You see, it's open,' Edita said.

Sure enough, we reached the shoreline at the mouth of the Cromarty Firth, and saw a tiny red-and-white passenger ferry approaching the end of a concrete ramp. It was so small that the green camper van took up almost the entire deck. We barely had space to squeeze our bikes alongside, and for the next 10 minutes I had no choice but to have a conversation with the driver, a cheerful Dutchman whose face was a metre or so from mine.

'I don't think I have ever been on a ferry this small before,' he said.

'It's certainly the smallest ferry that I've ever seen,' I agreed.

It was an interesting conversation.

Cromarty is a neat little village of Georgian merchant houses on the shores of the Black Isle (which, despite its name, is not an island, but a peninsula dividing the Cromarty and Beauly Firths). There appeared to be no way out of it that didn't involve cycling up a hill. For a change Edita was now the one feeling short of energy. It was 11.30, so we stopped for an early lunch of bacon, egg and sausage sandwiches in a cosy little café. We left refreshed and looking forward to the last few hours to Inverness, but the Black Isle had other plans.

The whole peninsula seemed to be on a big plateau. After a steep ascent out of Cromarty on cobbles, we were faced with another gentle climb onto the plateau. To our right we looked across ploughed fields to the factories and refineries on the shores of the Cromarty Firth. I put my head down and ground my way up the hill, but Edita was intrigued by the structures to our right, and cycled behind me asking questions.

Mark on the Nigg-Cromarty ferry, with
just enough room for a camper van

'I wonder what they make.'

'What they bake? Bread I guess. But this looks like oil.'

'No, *make*, not *bake*. Do they come from Inverness, I wonder?

'Who?'

'The workers.'

'I don't know. I guess some do.'

'Do you know who it's for?'

'Do I know if who's a whore?'

'No, who it's for. What are the industries here?'

I pulled up into a gateway and took a few deep breaths.

'Look, I'm too tired for this. Either we can have a conversation about the local economy – I don't know much about it – or we can cycle, but I can't do both.'

She looked hurt. Without answering, she wheeled back into the road and kept cycling. I tried to keep up, but she was too quick for me. It was some time before she stopped for a butt rest and I was able to draw alongside.

'I'm sorry. I didn't mean to upset you,' I said. 'I'm tired, and I couldn't answer your questions.'

'Why do you have to be grumpy like that? I was in a good mood, and now you've spoiled it for no reason,' she said.

Before I could respond, she was on her way again. For the next hour I felt sad. The cycle ride had broken me physically a few days ago, and I had never quite recovered. Now it seemed to be breaking me mentally too. I was no longer enjoying it, and my demeanour had changed. I didn't feel like I was being grumpy; it felt more like tired resignation. Yet despite the hardships, Edita had remained perpetually cheerful, and there were moments when her high spirits rubbed off on me.

She was the one ray of light, but now my ill temper seemed to be casting its shadow. I couldn't wait for this damn bike ride to end. Then at last I could get back on my feet.

The road across the Black Isle was one of the most tedious of the whole trip, consisting of long straight sections a mile or two in length, mostly on a slight uphill gradient. I cycled to the end of each one looking forward to a change of scene; the road would bend slightly, then I'd have to begin another one. But eventually all hardships come to an end. We took a sharp left, and there was a long gentle downhill section into Fortrose, allowing us to relax and freewheel for a long time. We were soon through the town and cycling alongside the Moray Firth.

I peered across the water to my left, and thought I could discern the spans of a large bridge about 10km ahead of us.

'Look!'

I slowed down and Edita pulled alongside me.

'What is it?' she said.

'It's Kessock Bridge, Inverness! It's Inverness Bridge, where we started two weeks ago. Do you remember waiting for that chap in an electric wheelchair?'

I was so happy I started punching the air with my fist.

'We're nearly there. Thank god.'

We turned inland and joined a horribly narrow, nerve-jangling two-lane road where traffic hurtled past us. With relief, we turned off onto a safer road through the village of Munlochy. On the other side we saw a narrow lane going up a steep hill into a forest. We stopped at the bottom to discuss our options. It was the sort of road that would have elicited a two-word grunt from me had Edita suggested cycling up it earlier in the trip, but now our perspectives were different. We were so close to the end, and we were prepared to do anything to avoid traffic.

It was our last hill and we tackled it willingly. It was bliss to be on a peaceful back road again. We whizzed down the other side, freewheeling through the forest. Suddenly we emerged through the trees, right onto the A9, which was now a busy dual carriageway. In some ways I found this encouraging. We just needed to get across the river and we'd be back in Inverness. There was just one problem: we found ourselves pedalling along a slip road into two lanes of traffic.

There was no cycle lane and no hard shoulder, and traffic was roaring past at 110km/h. It would be suicidal to join it on a bike with wide panniers; I might as well have pushed a wheelbarrow out there.

We stopped on the slip road and had a discussion. I knew there was a cycle lane on the other side that continued across Kessock Bridge and into Inverness, but how to get across the A9? There was a 5m grass verge between the north- and southbound carriageways, with a knee-high crash barrier running down the middle.

'I think it's much safer to cross over the road,' I said.

'But isn't that illegal?'

'I don't think so. Not if we wait for a gap.'

At that second there was a lull in the southbound traffic and I ran across to the verge in the middle, wheeling my bike. But Edita was waiting to cycle across, and she missed her chance.

While I waited for her to join me, I set about the next part of the operation. It's not easy to get a bike with two loaded panniers over a knee-high fence, but with the end so close, I was determined. Summoning up superhuman strength from somewhere deep inside, I lifted the bike over and propped it against the fence.

I had time to get my breath back before Edita's chance came and she ran across to join me. The strength was still with me; I lifted her bike over the barrier, and took my own. Perhaps the wheel gods were with us at last, because at that moment a gap opened up in the northbound traffic like the parting of the Red Sea. We took our chance and legged it across, laughing as we ran.

A huge wave of relief washed over me when we reached the other side. We were on a dedicated cycle path with no more hazards to negotiate. We had done it.

A few minutes later we reached the foot of Kessock

Bridge, where we had started our adventure 13 days earlier, and looked across the water to Inverness.

'Hi Mark, how is it going?' Edita said as I stared with yearning across the barrier.

She was pointing a camera at me. I was speechless, but after a short pause I was able to spill some words out.

'I'm fucked, but we are here. Five hundred miles. Five hundred fucking miles. I have a sore arse, but we are here.'

The video is now on YouTube if any TV producers are looking to recruit fresh talent for their cycling documentaries.

Later she took a shot of me shaking my fist in the air as I cycled across the bridge. It wasn't a confident shake of conquest, but a quiet shake of happiness, relief and perhaps survival. We retraced our route along back streets and cycle paths beside the river, and reached the bike hire shop, Ticket to Ride, at 3.30pm. The bikes had got us around with only one puncture. They were less wrecked than I was.

The feeling of relief as we unpacked our panniers is hard to put into words. It's a feeling I've felt a few times after coming down from a high mountain having reached the summit. It's a feeling of joy at finishing and being richer for the experience, and it's an overall sense of happiness at being alive.

We had completed the North Coast 500 on bikes, but one thing we'd failed to do was climb any mountains. For the next week we based ourselves in Ullapool with the aim of climbing Edita's first Munro.

There was a buzz about Ullapool. It's a tourist hub for the north-west coast, but it still had the feel of the sleepy fishing village it had once been. We found it welcoming – the most cosmopolitan place we had visited on our trip – and the European bar staff made it feel like London, the place that had been my home for 20 years. It was also a good base for the isolated peaks of Assynt that reminded me of Ecuador's highlands. I really wanted to climb them again. Stac Pollaidh, Suilven and Quinag were the iconic mountains of our trip. Further south were the majestic corries and ridges of An Teallach, the mountain we both wanted to climb most of all.

Anyone who has climbed extensively in Scotland will know that you can easily spend a week there, even in the height of summer, and not experience a single good day. A good day in Scotland doesn't have to be sunny; it just has to mean that the clouds are above the summits, so that you can see where you're going and you don't have to climb through a cold, grey soup.

There's no better way to forget that for two weeks your bottom has been spanked repeatedly like a piece of raw meat than to stand in the bow of a boat as a pod of dolphins surge in front, leaping out of the water in formation. I had never seen this wonder of the natural world before, but the day after we completed the North Coast 500 we spent a day of rest on a wildlife cruise around the Summer Isles. We saw seals, porpoises, and a fleeting glimpse of a minke whale emerging from the sea (which was so far away that, frankly, it could have been a kraken) – but the dolphins stole the show. Edita was probably wondering how such graceful animals surfing the waves like dancers on a stage could share the same planet as that lumbering oaf on a bike who had spent the best part of two weeks spewing forth a torrent of profanities.

I was in a better frame of mind now that I could stand on my feet again. The weather was awful the following day, and the forecast wasn't much better, but we went up Stac

Pollaidh anyway in rain that could have washed away the sins of a debauched bishop. I had forgotten how tiny the mountain is, not much bigger than a ruined castle, and from the road its outline was similar. Grassy slopes led up to the summit ridge like the ramparts of a mediaeval fortress. The jagged ridge was like a ruined curtain wall, with a series of broad pinnacles rising up like flanking towers.

'Does it remind you of Rucu Pichincha?' I said to Edita as we climbed a stone pathway that circled the back of the mountain on heather-clad slopes.

'Maybe a little. It's certainly cloudy enough.'

We had barely started heading up into the mist on rocky steps when we suddenly found ourselves on the summit ridge, staring through a thin veil down to the road snaking its way along the shores of Loch Lurgainn. We skirted rocky towers to get to the highest point. There was a hairy moment when we had to cling to the side of a smooth boulder and make our way around it, nothing but fresh air below us. For a pocket-sized peak, Stac Pollaidh has a tricky final section.

'Yes, perhaps this reminds me of the Paso de la Muerte route up Rucu Pichincha,' Edita said. 'There was some fun scrambling on that route. It was very exposed.'

Back at the car it hardly seemed worth it. Our clothes were soaked and our boots caked in peat. The next day was even worse, but we were determined to go up a hill come rain or shine (which meant come rain). We climbed Quinag, the trio of summits overlooking the village of Kylesku, which was where Edita had that memorable meal of langoustines hung from a mini gallows. It wasn't until our fourth day in Ullapool that the weather gave us the opportunity to climb An Teallach. When he became the first person to climb all the Munros in a single long walk in 1974, the hiker and outdoor writer Hamish Brown perused the visitor book at Shenavall bothy beneath An Teallach's southern flank on the evening before he was due to climb it. He shook his head in disgust at the one visitor who had described 'breasting The Maiden' (another Munro to the south), but he noticed a theme to some of the other entries. One of them talked about being 'pinned down here by storms, midges and inertia' and another misleadingly described how they had endured a 31-hour rain shower (a 31-hour rain shower is not a shower, but a bath).[29]

Sir Hugh Munro himself climbed An Teallach one Easter day in 1893, intrigued by the extravagant descriptions heaped upon it by earlier writers. An 18th-century traveller and naturalist called Thomas Pennant saw the mountain from the east side, and described seeing 'sides dark, steep and precipitous, with summits broken, sharp, serrated, and spiring into all terrific forms; with snow glaciers lodged in the deep shaded apertures'.[30] Opinion is divided on whether there were still glaciers in Scotland in 1772, but in those days the word *glacier* was less specific, and it's likely that what Pennant was describing was, yes, that's right… snow.

Munro didn't believe it either. His first view of the mountain was from a similar place to where we saw it as we cycled across the plateau on the fifth day of our bike ride. The peaks were hidden among storm clouds as he approached from the direction of the Fannichs, but the clouds cleared, and suddenly An Teallach 'stood out, black, snow-slashed, and jagged against a setting sun'.[31] In a 12-hour day, Munro and his companions completed an entire horseshoe of An Teallach: over a subsidiary top, Glas Mheall Mor; the two Munros; and all four black teeth of the jagged ridge we could see from the road, a peak known as Corrag Bhuidhe.

We bagged our reward, and Edita her first two Munros, when we completed a full traverse of An Teallach, climbing both its Munros in conditions that were far from perfect, but good enough. The view of Sgurr Fiona upon reaching the summit of Bidein a' Ghlas Thuill, and the sawtooth ridge of Corrag Buidhe disappearing into mist behind it, sent my sphincters fluttering in a way I didn't like. Beneath us the black waters in the corrie of Toll an Lochain looked more inviting. We climbed the two Munros, then traversed beneath the crags of Corrag Bhuidhe on a trail that was quite exposed enough for my liking.

The next day offered a more classic Scottish hill-walking experience when we bagged four Munros in a range of peaks known as the Fannichs. We had seen this cluster of mountains ahead of us as we crossed the plateau from Dundonnell to Ullapool. Most of the trails in the valleys were submerged under watery peat, and within minutes our boots resembled plant pots. Impenetrable mist veiled most of the ascent. Visibility was so poor that had I been wearing a pair of clown's shoes then I'd have been unable to see my toes.

To my embarrassment, I had forgotten to pack my compass, which in the Scottish hills is rather like arriving at the swimming baths and discovering that you've forgotten to pack your Speedos – embarrassment seems certain to follow. Edita came to the rescue with a GPS app on her phone called Maps.me. This marked no features apart from summits, roads and the occasional trail, but when used in conjunction with my paper Ordnance Survey map it was enough to get us from summit to summit, and find our way down off the correct side of the ridge.

Beneath our last summit we emerged from the clouds and could see the route ahead, but now we found ourselves slithering down heather-clad hillsides submerged in peat. You might think there's not a lot to say about a load of muddy old sod that makes hiking in the Highlands of Scotland more awkward than it needs to be, but in the course of writing his book *Landmarks* the nature writer Robert Macfarlane discovered dozens of ancient Gaelic words to describe the various nuances of peat. These included *bruach* (the word for a bank of peat), *carcair* (the layer of turf on the surface of a peat bank), and *bungel* (which is, I'm not kidding, a clod of peat for throwing at people). One of the most esoteric words is *caochan*, a narrow stream winding through peaty moorland that's been obscured by vegetation so that it's virtually invisible until you stumble into it. I've had my leg swallowed by a few *caochans*, and each time it's happened I've shouted out a much shorter word that also begins with 'C'.

But the most loathsome thing about peat bogs in summer is the midges. Midges are attracted to dark colours, and back at our dark vehicle they were waiting in ambush. In their thousands. As I peeled off my damp, sweaty Gore-Tex jacket, I could hear them purring with delight. I felt them crawling over my hands and up my sleeves. I had to throw the jacket on the ground and retreat to a safe location – where they soon found me removing my Gore-Tex overtrousers. It didn't take long before they were crawling over those too, so I had to leave them in an untidy heap on the ground and move elsewhere to change my shoes. I felt like some kind of peat-bog streaker casting aside his garments as he ran along. We packed everything up, threw it in the back of the car, and wound all the windows down as we hurtled off down the road with midges crawling down our necks.

Had it not been for the North Coast 500, the three things Edita remembered about Scotland would have been mist, peat and midges.

Before we left Scotland for Ecuador, we had a final appointment with my brother Perran, who invited us to his home near Aberdeen before we drove back to London.

The visit had two purposes. Edita had never met him before, and (far more importantly as far as I was concerned) he was also a keen cyclist. We couldn't miss the opportunity to get some tips from an expert before we headed off to cycle across Ecuador. Perran had a competitive side. He entered bike races, and once or twice a year completed multi-day cycle rides across mountainous parts of Europe. His posts on Facebook about the latter often included a few stats.

'Cycled 152km today with 4,000m vertical to finish line at Passo Gavia. That's half the height of Everest in a single day.'

I always assumed his references to Everest were a little dig at his brother, who had climbed Everest, but I was to discover that Everest had a special distinction in the world of cycling. On a bleak section of road across moorland south of Tomintoul – the place, if you remember, with Britain's highest National Lottery outlet – we passed dozens of cyclists pedalling up a big hill. It was the sort of hill that I would have ground to a halt halfway up before getting off to push. I had so despised these hills that I couldn't believe how these steep sections of road seemed to attract cyclists.

'That'll be the Lecht,' Perran said when I told him about it at dinner that evening. 'You can go Everesting there. It's about two hundred metres from top to bottom, so you need to climb up and down it forty-five times.'

Everesting, it turned out, is a popular activity among endurance cyclists that involves repeatedly cycling up and down the same hill until you've climbed 8,848m, the height of Everest. I did a quick calculation – we'd have needed to cycle up and down the Bealach na Ba no fewer than 14 times. Absolutely stark-staring bonkers, but Perran did give us some useful advice as well. I discovered that I'd been cycling with my saddle far too low, which meant I'd been putting in more effort than necessary (we later learned how to adjust it to the optimum height when we were out in Ecuador). He also gave some encouraging comments about the panniers when we told him how much we'd been carrying.

'Bloody hell, that makes a massive difference,' he said. 'I once cycled a hundred miles from Hull to Derbyshire with eight kilos on the back of my bike. That's a distance that would have been OK normally, but I was knackered.'

This was good news. We would have a support driver in Ecuador, and would be carrying nothing but a few snacks and water. But Perran's most useful advice came in the form of a gift that he produced at the end of dinner.

'Take this,' he said, holding out a tub of white cream. 'This isn't for eating. It's the Rolls-Royce of butt cream.'

'Does it do any good?' I said. 'We were smearing on butt cream every morning, but I still had a sore arse for most of the ride.'

'Where were you putting it?'

'What, the cream? On my arse, of course.' It seemed like quite a silly question.

'The best place to smear it is over the padding inside your cycling shorts before you put them on.'

I glanced at Edita, and she was looking as puzzled as I was.

'What, you mean you don't wear any underwear?'

Perran slapped his hand to his forehead and shook his head.

'You were wearing your undercrackers? You're not supposed to do that. I'm not surprised your arse was chafing.'

And with that vital piece of advice for novices, we were ready for Ecuador and our sea-to-summit challenge.

PART THREE

THE SEA-TO-SUMMIT ADVENTURE

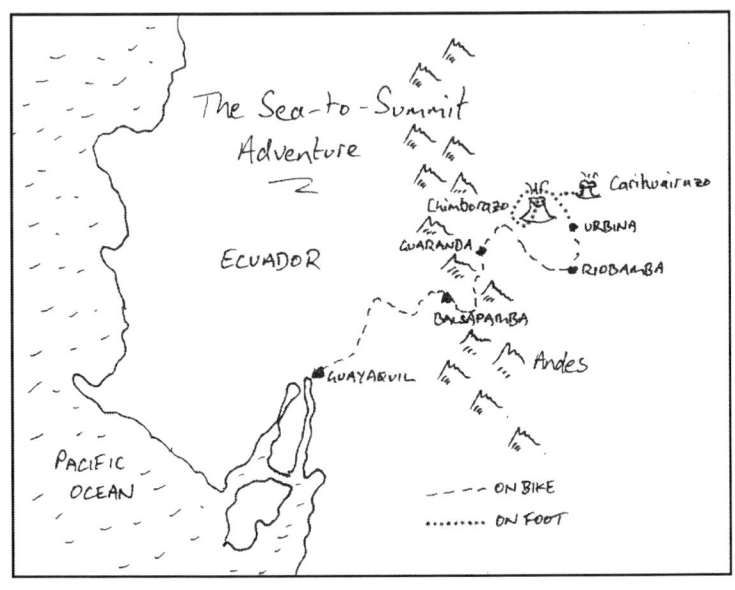

10 SINCHOLAGUA

It was a great honour to reach the arrivals hall at Mariscal Sucre International Airport, Quito, and see Javier waiting for us. Normally he would send a driver to welcome clients when they got off the plane, but when we saw the man himself standing patiently behind the bustle of people with named placards we realised that our trip must be something special.

Our own planning for the South American leg of our sea-to-summit adventure was minimal. In truth, Javier had done most of the work, but I had reread *Travels amongst the Great Andes of the Equator* to trace Edward Whymper's route through Ecuador. Although he went all over the Central Highlands, I wanted to follow his route to Chimborazo as closely as possible.

If you carry out a challenge like this – which may or may not be a world first that others will seek to follow or improve upon – it's a good idea to set down a few basic rules. In the highly likely event of someone accusing me of cheating, if I wasn't able to deny the accusation, I should at least be allowed to accuse myself first. Whymper had taken a river steamer from the port of Guayaquil on the Pacific coast to the town of Babahoyo 60km closer to the Andes. Clearly, it would be cheating for us to float up the river on a boat. On the other hand, it would be plain silly to complete this part of the journey in a pedal-operated pleasure craft just for the sake of saying that we'd done it under our own steam – especially given that the Babahoyo River was said to be alive with alligators.

We would have to take the road from Guayaquil to Babahoyo, but beyond that we could follow Whymper's route more precisely. He took a caravan of mules up through the Andes, passing through the towns of Balsapamba and Guaranda. Both of these places now lie on the main road. We could also climb Chimborazo by the south-west ridge, the route Whymper and the Carrels climbed on their first ascent. This was different to the route we took with Romel a year earlier.

One of the more remarkable things about Whymper's first ascent of Chimborazo was how easily he achieved it. As far as anyone knew, nobody had ever climbed that high before (well, there may have been Incas, but that's another story – and any such ascents went unrecorded). This meant that the effects of altitude were not well understood. Humboldt and Boussingault both claimed to have reached around 6,000m, but there were doubts about their ascents and nobody was really sure if it was possible for humans to get so high without dangerous consequences. Although Whymper's expedition ended up being something of a peak-bagging extravaganza, there was sufficient doubt that success would be possible that he had framed it as a scientific expedition to study the effects of high altitude.

Yet he landed in Guayaquil on 9 December 1879, and by 4 January 1880 he had marched through the Andes to Chimborazo's base, identified a route and climbed to the summit. With the main objective achieved so soon, he and the Carrels then spent the next six months bimbling around Ecuador, picking off further peaks. Even with my significant cycling handicap, we would find this even easier 130 years later. It was theoretically possible to cycle from Guayaquil to Carrel Hut on Chimborazo in three days, but clearly that wouldn't have been much of an adventure. In any case, you can't just cycle from the coast to the summit of Chimborazo in a single push without gasping from altitude sickness. We first needed to spend some time acclimatising in the Central Highlands.

After their first ascent, Whymper and the Carrels circled around the south and east sides of Chimborazo before taking the road north from Ambato to Quito. Before their second ascent, they also climbed 5,020m Carihuairazo, a collapsed volcano on Chimborazo's northern side with more vowels than should strictly be legal. It would be considered a substantial peak in its own right were it not dwarfed by its neighbour.

I thought that a full circuit of the mountain would be a more interesting way of climbing from sea to summit, spiralling back to our starting point on the west side in order to make the ascent of Whymper's original route. This would nicely sandwich a bit of hiking (which was more to my liking) in between the cycling and the climbing, and would give us an opportunity to climb Carihuairazo on the way. Our need to acclimatise before the cycle ride also gave us a good excuse to head up a couple more volcanoes that we hadn't climbed on previous visits. Whymper also made first ascents of Cotacachi in northern Ecuador, and Sincholagua, a mountain we were more familiar with due to its prominent position on the páramo grasslands directly between Cotopaxi and Antisana.

It's common for expedition books to begin with lengthy accounts about planning. I would love to bore you with a whole chapter about how we stored all the expedition vegetables in my father's garage, and roped in the local choir to help with boxing it up three hours before the ship was due to depart from Plymouth for its lengthy voyage across the Atlantic. Or how Edita's grandmother was charged with knitting socks for all the muleteers, and how her cousin's next-door neighbour drove them the length of the Pan-American Highway in a battered old Reliant Robin van that kept rolling on its side. Sadly, I can't pretend our planning was that elaborate. Of course, the romance is gone, but a reliable expedition operator in a foreign country makes the job of planning a bit simpler.

Before we left on our cycle ride around the North Coast 500, we had a conference call with Javier on Skype. It went something along these lines.

'I'm thinking we should follow Edward Whymper's route from Guayaquil to Chimborazo via Guaranda,' I said.

'Sure, the road goes that way, so that's easy,' Javier replied.

'Whymper also climbed Carihuairazo. Perhaps we can do a full circuit of Chimborazo between the bike ride and the climb?'

'That's a nice idea. I know a nice lodge on the east side owned by a man called Rodrigo. He's an interesting character, and also a trekking guide. He could guide the trek round the north side, and perhaps up Carihuairazo too.'

'That's handy,' I said. 'Let's do that then. And I'm wondering if we can acclimatise on a couple of the other peaks that Whymper climbed, such as Cotacachi or Sincholagua.'

'Sure, I can find a guide for both of those.'

'Great. Is there anything else you need from us?'

'Not really. I just have one other question about the bikes.'

'What about them?'

'Do you need any?'

'Any what?'

'Bikes.'

'Oh, yeah, that's a point. Yes, you're right. We're going to need a couple of bikes. And some helmets too, if you can get hold of them.'

'Sure.'

I may be simplifying things a little, but by the time we got off the plane and Javier greeted us at the airport it seemed like our entire sea-to-summit expedition had been magically arranged for us.

After breakfast on our first morning in Ecuador, Javier took us to the bike shop to test ride the bikes he'd hired for us. He parked up on a busy two-lane highway. The shop was tiny and cramped, and we squeezed past a technician carrying out repairs. Javier had arranged a pair of mountain bikes with much smaller wheels than the hybrids we took around Scotland. The bikes for our last trip had been brand new. These looked much older, but they had 3 rings and a total of 24 gears. Hopefully this would make them easier to ride up steep hills.

There were no hills in this part of Quito to test them on, but we cycled along the street for about a quarter of a mile until we reached Parque Aeropuerto. This had been the main international airport when I first came to Ecuador in 2009. When it first opened in 1960 it lay among cornfields on the fringes of a city of just 350,000 inhabitants, but over time the urban sprawl of Quito had swallowed it up.

On my second visit to Ecuador, when Edita and I had climbed Chimborazo, I was a bit disorientated when we arrived in Quito and I got out of the plane. I don't know if the Tardis has an 'I'm Feeling Lucky' button, but I felt a little how Doctor Who must feel if he ever falls against the button after a few drinks and steps outside. I had no idea where I was. On my previous visit, we'd flown right over the city and landed in its heart. But on my second visit I found myself standing on a massive plain in the middle of nowhere. I had no idea the airport had moved. There was a mountain rising a few kilometres away that might be Pichincha, but on the other hand it could just as easily have been Mount Olympus.

In fact, I was right the first time. It was Pichincha and I was standing on the Yaruqui Plain, where Bouguer and La Condamine had measured their baseline in 1736. Quito was hiding on a plateau 500m above me, shielded by a ridge.

By the time the new airport opened in 2013, there were 2.2 million people living in Ecuador's capital. Planes coming in to land had to fly low over the main city centre for large distances. Worse, the runway was only 3,120m long – not enough for large passenger aircraft to stop safely. The terrain and altitude didn't help. Planes landing in the thin air of 2,850m have to travel faster during landing, and it takes longer for them to take off. The mountainous landscape meant that there was a steeper angle of approach.

The airport became famous for 'runway excursions' – aviation industry parlance for shooting off the end. In 1984, 49 people died when a plane clipped some navigation equipment during take-off and took an unscheduled excursion into neighbouring homes. In 1998 another 76 people died when a plane failed to take off in time and rammed into the wall at the far end of the runway.

The new out-of-town Mariscal Sucre International Airport is 12 times the area of the old one, and, at 4,091m, the new runway is nearly 1km longer. This is big enough for an Airbus A380, one of the world's largest passenger aircraft.

The old airport has now been converted into a park. I liked what they had done with it. The old runways had been converted into cycle tracks, and trees had been planted on the grass verges in between. It was a park for active people.

There were several cyclists, but it wasn't too busy. The runways may have seemed small for landing aircraft, but to cyclists they were huge. There were long straight sections that enabled us to get up some speed and test all the gears. Javier knew more about bikes than we did, so he tested both our bikes himself. He decreed them acceptable – but made a few notes on minor issues for the staff in the bike shop to correct.

Mark and Edita try out their bikes at the Parque Aeropuerto

There was another special reason why Javier was uniquely qualified to assist us with this adventure. I had known that, before he took up mountaineering as a career, he was a talented cyclist and even an Ecuadorian national cycling champion for a time, but I didn't know anything more about this period of his life. He took us for lunch at a sandwich shop around the corner from his office, and I asked him about it.

'When I was thirteen years old, my cousin Pablo and I

were keen cyclists and we decided to enter a race,' he said.

'Really? And don't tell me – you ended up winning it,' I said.

'No. I came last, but that only made me more determined. I decided to train hard and enter the same race the following year. This time I won it. I entered more races over the next few years, and won several of those too. Eventually I was selected to represent Ecuador in the under-nineteens category at the Pan American Games. They were being held in Quito. I competed in the hundred-and-twenty-kilometre road race and won it.'

'Blimey, so you weren't just national cycling champion, but champion for the whole of South America?'

'For all of the Americas. But only in the under-nineteens. We were just kids. After that I went off the rails a bit.'

'That's when you drank a bit more and fell off a church tower?'

Javier frowned. 'It is when I took up mountaineering.'

This, I realised, was something that many people would regard as going 'off the rails', but before I had time to reflect on this, he continued.

'Pablo is a much better cyclist than me now. You will meet Pablo. He's a great guy. He is your rival.'

'My rival. Why, what have I done?'

'We think he is the first person to cycle from the sea to the summit on Cotopaxi. He wants to be the first to do it on Chimborazo too. He has agreed to support you in the vehicle.'

I paused with my hands either side of my mouth, and a half-chewed sandwich wedged between my cheeks.

'Yue as gweed tsports inzhe beekle?'

'Excuse me?'

I swallowed the mouthful and put my sandwich down on the table.

'I'm sorry. You say he's agreed to support us in the vehicle? You've arranged for us to be supported on the bike ride by someone who wants us to fail because he is our rival for the Chimborazo sea to summit?'

'No, that's not quite right. He wants you to succeed. As I said, he is a great guy.'

We could only wait and see, and trust Javier that he wouldn't assign us a support driver who wanted to stitch us up. I was just glad that we had a support driver at all. In truth I was nervous as hell about the cycle ride. After all those hills on the North Coast 500, I doubted if it was even possible for me to ascend 4,000m through the Andes with or without huge saddlebags attached to the bike. Having a native Ecuadorian to accompany us – especially one who knew how to fix a bike and had completed such a challenge before – boosted my confidence a lot. In the worst-case scenario, at least I could sit in the back of a vehicle and enjoy the view.

Before we could begin our bike ride, we had our acclimatisation programme to complete. We hiked up Rucu Pichincha without a guide. Having both climbed it before, we managed to find our way up through the mist, which Edita said reminded her of Scotland. Javier took us to Cotacachi (4,944m), a complex peak in northern Ecuador whose crumpled terrain Whymper had described as 'not very unlike that of a biscuit which has been smashed by a blow of the fist'.[32] I don't know what type of biscuit he was referring to when he made this arresting statement, but when I tried to simulate it with a Chocolate Digestive, it simply bounced off the table and landed a few centimetres away, leaving a trail of crumbs in its wake. Not wishing to waste further biscuit, I decided the best course of action was just to eat it.

Alas for us, the mountain gods had stamped their fists firmly down on Cotacachi's summit, to say do not climb. We struggled through high winds and mist over icy rocks before turning around, defeated, at roughly 4,700m. There was a sobering moment during our drive back to Quito. We passed an ambulance parked beside the remnants of a road accident. The driver's corner of a vehicle had been completely crushed, as though someone had dropped a concrete slab on it, and it was impossible to believe the driver could have survived such a devastating impact. Drivers slowed to stare in ghoulish fascination. It was a shocking reminder of the risks we would be taking on our bike ride. How kind were drivers to cyclists in Ecuador? We could only wait and see.

The next day we met Javier's cousin Pablo Montalvo. It was a key moment in our journey, for I knew that Pablo carried it within him to make or break our sea-to-summit challenge. Javier had told us much about him. We knew that as well as being his cousin, Pablo had been Javier's best friend since childhood. He was a trekking guide who had maintained an interest in cycling throughout his life as Javier gravitated towards mountaineering.

As far as anyone knew, Pablo was the first person to travel from sea to summit on Cotopaxi, and we knew that he wanted to be the first on Chimborazo too. If anyone deserved that accolade, he was the man. Yet here were two gringos, interlopers from a foreign land, keen to pip him to that achievement – two people, moreover, who had no interest in cycling, one of whom could barely ride a bike. He was being asked to support us, and help us to achieve our goal. It was like asking a rooster to share his harem.

I wondered what sort of person Pablo would turn out to

be. Javier had described him as a great guy, but he was Javier's friend, so he would say that, wouldn't he?

Pablo would also be guiding us up Sincholagua, our last acclimatisation peak before the cycle ride. I was relieved when he arrived at Javier's house after breakfast. We shook hands as he stood inside the door.

'Pleased to meet you,' he said.

He had a vice-like grip, but was smiling from ear to ear.

'This is your cousin?' I said to Javier.

I had noticed the smile right away, but Pablo had an even more distinctive characteristic that I couldn't fail to observe: his size. Javier was muscular and powerful, but in height he barely came up to my shoulder. By contrast Pablo was tall and wiry, well over 6ft, and he towered over me. Could these two men really share the same grandparents?

I looked from one to the other in exaggerated fashion.

'We grew in different directions,' Pablo said, still smiling, 'but as you can see, Javier got the looks.'

Javier frowned.

'Pablo is your rival,' he said.

I laughed. 'We are no rivals. We will be asking him for advice all the time.'

'Just take it slowly,' Pablo said. 'There is nothing to worry about.'

Their reactions had revealed another notable difference between them.

Javier was a man with a deadpan sense of humour, who remained inscrutable even when he was telling a joke, but Pablo's manner was more genial. I could see at once that he wasn't smiling through gritted teeth. He looked to be a genuinely cheerful character, open and kind-hearted – someone we could rely on to help us in any way he could.

Or so I hoped. Only time would tell whether this observation proved to be true.

As he drove us to Cotopaxi, where we would spend the day before attempting Sincholagua, I took the opportunity to ask Pablo many questions. I explained that we were cycling novices, and although we were physically active and believed that our fitness from hiking and mountaineering would enable us to complete the challenge, we still had a lot to learn about bikes.

'It's going to be painful,' I said. 'We spent two weeks cycling around Scotland, and I found it hard. I'm not used to being on a saddle, and my cheeks were very sore by the end of it.'

Pablo nodded knowingly.

'But we'll be OK this time,' I continued. 'My brother is a keen cyclist. He gave us some useful cream. And he gave us some other advice, but I don't know whether to believe him…'

'You're not supposed to wear any underwear,' Pablo said.

I gave him a puzzled look. 'How did you know I was going to say that?'

He roared with laughter. 'You were. You were wearing underwear, weren't you?'

'So it's true. You're supposed to cycle commando-style?'

'It's true,' he said. 'It's much more comfortable that way.'

As we travelled south from Quito on the busy Pan-American Highway, I was reassured to see a metre-wide cycle lane on each side of the road. Pablo explained the best way to use them.

'Don't keep right up to the verge,' he said. 'Then drivers will ignore you, and you have nowhere to go if they drive too close. Instead, keep to the left, just inside the white line. Then drivers will notice you and beep their horns. If they beep then that's a good thing. It means they have seen you, and you can move to the right to give them space.'

It was good advice, and the opposite to what I would have done without it. It seemed more intuitive to keep as far away from traffic as possible, but I could see that Pablo was right.

'And another thing. Don't drink when you are super thirsty after a steep climb, as you will gulp down too much water. Instead, wait for a few minutes and then have a drink.'

We drove around the south side of Rumiñahui to approach Cotopaxi from the west, up a smooth road among forest. At the national park gate Edita bought a box of maize kernels coated in brown sugar to eat on the trail the following day. Pablo told her with great delight that these were known as *caca de perro* ('dog shit') in Ecuador. He declined her offer to eat some, but I actually found them quite tasty.

A sign next to the visitor centre provided some rules to follow if Cotopaxi erupted. One of these was to 'Keep always close your emergency backpack' (I guess they must have used Google Translate to convert it into English).

'What does an emergency backpack do?' Edita asked, the trace of a smile forming at the corners of her lips.

'Oh, I think you are supposed to carry things like water, a flashlight and first aid kit,' Pablo replied. 'I don't have a dedicated backpack, but I think we have those things somewhere in the vehicle.'

Edita feigned disappointment. 'Oh, I hoped you would have something like a jetpack or a wingsuit ready, so that we can fly back to Quito.'

Pablo roared with laughter. 'Do you have one? That would be wonderful.'

As we reached the Limpiopungo Plain, the boulder-strewn plateau stretching between Cotopaxi, Rumiñahui and Sincholagua, grey cloud framed the great cone of Cotopaxi, but we could just see the summit. Though it was Edita's first time here, I remembered it well from my visit eight years earlier. I pointed out the red roof of the refuge high up on Cotopaxi's slopes, a short distance below the snout of the glacier.

Pablo drove across the plain and began ascending the zigzag dirt track up to the car park at 4,600m. We could tell it was going to be busy with sightseers. Yellow Quito taxis were on their way up. One hadn't made it up the rutted gravel surface and had parked beside the road. A little higher, a tourist with a tripod was trying to hitch a ride. We even saw someone trying to cycle up – a man after my own heart, who had followed my example and got off to push. It was already too steep for my liking, but the deep gravel must have made it an order of magnitude harder than the roads we cycled up in Scotland.

'This gravel is very difficult to cycle down,' Pablo said. 'You have to really know which brake to use.'

This was my cue.

'I know this is going to make me sound like an idiot, but when should I use the front brake instead of the back one?'

'You are joking?' Edita said.

'Actually, that's a very good question,' Pablo replied. 'I need to remind you that the brakes are on the wrong side.'

'What, you mean they are underneath the handlebars?'

'No, I think that in the UK you are used to operating the front brake with your right hand? But here in Ecuador, and most places in the world, the front brake is on the left.'

'That won't be a problem for me,' I replied. 'I haven't got a clue which way round they were in Scotland.'

He laughed nervously. 'Well, anyway, to answer your question, if you only use the back brake then sometimes you will not stop. You will just keep going in a straight line. The front brake is really for stopping. You should try to use it as often as you can, but you need to be careful. If you use it in the wrong place then you can lose control of the bike and fly over the handlebars.'

'Yes, that's what they told me in school. That's why I always use the back one.'

'But on hills, you should pump the brakes. Lean back and put your weight behind you, and try to use both brakes at the same time.'

'That's what I was doing,' Edita said. 'It's easy. It's obvious.'

For the ever-practical Edita I expect it was, but I could see that it was going to take some practice.

Above the car park, at the start of the trail up to José Rivas Refuge, we walked past some mattresses ready to be carried up. This seemed a clear indication that Cotopaxi was going to be opened for climbing soon. Halfway up the trail we met the manager of the refuge, who told us he hoped it would open next week.

'You can go upstairs and see the rooms if you like,' he said.

'Yes, let's do that,' Edita replied. 'Call me when you open. I want to climb it.'

We took the direct route up a sandy scree slope to get to the hut. It was decidedly steep and we walked slowly.

'I once cycled up this trail,' Pablo said.

The hut was much improved since my last visit in 2010. I still recognised the downstairs dining area, but the upstairs dorms were completely transformed. I recalled the rickety old triple-decker bunk that shook like an earthquake every time one of us rolled over. Now there were three rooms with spacious double bunks. It looked so much more conducive to a good night's sleep. The downside was that I could only count 50 beds in total.

'You can have two hundred people climbing here on

busy nights,' Pablo said.

We stayed for lunch of *locro de papa* (potato and cheese soup). The walls of the dining room were adorned with photographs of Ecuador's volcanoes by the well-known mountain guide and speed climber Karl Egloff. Born and raised in Ecuador to a Swiss father and Ecuadorian mother, he is best known for what in modern running parlance are termed Fastest Known Times (whose acronym, FKT, coincidentally describes the state of the participant at the end of the challenge). He came to international attention in 2015 after breaking two of Kilian Jornet's speed climbing records on Kilimanjaro and Aconcagua. At the time he was hardly known outside Ecuador, but his father was a mountain guide, and he had been climbing mountains from a young age. A natural athlete, he broke the record for a speed climb of Cotopaxi in 2012, going up and down in just 1 hour 37 minutes. At age 26 he took up mountain biking; within a year of his first race he was racing for Ecuador's national team.

This combination of mountaineering and cycling led us into a conversation about our Chimborazo sea-to-summit challenge. We still didn't know whether anyone had done it before, but if anyone had, then Karl Egloff would seem to be a likely candidate. Performances such as his emphasised to me that, even if I ended up being the first, I'd be something of a fraud. It was only my third time in Ecuador and I could barely ride a bike up a hill without collapsing like an elephant seal reaching the top end of a beach. Karl Egloff could probably achieve what we were planning in a fraction of the time, on a unicycle, with one leg tied behind his back.

I asked Pablo about his Cotopaxi adventure, when he and his American friend Steve Tober travelled from Pedernales to the summit in six days.

'The weather was terrible,' he said. 'Only two of us

completed the challenge by climbing Cotopaxi. Steve was leaving Ecuador, so he was really determined. He was exhausted. Our guide Marco was on one end of the rope and I was at the back, and we had to work hard to keep him on his feet.'

'So you and Steve may have been the first on Cotopaxi,' I said, 'but do you know anyone else who may have done it on Chimborazo?'

'Hmm, well, there's Santiago Quintero. He's an extreme climber who does lots of crazy stuff. I once cycled up to the refuge on Cayambe. When I arrived I asked the warden if anyone else had cycled up. "Oh, yes, Santiago Quintero," he said. Apparently Santiago cycled to the refuge from Quito in a day, then climbed Cayambe.'

'So he might have done Chimborazo on a bike too?'

'I don't think so. He's not much into cycling.'

Determined to follow up this lead, we drove down to Tambopaxi, the lodge on the Limpiopungo Plain where Pablo had stayed during his sea-to-summit adventure. I had stayed there myself in 2009, and had fond memories of its comfortable dining room with a huge glass window looking south towards Cotopaxi. To the east, Sincholagua was free of cloud now, and we could see quite a lot of ice below the summit.

We found Wi-Fi downstairs in the bar, and they were serving *cerveza artesanal* ('craft beer'). It seemed like a good opportunity to investigate Santiago Quintero's website. He was a sponsored athlete of some renown, and among the sponsors' logos I noticed many references to the extreme routes he had climbed on high mountains throughout the Andes and Himalayas. One of these included a circumnavigation of the inside of Cotopaxi's crater, which was presumably the 'crazy stuff' that Pablo had alluded to. In case anyone wondered what this involved, there was even an aerial shot looking down into the crater with Santiago's route drawn on as a red line.

At first I saw no obvious references to cycling, but then my heart missed a beat when I came across a video entitled *Pedaleando por un Sueño* ('Pedalling for a Dream'). Within a minute of the start there was footage of Santiago on a mountain bike talking about Chimborazo. The video described a cycling trip from Quito to Cuenca in southern Ecuador, and finishing at Guayaquil down by the coast. He also climbed to the summits of Cotopaxi and Chimborazo in the 15 days the journey took him. While some people might argue this was a tougher challenge than ours, with even more ascent, I basked in a feeling of smug satisfaction that it involved a net *loss* of 2,850m, instead of the 6,310m altitude *gain* that we were hoping to complete.

'It's a piece of cake,' I said to Edita as we watched it on my phone. 'He's actually going downhill most of the way.'

As we carried out this important research, Pablo was out on a mission of his own. He said that the last time he and Javier came here they found the road up Sincholagua to the start of the trail blocked by a fallen tree. This would mean a long day for us with a few extra hours of walking from lower down. Pablo drove off to see if he could get the Toyota Land Cruiser up to the trail another way. Just before dusk he returned triumphant, believing he may have found an alternative route – provided it wasn't blocked again by the park rangers before we arrived there tomorrow.

At 5.30 the following morning we had breakfast and made sandwiches as we waited for the sun to rise. At first light, the signs were ominous. Thick clouds billowed over the summit of Sincholagua, threatening to engulf the mountain like a

tidal wave. It looked horribly windy up there, but we were determined to give it a go.

We left at 6.15. As we drove north and out of the national park, we looked behind and saw a cloud rising vertically above Cotopaxi's crater – a cloud that looked suspiciously like a small eruption. This was exactly the hour in the day when climbers would be reaching the summit, having climbed through the night. They would be standing right next to the explosion on the north side of the crater. We could see from our vehicle that prevailing winds were taking the gas cloud south-west, away from climbers, but a sudden gust or change in the wind direction could engulf them in sulphur fumes. I wondered about the wisdom of opening Cotopaxi again so soon.

Focusing once more on Sincholagua, we travelled away from the mountain for several kilometres until Pablo turned right up a farm track. There was a gate at the end, but it was open, and Pablo continued for some distance, passing farms on either side. The track descended into a river valley and crossed the dry river on a flimsy-looking bridge made out of tree trunks. There was another gate at the end, partially blocked by a large boulder, but we were able to get past.

'Wonderful. We are through the gates,' Pablo said. 'Now I'm confident we can drive up the track to Sincholagua. We just have to hope the gates are open when we come back.'

It still took us a while to find the track despite Pablo's confidence. We eventually did so using Edita's magic app, which took us on an impossibly rutted road up through a pine plantation. Pablo was in his element. The first section rose steeply with trenches a metre or more deep.

'You're never going to make it up there,' I said.

'You'll be surprised. This vehicle is like a tractor. It can do much more than this. Watch.'

I leaned forward, expecting him to press a button on the

dashboard, like Q in the James Bond films, and to see the vehicle sprout a pair of wings that would flap us up the mountain.

But I was disappointed. Instead, Pablo drove with care, the vehicle rocked slightly, and we eased our way up the huge trench without a hitch. We passed through the pine plantation and started heading up a grassy hillside. Sincholagua disappeared from view, but the vehicle track just kept on going, past a radio antenna, and on through grasslands. Every time I thought it would be too steep to continue, Pablo changed gear and up we went.

We eventually came to a halt where the grass slope ended and a rocky ridge began. Sincholagua was now visible rising into clouds at the end of the ridge – we couldn't see much of it, but at least we were able to start our walk below the mist. As for that torrent of clouds billowing over the summit, we would have to wait and see. It was eight o'clock and Edita's altimeter read 4,200m. Pablo's reconnaissance and his careful off-road driving had saved us several hours of walking.

With the summit now just 693m above us, some people might consider us to have cheated. But it's worth pointing out that when Whymper and company made the first ascent of Sincholagua in 1880, they took horses (the Toyota Land Cruisers of their day, and more besides) to more or less the same point we had. They had found the grassy slopes that Pablo had driven up in the vehicle a little on the boggy side – so much so that Louis Carrel and his animal became stuck in 'deceitful ground' and had to be dragged out by the rest of the team. Whymper observed that 'any spot that is especially verdant is sure to be swampy'[33] (I expect he based this assertion on experience of Scottish peat bogs).

For the next hour we walked along the ridge. The ascent was so gentle that it hardly felt like we were climbing at all.

At the end of the ridge we began ascending the main shoulder of Sincholagua: a steep but non-technical trek. The weather seemed to be improving. We kept expecting to ascend into cloud, but as we climbed the clouds kept rising too. The ridge steepened into a wall of loose rock, rising to the first summit, but the route traversed beneath it to the left.

The loose stones were hazardous. Cliffs rose above us on the right and we put on helmets to protect us from rockfall. I say 'protect', but if a large rock did fall and strike any of us, it wouldn't be much fun. The helmets might protect us from death, but brain injuries were still on the cards – something I was keen to avoid. To our left the terrain sloped steeply. It was like walking across a pitched roof heaped with loose tiles. We tiptoed across it carefully, trying not to dislodge rocks onto each other.

I relaxed when we made it across without mishap, but the dangers weren't over. Behind the first summit we stopped to discuss the route. Cairns led to the right, but Edita's app suggested an easier route up a boulder field to a col between the first and main summits. We took this one, up into a fine mist.

Though we were following the same route that Whymper and the Carrels had taken in 1880, at around this point in the ascent our experiences diverged in much the same way as a tent diverges from a mansion. We were about to ascend into a fine mist, but were conscious that the main summit couldn't be far away and conditions weren't going to get much worse. Whymper and company were climbing happily when they were ambushed by a hailstorm of Biblical proportions. Half-inch balls of ice sent them cowering between cracks in the cliffs. They desperately shielded their faces with their hands. To add insult to injury, the ice ricocheted off the rocks with such force that real stones were dislodged onto them. It was as though the weather gods were flicking V-signs at them for having the gall to cheat by taking horses.

But there was worse to come. After a lull, thick flakes of snow began to fall instead. This was a signal for them to leave their hiding places and resume the climb. In one respect they had it easier than we did: there was still a glacier on the summit ridge, which has now disappeared. As they ascended the slope of snow and ice, forks of lightning stabbed at the mountain and the metal of their ice axes fizzed with electricity. It would have put the willies up most sensible people and sent them retreating down the mountain, but Whymper and the Carrels continued doggedly.

The ridge became steeper. They couldn't see the summit through the clouds, but they were very close. The last few metres were so steep that the man in front had to reach above his head with his axe and hook himself up (Whymper didn't say which of them it was, but Jean-Antoine Carrel was known to be the best climber). The actual summit was too small to stand upon; they all got as near as they could, then immediately descended, facing into the slope to go back down the steepest part. It must have been a pretty scary descent. Somehow they managed to get down safely without anyone being skewered by a lightning bolt.

Had lightning been forecast for the day we climbed Sincholagua then nothing, not even a giant piece of chocolate cake with lashings of rum sauce, could have induced me to go up. Whymper had no weather forecast, and the hailstorm surprised them with its suddenness ('Heaven knows where it came from,' was Whymper's comment when it arrived. Heaven perhaps?). By then, they were so close to the summit that they were in a bit of a pickle anyway. Had they turned around immediately – as any half-sensible person would – they would still have been most of the way up a mountain in a lightning storm. They were the extreme sportsmen of their day; the ones who only appreciate their good fortune if they eventually make it to old age. They continued onwards, bagged the first ascent, then made it down alive.

We were soon at the col, and knew the summit couldn't be far away as we began the climb up the summit ridge on terrain that was a combination of scrambling and loose scree. This was totally different to the snow-covered glacier that Whymper described. Had the glacier still existed then it would have been much easier to walk up with crampons; this scree was so steep that it almost warranted crawling on hands and knees. People often describe this sort of terrain as 'two steps up, one step back'. This was more like 'two steps up, three steps back'. I felt like we were moonwalking. I pulled my helmet down over my forehead like a top hat and imagined Michael Jackson walking beside us. I thought about twirling my trekking pole around in the manner of a cane, but then I realised I would look like a dick.

Our ascent came to an abrupt halt 30m below the summit. The scree ended at a rock wall. It was still possible to scramble upwards without a rope, and Pablo led the way up a narrow couloir of loose rock, followed by Edita – but she became stuck at the top end. I was following behind her and could find no way of climbing past unless she moved, but neither could she come back down unless I did. It was a Mexican standoff. To compound matters, the rock was so loose that I found myself pulling off great flakes of it whenever I grasped for handholds.

I looked up and could see Pablo waiting for us. Above him the wall continued to steepen into mist, with rivulets of snow wedged in cracks in the rock. It didn't look at all inviting. We had been warned that the last 5m were extremely steep. Pablo had described them as vertical, but Javier had been more bullish about us being able to make it up.

'Let's go back down and regroup,' I said, not as bravely as I could have done.

'Yes. Let's have a sandwich and make up our minds,' Pablo replied.

A few minutes later, we found ourselves sitting at the top of the scree slope beneath the summit cliffs. As I munched away on a sandwich, I explained our situation to the others.

'I read the route description in a climbing guidebook down in Tambopaxi. It said there were twenty-five metres of scrambling, but the last five metres were even more difficult, and we'll need to abseil off the top.'

'I don't have a rope,' Pablo said. He was a trekking guide, not a mountain guide.

'So how do we get down then – do we jump?' Edita said, a little unhelpfully I felt. She gave a little chuckle.

I could only assume that Javier must have thought that because we had both climbed Everest, then we were better technical climbers than we were. The summit was there for the taking, but there was no way I was going to ascend those last few metres without a rope and climbing guide. There would be no view from the summit in this cloud anyway.

'I think we're screwed,' I said after a pause.

'Yes, but we can come back another time with all the gear and a climbing guide,' Edita said.

'I am sorry,' Pablo said.

He seemed sheepish, but it wasn't his fault. He was a trekking guide, and we needed him for the cycling. There were other guides who could help us get up those last 5m.

Any lingering doubt vanished on the way down as we approached the vehicle. Behind us the clouds lifted off the summit and my mouth opened wide.

'Look at that!' I cried.

Edita turned and looked up. 'Wow.'

We were looking east to a wall of rock crowned by three summits that would have had rock climbers licking their lips. The two summits on each side were moderate, but the one in the middle – which was clearly the highest – was certainly not. It was like a sharpened tooth rising to a fine point and runnelled with ice.

'It's a needle. The summit's a sodding ice needle.'

My voice had raised to such a high falsetto that I could have passed an audition for the Bee Gees.

I was happy then. I knew that I wanted to come back and climb it, but today wasn't the day. We had achieved our objective, which was to climb as high as we could and acclimatise for our sea-to-summit challenge. Now we were ready for the cycle ride.

11 INTO THE ANDES

I was nervous as we sat around Javier's breakfast table, waiting for Pablo to arrive to take us to Guayaquil.

'There is some risk with what you are doing. We have never done it before.'

I closed my eyes briefly and tried to calm my thoughts.

'But I think you know that,' Javier continued. 'You are athletes.'

My toast didn't agree, and expressed its disdain by attempting to re-emerge from my throat. I began coughing.

'Athletes, my arse. I need a rest just thinking about this bike ride.'

'You are athletes. You may not believe that you're the best—'

'No shit.'

'But it's all about determination. I know that you can do this if you want to. You are mountaineers. You have climbed Chimborazo before. You are strong at altitude, and now you are acclimatised. The hardest part is no problem for you.'

'Javier's right,' Edita said. 'You're worried about the cycling, but you managed the North Coast 500, no problem.'

'I wouldn't say "no problem". You've got a video of me sleeping by the side of the road.'

It's true that the part of the expedition most people

would find most challenging – climbing Chimborazo – didn't worry me at all. We'd done it once before and I knew we could do it again. You are always more confident about climbing a mountain for a second time. The bike ride bothered me because I'd never done anything like it before. We'd got around the North Coast 500, but now we had to cycle to well over 4,000m. That was tough, and I also had concerns about drivers in Ecuador – I didn't know what to expect from them.

Two things concerned me in particular: death by lunatic driving, and day two of the bike ride. The first of these is self-explanatory, but the second needs a bit more detail. Ever since Javier had emailed us his recommended itinerary, I had picked out day two, from Babahoyo to Guaranda, as the crux of the whole enterprise. Not only were the 116km we were due to cycle that day 36km further than our longest day on the North Coast 500, but we would be climbing 2,600m. How the hell did I think I was going to manage that?

But Pablo had a solution to both problems.

'I've been thinking,' he said when he arrived to drive us to Guayaquil. 'The cycle ride tomorrow from Guayaquil to Babahoyo is much too short. The day after is very long. Tomorrow we can push on to Montalvo, maybe even higher into the Andes. It will make the second day much easier.'

Javier rolled out a map and we looked at the route. As the crow flies, Babahoyo did indeed look equidistant between Guayaquil and Guaranda, while Montalvo looked much closer to Guaranda. But Pablo explained that Montalvo lay right at the foot of the Andes. The road from Guayaquil was completely flat. We could easily cycle it in a day, and reduce the second day's distance by over 30km.

'After Montalvo, the road goes up into the mountains,' Pablo said. 'Depending on how you feel, we could even keep going a little to get some of the climbing out of the way as well.'

'I like it,' Edita said. 'You know how Javier thought we could climb up that sheer rock face yesterday without a climbing guide? Well, he thinks we are professional cyclists as well.'

We laughed.

'Professional cyclists? Pablo had to give me advice on which brake to use,' I said.

'I didn't say *cyclists*,' Javier pointed out, 'I said *athletes*. It is a very important difference.'

Pablo had made his suggestion unprompted, and it looked to be a possible solution to one of my deepest fears about the challenge. He went on to suggest something that might solve my other fear about the safety of the roads.

'If you like, we can drive that way today. Instead of taking the direct road from Quito to Guayaquil, we can drive past Chimborazo and take the road we intend to cycle up. This would give you an opportunity to see how much of the road has cycle lanes, and identify the difficult sections where traffic might be a problem.'

'We have time?' I said.

'Yes. We have all day to get to Guayaquil.'

'I think it's a great idea. Let's do it,' Edita said.

We left Javier's house at nine o'clock with both our bikes, a spare bike, and all our kit in the back of the Land Cruiser. We had only a few hours left for Pablo to give us all the advice he knew about cycling. As we sped along the now-familiar road out of Quito, with volcanoes rising on either side, he started with the subject of dogs and how to avoid them.

'There will be times when dogs chase you,' he said. 'First,

there are the friendly dogs that just want to tell you that you are on their territory. They will wait till you are near then bark at you. Their tails wag to tell you they are friendly. You can just ignore these dogs and cycle on.

'Then there are the aggressive dogs who want to attack you. They will run towards you with their tails erect. Whatever you do, don't be aggressive back to them or they will attack to defend themselves. The best thing to do with these dogs is to stop right in front of them, then stare at them. They will know that you are not frightened, and they will move away.'

Clearly Ecuadorian dogs behave differently to British dogs. If a dog ran barking towards me at home, I would simply run towards it barking back, and expect it to turn on its heels and run away. In Britain, people keep dogs as companions, not as guards, and only the biggest dogs give me any cause for alarm.

But now the tables were turned. I glanced at Edita and could see that she was deep in thought. She is one of the bravest people I know – fearless as a tiger. The cycle ride didn't worry her at all. What Pablo didn't know was that she was afraid of dogs, and while his advice may be helpful, it had dented her confidence.

We sat silently for a few minutes. The three summits of Rumiñahui passed to our left, forests rising up their flanks. I could almost hear Edita's brain buzzing in the seat in front of me, and before long she returned to the subject.

'Should I wear long cycle pants instead of shorts, to protect myself from bites?'

'You don't need to worry about being bitten,' Pablo said. 'I have ridden a lot in the lowlands, and I have hardly ever been bitten.'

'Really?'

'You have repellent?'

'What, dog repellent? I didn't know it existed.'

Pablo started laughing. 'Ah, you are talking about dogs again. I thought you were talking about mosquitoes.'

He paused, then spoke again. 'Actually, if nothing works and you really are attacked, get your water bottle and squirt water in its face. Dogs hate getting wet.'

From Ambato we took the road up to the Gran Arenal that we had driven with Romel a year and a half earlier. Chimborazo rose up like a citadel, and although it was framed in grey clouds, we could see all of it. It held no fear for me, but the road ahead to Guaranda carried more questions. It descended 1,700m over a distance of 31km. Yet it was quite a pleasant road – quiet, with a smooth surface and a wide cycle lane. I would be comfortable cycling up it, I thought to myself. It was from Guaranda onwards that things became scarier. Guaranda did not seem like a pleasant town for cyclists. Streets slanted steeply like harbour slipways, with traffic squeezing between tiny gaps and pumping out petrol fumes as drivers sounded their horns. Then there was a 14km section from Guaranda to the next town, Chimbo, that had no cycle lane. It was busy when we drove along it, with many cars overtaking. On a bike we would be at risk from cars in both directions – we'd need to keep our wits about us.

I was nervous already, but what I didn't know was that we'd just driven the easy bit.

In Chimbo, Pablo stopped to ask for directions, and learned of a shortcut that would shave off many miles. He asked one of the locals if this road had less traffic, and they gave him the thumbs up.

We took this route. To begin with things looked promising. It had a cycle lane, and there was hardly any traffic at all.

We soon found out why. The road *climbed* for another

300m.

'Why are we climbing?' I asked Pablo. 'Aren't we supposed to be going down?'

And then, of course, there was another thing that's really obvious when you think about it: a shorter road also means a steeper road.

We emerged at the top of a precipitous, forested ridge, with views to the lowlands over 2,000m below. It was spectacular, but I found the thought of cycling up it terrifying. The road dropped in horrendous zigzags. Pablo had to descend in low gear because he was afraid of wearing out the brakes on Javier's Land Cruiser. The road turned into a rough dirt track for about a kilometre – a surface that would wear out the tyres on our bikes and the skin of our buttocks.

'You've got to be kidding me,' I said. 'There's no way on earth I can get up this thing.'

'It's wonderful. I would love to cycle up it some time, but I will need to train,' Pablo said.

This sort of challenge would normally get Edita excited, but instead she sat in the passenger seat laughing as the road hurtled down, down, down towards the lowlands.

By the time we completed our plummet down the Hill of Death and rejoined the main highway at Balsapamba, we had descended 2,000m over the course of 20km. Pablo was still astute enough to manage a spot of basic mathematics.

'That's an average gradient of ten per cent – for twenty kilometres,' he said as he shook his head. 'That's some road.'

'Just to be clear, then: we're taking the main road,' I said.

They roared with laughter.

'We have no choice,' Edita replied.

Her altimeter read 900m as we passed through Balsapamba. The road continued to descend, but less steeply.

'We can try to reach here tomorrow,' Pablo said, 'to give us less mountain to climb the following day.'

I was sceptical, but we soon reached Montalvo, and from then on, as Pablo had told us, the road was completely flat all the way to Guayaquil. It gave me a lot of confidence.

We were driving through an Ecuador that I'd not seen before. One of the country's biggest exports is bananas. They come in all shapes and sizes, from green savoury plantains to the sweet ones we buy in supermarkets. But where did they come from? I'd never seen any growing up in the highlands, and now I learned the answer as we drove past mile upon mile of banana plantations. Where they weren't growing bananas, we passed flooded rice fields.

I was happy to see that the road had a cycle lane for most of its length. There was more traffic the other side of Babahoyo, and a short 10km section of dual carriageway with no cycle path. I could imagine huge trucks haring past me with inches to spare, a waft of warm air tickling the leg of my tights. It wasn't going to be a pleasant sensation. I breathed a sigh of relief when this section ended and the cycle lane resumed.

We turned off the road to join a five-lane highway into Guayaquil. Traffic congested every lane, and this worried me, but we hadn't gone far along it when Pablo gave a cry.

'There's the bridge.'

And there it was – the bridge over the Babahoyo River where we would start our ride. I couldn't believe it. There was hardly any of Guayaquil to cycle through. We'd be out in the country in no time and heading along a road with a wide cycle lane. This was going to be safer than many of the roads we'd pedalled along in Scotland.

Guayaquil's huge river-cum-harbour was impressive. Two rivers – the Babahoyo and the Daule – joined to form the Guayas River that fed into the Pacific. Between the rivers was a long peninsula attached to either side of the Guayas by two long road bridges. The first bridge was huge; the second was a little shorter. The two bridges were completed in 1970 and, combined, are known as the *Puente de la Unidad Nacional*, or National Unity Bridge. Together they span a total length of 2,186m. It was going to be the perfect place to start our sea-to-summit adventure the following day.

We reached the main commercial centre of Guayaquil via a tunnel under a small hill guarded by a statue of a giant monkey. Javier had booked us into the Grand Hotel, which backed onto Guayaquil's main cathedral. We had dinner on a terrace beside a swimming pool, underneath a statue of a giant iguana. The day's drive had been good for me. Tomorrow would be fine, and then we would be a quarter of the way.

We met promptly for breakfast at six o'clock, aiming to start the cycle ride at seven, when we hoped the roads would still be relatively quiet. I was concerned about the distance we had to cover, but Edita was bullish that with such an early start we could complete the 100km to Montalvo by lunchtime.

My first job of the day was to smear my cycling shorts with my brother's gift of the 'Rolls-Royce of butt cream'. It was clearly posh, because it was described on the tub as *chamois crème*, including an accent over the word *crème*, instead of the more prosaic *cream*. But in case you're thinking that some poor mountain goat has had its teats squeezed to produce an ointment to smear on my backside, I should explain that it's called chamois cream not because it comes from the milk of a chamois, but because, in the old days, the padded insert that cyclists wore inside their shorts was made from chamois leather. Before the advent of chamois inserts, legend has it that riders used to shove steak down their pants to help prevent sores. The meat would become tenderised so well during the ride that some cyclists would even eat it later in the evening.

The cream was antibacterial and was supposed to reduce friction. Happily, in Scotland the only saddle soreness I experienced was gentle bruising, but the less pleasant type results in skin abrasion, inflammation of the hair follicles, and ultimately the build-up of pus under the skin (known as an abscess). This was not to be contemplated. I took a big scoop out of the tub and smeared it generously over the padded part of my cycling shorts. This was so much easier than performing contortions in a tent while trying to smear it onto myself. I felt a cooling sensation as I pulled on my cycling shorts, but I was pleasantly surprised to discover that wearing them commando style didn't feel as odd as I had expected.

The hotel breakfast was excellent. I feasted on scrambled eggs, fried beef and empanadas, but I dropped a Danish pastry and bowl of yogurt on the floor. I hoped this wouldn't prove to be an omen. We left the hotel in good time, and Pablo drove us the short distance across the two bridges and found a lay-by to park in just beyond. Edita and I cycled onto the bridge to take photos and start the ride. I filmed a short video from the cycle lane, shouting loudly above the roar of the traffic.

'Here we are at the Babahoyo River in Guayaquil, about to start off on our sea to summit. This is at sea level... Edita is ready to go and we're going to cycle that way... Edward Whymper when he came took a riverboat to Babahoyo, but we're taking these bikes along the main road.'

Edita pushed off and rolled her bike back down to the foot of the bridge. I followed along behind, and soon we were pedalling along the five-lane highway out of Guayaquil. It was already busy; I pedalled nervously with four lanes of traffic outside me. My biggest fear was getting steamrollered by a bus. I imagined being flattened pancake-fashion, like some cartoon character with my four limbs akimbo, ready to pop back up like a spring and resume my 3D shape at the first gap in traffic. It would be an interesting start to our adventure, but not one I was keen on.

Drivers seemed to be aware of us and treated us with respect. Nobody tried to share my lane, though I often felt a vehicle slowing down behind me and an engine rumble tickling the hairs of my neck. Every so often I glanced back to check Edita was still there. I soon gained confidence as we left the city behind us. After a couple of kilometres the five lanes dropped to two. We cycled under the main road north to Babahoyo, and I turned right onto a slip road that looped clockwise to bring us up onto it.

Now we were on safer ground – just two lanes of traffic with a wide cycle lane. The next 60km were flat and monotonous, but we made good time. We regularly passed electronic speed checkers bearing the legend *su velocidad* ('your speed'). If I see one of these when I'm driving a car, I tend to squeeze the brake abruptly and annoy the driver behind. Only when he gives me a loud 'up yours' blast on the horn do I realise I'm already driving well below the speed limit.

This time, however, the lights of the speed checker flashed like a challenge.

'Show us what you're made of, NC500 Boy,' they screamed.

I put my head down and pedalled like a lunatic, feeling the veins of my neck tense as I shot past like a bullet from a gun. Well, like ketchup from a bottle anyway. I looked up and the sign read 28. Was that any good? I had no clue, but a few kilometres later I had another chance. I took a deep breath and gritted my teeth, legs rotating frantically like a hamster's as it hurtled round a wheel. My efforts were just as futile: 27, the sign read. I was livid, but I had a third chance. This time I started my sprint for the line several dozen metres early, imagining Mo Farah on my shoulder. There was no way I was going to let him past. Thirty-four – thirty sodding four. I shook my fist in the air... and abruptly put it back on the handlebars when I felt the bike lurch towards the verge. I was exhausted when the fourth speed checker came and I could only muster a paltry 24.

Luckily Edita was ahead and couldn't witness my feeble antics. But perhaps her prediction of reaching Montalvo for lunch didn't look so silly. I decided to ignore the fifth speed checker, and took up the more leisurely pursuit of monitoring our progress by the green signposts by the side of the road that marked each kilometre. When they reached 60, we would be nearly in Babahoyo and well on our way.

We saw Pablo a few times. Sometimes he drove past us and stopped in the wide dusty roadside verge to offer us snacks and check our bikes. On one occasion we passed him birdwatching across flooded fields with a pair of binoculars in hand. We stopped for water and snacks, then sped on. The short section of dual carriageway before Babahoyo passed without incident. Traffic was quiet. We reached Babahoyo at only 10.30. I couldn't believe it. Pablo was right – it would have been ludicrous to stop there for the day.

Whymper arrived in Babahoyo at midnight by river steamer. He had arranged mules in advance and left the town at one o'clock the following afternoon. At the time, it was a small port of 2,000 inhabitants where goods were brought upriver from Guayaquil in transit to Quito. He described how many of the houses were built on stilts because in the rainy season the river flooded its banks and the town became a lake.

Babahoyo is now a trade centre for the surrounding agricultural area, trading in rice, sugar, balsa wood and fruit. It has grown to over 100,000 inhabitants, but many houses are still built on stilts. We passed beside a long row of them as we took a main road lined with palm trees. The road had been built on an embankment so that water could drain underneath. Below us, the houses looked surreal. I wondered if the owners also wore stilts. Perhaps the homes belonged to a family of circus performers. I cast my eyes up and down the street, expecting to see absurdly tall people in top hats, buttoned coats and exceedingly long trousers parading up and down, removing their stilts to climb onto their front verandas in much the same way you and I would remove our shoes.

I shook my head and came back to my senses. Perhaps I was more tired than I realised.

The 30km stretch between Babahoyo and Montalvo was much quieter. The land remained completely flat as we passed between empty fields broken only by the occasional hedgerow and clusters of thorn trees. The monotony of it all started to tire me, but as we approached Montalvo the landscape at last began to change. Up ahead, we could see the Andes beginning abruptly with lush forest rising into the clouds. Though we were approaching the moment of my worst fears, it had been an encouraging start – I would never have believed we could cycle 100km before lunch on the first morning. Cycling is so much easier when you are riding on the flat, unburdened by weighty baggage.

The town of Montalvo is named after the 19th-century political writer Juan Montalvo, who was born in Ambato, but spent much of his life in exile for writing pamphlets criticising the government of the day. The town's coat of arms still bears a picture of his face. By a strange coincidence, Montalvo also happens to be Pablo's surname, but when we arrived in the town at 12.30 and cycled through, he was nowhere to be seen. Perhaps he was expecting to be mobbed by adoring fans and bowled over by a hail of underwear thrown from the pavements.

We reached the far end of the town, where the road started climbing up into the Andes, and could see no sign of Javier's Toyota Land Cruiser. Edita gave Pablo a call and put him on speakerphone.

'Where are you?' a worried voice came over the line.

'We are in your town.'

'You are in Montalvo already? I can't believe it. I am still waiting at the far end of Babahoyo. I am parked sideways so that you can't miss me when you cycle past.'

'It's a bit late for that I think, Pablo.'

'I will come right away.'

We found a basic restaurant and ate chicken soup as we waited for Pablo to join us. I had somehow managed to pedal 100km in a little over five hours, but as soon as I got off the bike and sat down to eat, I felt shattered. My limbs creaked like an arthritic skeleton in need of a squirt of WD-40 and it wasn't easy getting back on the bike to resume our ride.

It took us another two hours to cover the remaining 14km to Balsapamba as we started our climb into the mountains. Bleak forest and mist lay ahead of us. The road was steep – this gradient would have killed me in Scotland. But with better gears, stronger legs and, above all, no heavy panniers, we were able to pedal slowly without undue strain. Edita seemed to be the better pace setter. She pedalled more frantically than I did, in a lower gear with her legs rotating rapidly, but her pace was gradual, and I could follow behind her with a more sluggish turn of the pedals. In cycling parlance, this pedalling rate is known as a cyclist's *cadence*.

In my case *decadence* would perhaps have been more appropriate. I felt like a glutton crouching over a fondue as I sweated in the humid, overcast conditions.

Pablo drove ahead to scout out possible places to stay the night. He returned only once, to give us directions. We reached Balsapamba at four o'clock. Cutting across a little square, we saw Pablo standing outside the hotel with its owner, a cheerful old man who could have been no more than 5ft high. Pablo towered over him like a giraffe with a guinea-fowl companion.

Our room may have been basic by some standards, but it had a hot shower in a bathroom the size of a cupboard. This worked well for me, given that I was stooping like a centenarian. In the evening Pablo drove us to a restaurant at the bottom end of the long, sprawling town. Edita wanted to walk – she considered it cheating to get in a vehicle – but I had to overrule this when she said she wasn't willing to carry me back up again. I was too tired to talk as we tucked in to a bowl of soup with a large chicken leg floating in it.

The day had gone better than I could possibly have hoped. We had pedalled 114km and climbed 720m. My confidence was flying, even as my body creaked.

The killer day had come, but thanks to Pablo we had been able to shorten it significantly. We had 70km to cover with a climb of 1,900m to the town of Guaranda at 2,600m. We left without breakfast at seven o'clock and cycled 100m up the road to a pleasantly clean café at the bottom of the Hill of Death, the preposterous shortcut we had plummeted down in our vehicle two days earlier. Pablo recommended fried egg and *bolón de verde* ('green balls'), a crispy ball of plantain with bacon bits in it, which tasted much nicer than its name suggested.

After breakfast we cycled under a big green sign that read *Zona Montañosa* ('mountainous area'). It wasn't kidding. We immediately began climbing through jungle on endless zigzags, with occasional glimpses of the trees and villages below. The roadside markers were now counting down the distance to Guaranda – conveniently, as this was our destination for the day. Convenient it may have been, but encouraging it most certainly wasn't. The markers started at 70km, but after ploughing up the zigzags all morning, by midday we had cycled only 22 of the 70.

We ascended into fog, and had to be more careful of traffic. Buses rolled by on the other side. Every few seconds we heard a loud *phussshh* as the driver touched his air brakes. I wondered how often the brakes on buses wore out, and how easily a cyclist could evade one if they did. Edita and I settled into different styles of climbing once again. We stopped to rest every couple of kilometres, when Pablo overtook us in the vehicle, but unlike in Scotland, I never had to get off and push.

Eventually we crossed what appeared to be a pass, and sped downhill for a short distance to the first village we had seen since leaving Balsapamba. Pablo was waiting at an open-air restaurant beside the road. It was basic, but that was to be expected now. Again we were treated to chicken soup with a chicken leg floating in it. I use the word *treated* in the sense that you are treated for an illness. Pablo wolfed down his food, but the constant diet of boiled chicken was starting to make me feel queasy. It seemed impossible that so many chickens existed in such a small country as Ecuador, but the evidence was there before our eyes.

Pablo asked the lady at the restaurant for the names of the towns coming up on the next stretch of road.

'San Pablo, San Miguel, Chimbo, Guaranda… páramo,

Ambato,' she replied.

'Páramo? That's not a town,' Edita said.

She was right. In many ways páramo was more pleasant than a town, but in one crucial respect it felt much worse.

'No, it's not a town. It's the bleak, blank emptiness that creeps across Ecuador's highlands,' I replied, staring at my chicken leg as it floated across the bowl. 'Stretching endlessly as far as the eye can see.'

Pablo started laughing. 'Come on. It's not so bad. You are doing really well. I know that you can cross the páramo easily.'

But the lady had underlined what we already knew from our drive two days ago – that there was nothing but grasslands between Guaranda and Ambato – around 100km across some of the highest parts of Ecuador. Edita's altimeter was more encouraging. It showed that we had climbed 1,500 of our 1,900m, and were now at 2,200m. This gave hope that the afternoon's ride would be flatter, but we were soon to be disappointed.

The Andes – as you probably know – is not a single mountain, but a whole range of them. And the problem with ranges is that not only do they go up, but they go back down again. And then, when they've finished going down – that's right – they go back up. Up, up, up went the road after we left our lunch stop, 300m more before we whizzed 200m down a hill into San Pablo. I zoomed past Edita, enjoying the sensation of lifting my buttocks off the seat, but cursing the wasted climb that the road had so carelessly tossed away without even asking.

The rest of the afternoon became a race to reach Guaranda before nightfall.

'Do you have head torches?' Pablo said at our next rest stop.

'What for?' I replied.

I already knew the answer and it sent a chill down my spine. Ecuador's position on the equator means that daylight hours are quite simple: for most of the year the sun rises at 6am and sets at 6pm. The afternoon was seeping away and we were barely halfway to Guaranda. The thought of cycling that busy road in darkness, with just a climber's headlamp to indicate our presence to oncoming motorists, didn't bear thinking about. We had to make it by six, but how much climbing did we still have to do?

Then something happened that I never expected: for the first time in our adventure, Edita started to have problems.

She was standing up on the pedals and changing gear when I heard a loud crack and she juddered to a stop. She stamped down on the pedals like a motorcyclist trying to kick-start an old-fashioned motorbike, but the bike didn't move. She tried several times, each time stamping harder as her frustration welled.

'Why did they give me this shitty bike?' she cried between gritted teeth.

Edita doesn't swear very often, even less frequently than she laughs at my jokes. It's a rare sight to even see her angry, but here she was, spitting profanities at an inanimate object. I didn't know what to do. I had no idea how to fix the bike, so I tried to calm her with soothing words.

'It's a nice bike. It's just tired.'

Not for the first time, this seemed to be the wrong thing to say.

'Don't be stupid. Bikes don't get tired. It's a shitty bike. I told them it was shitty when we tested it. They were supposed to fix it.'

I fell silent. I didn't want to be the annoying guy, but I had a feeling I already was. Luckily, we didn't have too long to wait before Pablo arrived in the vehicle. He was better in these situations then I was. Not only was he able to keep his foot out of his mouth, but he had practical skills. He examined the bike, but could find nothing wrong. He gave Edita some helpful advice about changing gear and we were on our way again.

But we made fitful progress as the road continued to climb. Every so often I would hear another crack behind me and those dispiriting words.

'Nngggg… shitty bike.'

Edita fights with her gears as she climbs up through the Andes

I was concerned about the time. The road ahead did not look promising – it contoured slowly up a hill towards what appeared to be a pass. Who knew what lay the other side?

'We need to get a move on,' I said.

'It's OK for you. I'm trying,' Edita replied, her brow furrowed in frustration.

'I'm sorry. I didn't mean to blame you. But I'm worried about the time.'

Edita was right. She was struggling, but I seemed to be

flying. I was like Chris Froome powering up the Alpe d'Huez, albeit a fatter, older version without as many screaming fans. Throughout our travels, Edita had always been the strong one. When I became frustrated, she never lost heart. When I stuttered to exhaustion and lay down for a long rest, she never seemed to run out of energy. And when I became disheartened, she remained optimistic. It was a shock to find our positions reversed. My mind returned to that moment near Brora, when I looked up in exhaustion to see a vehicle overtaking just a few metres in front of me. Imagine if that happened during darkness. We had no lights. The driver wouldn't even know I was there until the moment we collided.

Worse still, what if it wasn't me who was struck, but Edita? I imagined a screech of brakes in the darkness and a loud thud. I could hardly think about my reaction, knowing the worst had happened and being helpless to prevent it. The thought was unbearable. We had to reach Guaranda in daylight.

We continued slowly to the pass, where Edita's altimeter read 2,800m, and a roadside marker told us we were 26km from Guaranda. It was 4pm, and even my brain could do the numbers. We had two hours of daylight: that made 13km per hour. On a normal road it would have presented no problem for us, but this road was as normal as a bike with square wheels. We hadn't managed anywhere near that pace today.

But there was hope. We zoomed down 500m to the town of San Miguel, covering 5km in just 10 minutes. The road to Chimbo undulated. Chimbo was the place where we left the main road to descend the Hill of Death on our journey out. It was known locally as *La Olla* or 'The Pot', because it lay in a deep valley with a road circling around its rim. We were somewhere down in the stew and had to climb back out.

Pablo met us at the 14km stone at the bottom end of town. It was 4.45, and we had just enough time if the road was kind to us. I grimaced my way up the steepest hill of the day, up through the town and out the other side. The road to Guaranda was relatively flat and we made better time. It was quiet now and Edita was digging deep. I could hear her gears rattling like a train. She struggled on and I waited for her often. On one occasion she saw me cycle past an angry dog, and called out for me to come back.

The light was fading, but relief brushed over me like a fresh breeze in scorching heat. The worst day of the trip would soon be behind us – and we were still alive.

We reached Guaranda just before dark. The streets of the town were laid out on a grid pattern with steep inclines. To add insult to injury, the surface of the streets were lined with bricks. I rattled along like a skeleton in a cement mixer as we squeezed through traffic on the narrow streets.

We were both on the verge of collapse when we reached our hotel, the Hostal Bolívar. Pablo was standing at the entrance with a camera, and we wheeled the bikes inside to a central courtyard. I could feel the relief oozing through our veins as Edita and I embraced. Somewhere in my heart it was mixing with happiness, curing the anxiety that had gripped me for most of the afternoon.

Although we were both shattered – and my joints creaked like an ancient rocking chair – it had been a positive day for me. I expected this day to be the hardest of the whole adventure, but I had coped much better than I imagined, gliding up the hills like a true mountain climber. We had a rest day tomorrow for my muscles to recover. I no longer had anything to fear from the final two days of the bike ride.

For Edita it had been much harder. Her gears were a concern. For the first time since I had known her, I was the stronger one.

Later that evening we wandered a couple of blocks up the road to Parque El Libertador, Guaranda's main square, a pleasant place with a cathedral and palm trees. We found an Italian restaurant in one corner, where I ordered a delicious pizza with every ingredient in the kitchen. Every ingredient – except boiled chicken.

I was looking forward to our rest day. But the cycling gods had been stuffing themselves with pizza too, and they were preparing themselves to let rip in my face.

12 THE GRAN ARENAL

I woke up with the taste of vomit in my mouth.

This was alarming, and hadn't happened since my student days. Jimi Hendrix is widely believed to have died by choking on his vomit. If it happened to me in a hotel room in Guaranda, I doubt I would be remembered for quite so long.

To my relief, there was no sign that I had actually thrown up, but my stomach was churning, and I had an immediate need to visit the bathroom. It seemed that my body was paying me back for the abuse I had given it yesterday. When I woke Edita during one of my many subsequent toilet visits, she suggested that I might have food poisoning.

At six o'clock, after very little sleep, I was back on the toilet passing several gallons of liquid when my stomach decided it was an opportune moment to present me with the pizza for a second time. What to do? I somehow needed to complete both tasks simultaneously. This isn't an easy situation to deal with cleanly, and may very well be the exact scenario that caused the ancient Greeks to invent the word 'dilemma'.

Luckily the bathroom had the dimensions of a broom cupboard, and I was able to lean over and project my vomit onto the shower floor at the same time as evacuating my bowels. This action suggested that Edita's diagnosis had been correct. A few explosive seconds later, I found myself studying a tapestry of molten cheese, mushrooms, onions, red pepper and little slivers of meat. The pizza no longer seemed so mouth-watering. I'm not a doctor, but at that moment I felt confident of my diagnosis that the delicious pizza had been the cause of my ailment.

The one consolation was that I didn't have to get back on the bike and pedal up to Chimborazo. We had a rest day ahead of us, and I spent most of it lying in bed, feeling as if my stomach had a 40-ton juggernaut passing through it. I had no energy – and, despite having ejected all my food by two different methods, I had no appetite either. Pablo came over with simple, digestible food, including bananas, apples and crackers, and Edita mixed me some rehydration solution to drink. I hadn't peed at all during the bike ride the day before, and it wasn't until mid-afternoon that my waterworks resumed normal service. Happily neither Pablo nor Edita were suffering. Like me, they had both eaten pizza, but not the sumptuous, multi-layered feast that I had enjoyed, with more ingredients than you'd see on the final of MasterChef.

Our day off gave Pablo an opportunity to look at the gears on Edita's bike. He took it out around the town and discovered that the two top gears on the bottom ring were sticking.

'The rest of the gears are OK,' he said. 'and you can still use the equivalent gears on the middle plate.'

This was annoying, but as long as Edita remembered not to use the broken gears, the bike was still usable.

She went for a walk around the town, but returned after less than an hour.

'I don't like this place,' she said. 'I feel like everyone is staring at me.'

With her blonde hair and pale skin, Edita certainly cut a striking figure in Guaranda, where everyone else was darker. But even so, this seemed a big statement from someone who had spent many years of her life working in the developing world. It emphasised that we were in a backwater, untouched by tourism. Pablo scoured the town trying to find a restaurant that didn't serve the staple of chicken soup with a floating leg of chicken, a dish whose ubiquity was starting to make Kentucky Fried Chicken seem appealing. It took him some time, but he found one, and at 6.30 I tried to force down some steak and chips. It was 24 hours since my dodgy pizza, and I was still feeling nauseous.

Food poisoning doesn't usually last much longer than that. I hoped I would feel better by the morning, but by 6am I was still passing red pepper from the meal two days earlier. We had another 1,700m to ascend that day, over a distance of 41km to the high point at Chimborazo park gate, where the road topped out at 4,300m. But that was only half the distance. We then had a 41km descent to Riobamba at 2,750m. All of the confidence I had gained from the ascent to Guaranda had been ejected by my stomach and was now watering the town's sewers. It seemed inconceivable that I could do that all over again – at an even higher altitude – in the frail condition that I now found myself in. But I had no choice.

As King George V lay on his deathbed contemplating a visit to the seaside town of Bognor Regis, he uttered the famous last words 'bugger Bognor'. I wasn't quite on my deathbed, but as we left Guaranda I had a similar phrase running through my mind – namely, 'fuck Guaranda' (perhaps reflecting my more plebeian upbringing). I had spent almost my entire time within its confines lying in bed or sitting on the toilet.

Gloomy grey clouds hung over the town as we continued our journey to Chimborazo. Guaranda was known as the Rome of the Andes for the simple reason that, like Rome, it's built on seven hills (and it's in the Andes). Other comparisons with Rome end there. As you have seen, the town's cuisine is not up to Roman standards. Nor are there many cultural sites of note. When Whymper passed through it in 1879, he told his waiter, perhaps a little tactlessly, that it was 'dull'.[34] The waiter went a step further, describing the town as 'deplorably dull'.

The gloom reflected my mood and the lousy feeling in the pit of my stomach. I longed to see Chimborazo, and breathe the fresh mountain air of the higher altitudes, but escaping Guaranda proved to be a lengthy purgatory. The streets were already choked with traffic at 6.30 when we left the hotel. To reach the main road, we first had to negotiate the precipitous streets of the central grid, with their brick surface that juddered underneath me and churned my insides. We had only passed a couple of blocks when a cobbled street went up a hill sloped like the sides of an equilateral triangle. I put my bike into the gear labelled 'tortoise on treadmill' and tried to cycle up, but we found ourselves in a sea of traffic, crawling between cars at a speed where the tortoise could find himself rolling backwards on the conveyor until he falls off the end.

I came to a halt. Ahead of me Edita was gamely standing up on her pedals, which enabled her to keep the bike vertical despite not making any forward progress. In cycling terminology this is known as a *track stand*. If that doesn't mean anything to you, in a helicopter it would be called *hovering*, while swimmers call it *treading water*. In all three situations, it's usually done deliberately, but not this time.

'Bugger sodding Guaranda,' I said to no one in particular (though King George may have smiled at me if he were listening). Then I did something that I hadn't done since those heady days in Scotland: I got off and started pushing my bike through the traffic. It was the only time in Ecuador that I had to get off and push, and I was annoyed about it.

Gradually the gradient lessened, but Guaranda showed no sign of letting me go easily. We found ourselves on a long hill out of town. The pollution was intense. Public buses spewed out black clouds as dense as volcanic ash. They were particularly annoying when they stopped in front of me to pick up passengers. I had to cycle behind them for a short distance, and they invariably waited until I was in the process of overtaking before pulling out again. This gave me a second opportunity to inhale the waft of petrol before they disappeared up the road. I swallowed deeply and thought of Darth Vader scything Obi-Wan Kenobi with his lightsaber, ducks skidding across a frozen pond, Elton John playing 'Candle in the Wind' on a Baroque harpsichord accompanied by an indigenous Australian on a didgeridoo – anything really. Anything my mind could conjure up to take it off pizza.

Chimborazo revealed itself for the first time across green hills to the right when we reached the main road. It was wreathed in clouds that resembled the fug of an exhaust pipe. This seemed fitting. I couldn't wait to bask in its foothills, but Guaranda kept sprawling.

We were still in the town when we saw Pablo's car parked outside a café. In his poem the *Inferno*, Dante and the poet Virgil escaped hell by climbing down into Satan's genitals and emerging in the southern hemisphere at a place called Mount Purgatory. Somewhere on the fifth terrace they encountered the souls of the prodigal face down on the ground, unable to move – a state I was in imminent danger of finding myself in. Was Chimborazo Mount Purgatory and Guaranda its fifth terrace? It seemed likely to me that I was being punished for my useless ambition. We still hadn't left Guaranda and I was shattered already. I almost fell asleep at a table. I chewed on a cheese sandwich for a few mouthfuls and stared at a mug of black coffee. As Pablo helped Edita change the saddle on her bike, I was forced to listen to a loud TV set playing some irritating South American game show.

It was nearly 8.30 by the time we emerged from Guaranda into fresher mountain air. I felt better out on the open road, but we still made slow progress for the first 10km. At 2,600m the land was still green. Trees lined the grassy roadside, and the road slanted through lush farmland fringed with eucalyptus trees. Green kilometre markers by the side of the road counted down the distance to Ambato and kept me motivated. They read 70 as we left Guaranda. I focused only on the 30km we had to ascend to the plateau, where I hoped things would get easier.

We stopped frequently for snacks, and I ground my way uphill on a diet of miniature Ecuadorian bananas. They seemed to be doing the job as I sped up the road and left Edita behind. Every 2km I stopped and waited for her. I didn't do this on purpose – lord knows it wasn't a race – but it was easier for me to go at my own speed, and get the job done, than cycle at Edita's more controlled pace and eventually drop behind her.

By 10.30 we had climbed 1,000m and covered half the distance. As we climbed, the vegetation became increasingly sparse and the trees more isolated. The bell shape of Chimborazo dominated the road ahead. With light traffic, a smooth surface, and the security of a wide cycle lane, I might even have enjoyed this stretch of road had I been in better shape (or a half-decent cyclist). My brother – and all those other peculiar people who like to cycle up massive hills – would have loved this section. It was one of those days when the sun seems to blast a way through an overcast sky and light up the land.

We were ascending a broad valley. Folds of hillside extended to our right, and we could see our road for many miles as it contoured up the valley ahead of us, slowly gaining height. Gradually we left the green world behind, and entered the barren landscape of the Gran Arenal, the desert plateau on Chimborazo's western side. I had made a promising start under the circumstances, but how long would it last? I was still unable to eat much. I tried to force down bananas, tangerines and cereal bars, but my stomach remained fragile. With every turn of the pedals I was becoming weaker.

Things started to get much harder as we crept up to 4,000m. I was still going uphill more quickly than Edita, but I was weakening, while she remained sprightly and cheerful. At a roadside marker I stopped and waited for her. Her smile stretched from ear to ear, and she took out her camera to take some video footage.

Chimborazo peers through clouds during the ascent to the Gran Arenal

'Wow, Chimborazo! How high are we, Mark?'

I shook my head and stared at the ground as I leaned against the handlebars. I must have looked like I was about to collapse. It wasn't the ideal time to have a camera thrust in front of my face, and I didn't even have a comb.

'No idea,' I said, unable to muster more than a few grunts.

'I think it's four-one-something,' Edita continued into her camera. 'Wow, so far we came. This is amazing. What a view. Still a bit to go today, but we're making good progress.'

As the vegetation thinned into alpine desert, with tufted grassy patches among stony ground, the hills became longer and steeper. I gritted my teeth and cycled on up. Now I experienced a strange phenomenon: passing motorists started beeping their horns at me. The first time it happened, just as the vehicle was on my shoulder, it made me jump. I couldn't understand the reason. I was cycling well inside the wide cycle lane, and causing no difficulties for passing traffic. My temptation to use the two-fingered gesture that I might have used at home was suppressed by the knowledge that it's not well understood outside the UK. Perhaps the middle finger might work better?

A loud parp echoed behind me, and I was just about to raise my hand in anger when the vehicle passed and I looked up. Somebody was smiling at me out of the back window and giving the thumbs up.

They weren't beeping because they were annoyed with me, but as a gesture of support.

I was nearing the Chimborazo plateau, close to the apex of our climb, and these motorists were congratulating me for cycling all the way up. It made me feel like a superman; I was even wearing tights. It was a nice moment. From then on, at the sound of every horn, instead of raising my hand

and flicking them a V-sign, I gave a friendly wave.

If only these supportive gestures could have acted like a drug then all might have been well. But, in reality, I was digging deep. Very small bananas are good for many things – making a banana milkshake or a very small banoffee pie spring immediately to mind – but to power a vigorous cycle ride up through the Andes they're somewhat inadequate. My energy levels were depleting more quickly than an iPhone after the latest software update; but while I continued to pedal, I didn't notice that many gigabytes of my potent man-force were draining away in the background.

The road flattened out as we reached the Arenal. I could see Chimborazo through bands of cloud, its snow-clad summit staring at me like an eye through a letterbox – with, I swear, an evil glint. I had watched our road slanting up the hill towards the plateau. When we reached it, I hoped for some respite to rest my weary legs. I had pedalled up for many hours, the volcano growing as we approached it. But a merciless headwind slammed into me the moment the winding hill became a long flat section of tarmac stretching into the distance. Along with drawing pins on the road (and an abscess up your rectum, obviously), a headwind is one of the worst things a cyclist can experience. As it winked at me through the cloud, I was sure that Chimborazo knew this.

I was just about to swear at that winking eye – a sure sign of madness – when Pablo drove past in the support vehicle, bringing me back to sanity. He slowed as he passed me and slid down the window.

'There is a restaurant in one kilometre,' he shouted. 'I will wait for you there, and we can have some lunch.'

This was music to my ears and I pushed down harder on the pedals. The thought of food gave me a burst of energy. In addition to very small bananas, Pablo had been carrying all manner of tasty snacks, such as tangerines, energy bars, chocolate and peanuts, but my body hadn't been tempted by any of them. I hoped that a proper meal of hot food in a restaurant would make my stomach realise what it had been missing.

I followed Pablo's Toyota Land Cruiser to a place 1km before the junction. Here the road to Chimborazo's park gate turned off the main road from Guaranda to Ambato, and a cluster of half a dozen houses lay either side of the road. The setting was bleak.

Outside a small thatched bungalow, a red sign advertised *desayunos*, *almuerzos* ('breakfast, lunch'). Next to a photograph of a dreary plate of beans, some chickpeas and a fish, the words *carne, pollo o chuleta* ('meat, chicken or chop') exploded. The words were definitely more exciting than the pictures.

Grey clouds hung overhead, obscuring Chimborazo from view, and the wind gave a chill to the air. The landscape was a drab brown. Even the dry clumps of grass failed to provide any colour. Nothing about this gloomy setting gave any reason to be cheerful – not even the restaurant.

Pablo was standing outside the vehicle. His face looked grim.

'It's closed,' he said.

It was 12.30, and we had made it to 4,100m, but I was exhausted, and the only things that could revive me were rest and food.

'Have you seen the statue?' Pablo said.

Beside the entrance to the restaurant was a statue of a man in old European dress from the Victorian era. He looked very serious. Or was he sneering? Either way, I didn't like his expression.

I recognised him immediately. He was an old friend, and I'm sure you know him by now too.

'And you can fuck off, Whymper,' I shouted.

It didn't matter who he was. He was sitting outside the restaurant; it was cold, windy, and the restaurant was closed. It wasn't much of a welcome.

A moment later, somewhat sheepishly, I decided to take a photo. Luckily he didn't object.

Edita cycled up behind me. She was shaking her head and smirking a little. In fairness to her, this wasn't the first time she had seen me act like this on a bike.

'He's a statue. He can't hear you,' she said.

I swung my leg off the bike and propped it against a wall (the bike, not my leg, you fool). As I shuffled over to the Land Cruiser, I suddenly realised how exhausted I was. I could barely walk. I opened the door and slumped in the passenger seat, breathing heavily. I tried to lie down and sleep, but there wasn't enough room to stretch out. It didn't help that a gear stick was prodding my ribs.

It was cold outside. We were above 4,000m, which meant temperatures around 25°C lower than at sea level three days ago. It occurred to me that a diet of small Ecuadorian bananas alone might not have provided the energy that I needed. Perhaps I should eat more salt and sugar. I tried to eat a bag of crisps, but could only get halfway through before I had to give up. Then I tried eating a Snickers bar, but managed only half of that, too.

A Snickers bar – what kind of man can't even eat a whole Snickers bar? That's like choking on a lettuce leaf or burning with pain while trying to swallow a yogurt. What poison did that pizza from hell contain if it could not only turn my stomach into a mediaeval siege weapon but also destroy my appetite for chocolate?

After a few minutes I started shivering.

'There's not far to go now. You're doing amazing,' Edita said.

But I knew we still had over 50km to cycle to Riobamba – and, although mostly downhill, it seemed inconceivable that I could manage it in my present state. My consolation was that I knew the entrance to Chimborazo Wildlife Reserve was four, maybe five kilometres away. This was the high point on the road; beyond it we would be largely freewheeling.

'The next eleven kilometres will be the hardest,' Pablo said. 'You are dehydrated and at your weakest. After that, it's all downhill.'

'Another eleven kilometres?' I said.

He nodded. 'It will be tough, but you can do it. There is another restaurant at the gate.'

This was a killer blow. I had put all my energy into reaching this point, believing that soon I would be able to stop. And if I hoped I would be leaving our lunch break strong and refreshed, that hope was gone too. I'd eaten next to nothing and sat in the passenger seat panting and shivering like a man waiting for the gallows. When we left the vehicle for the next leg of our journey, I was still weary, and those 11km loomed large.

A cold wind blew across the plateau when we set off at one o'clock. I wore an extra layer, but still I was shivering. We turned off the main road 1km later to continue up the plateau to the park gate. The road from Guaranda to Ambato had been as smooth as a billiard table, but the surface changed as soon as we turned off to Riobamba: it was still made from asphalt, but it had become much rougher, with a lining of stone chips that provided friction for the bike. I had to pedal harder for every rotation of the wheels.

The plateau was desolate, with long stretches of road disappearing into the distance. Even the vicuñas grazing beside the verge failed to spark my enthusiasm. I knew from previous journeys that we were cycling directly beneath Chimborazo, but the mountain was now in cloud. I dug deep, but my stops were becoming more frequent, and I could no longer reach the next roadside marker without stopping. At each rest I leaned on the handlebars and tried to recover my breath.

I really wanted to lie down on the soft verge, like I had in Scotland. Those stops, when I had fallen asleep for a few brief moments, had revived me and enabled me to continue slowly. But here the verge was not so inviting; all around were miles of rocks and sand, with no comfortable bed to lie on.

This wasn't my only discomfort. Perversely, despite having barely eaten, I was seized by an uncontrollable urge to relieve my bowels. I'd purged the diarrhoea in our hotel room that morning, but now it seemed to be coming back. It felt like all the chicken legs that I'd eaten over the last few days were stampeding through my colon and trying to force their way out of my ringpiece.

I looked around for a place to go, but all I could see was featureless desert. There was nowhere to crouch down without being an art display for passing motorists, a break from the monotonous miles of sand. I've never been much of an exhibitionist, and my curiosity value would have been greatly enhanced by the fact that I was wearing my wrestler's outfit – a pair of Lycra cycling pants with shoulder straps that went on under everything else. I vowed that I would never wear such a ludicrous item of clothing ever again. There was no way to drop them without first removing my two shirts. I would effectively have to strip naked and turn my cheeks into the howling wind.

To me this would be mortifying; I would be unable to finish quickly enough. Traffic was scarce on this remote mountain road, but that didn't matter. I could guarantee this would be the moment that the Ecuador branch of the Harley-Davidson Riders Club passed by in convoy on their annual members' road trip. Defecating al fresco in front of an audience as 'Ace of Spades' by Motörhead echoed in my ears was not on my bucket list.

And how was I going to wipe my backside afterwards? By scraping it clean with rocks? Pablo had toilet paper in the support vehicle. Perhaps I could fall asleep and wait for him to arrive?

Since lunch, I had struggled for 6km along a road rising gently over long straight stretches, but now it rose steeply on a sharp hairpin. There were just five more kilometres to the park gate, but my stomach was screaming at me. How on earth was I going to get there without my bowels exploding like a volcano?

Edita spied a grassy area just inside the hairpin.

'Why don't you take a rest here? When you are better we can go on.'

I didn't need any persuading. Within seconds I had parked my bike and was lying on my back. Although more comfortable, I really needed half an hour's sleep to get my body back on track.

After two minutes I heard Edita again.

'I need to go. I'm getting cold here.'

'OK, in that case, please can you call Pablo.'

'What?'

'Please can you call Pablo. I'm going to get in the support vehicle.'

'You're giving up?'

'I don't care.'

'I will call him, but then you should try to get back on the bike. It's not far now.'

Not far? There were still over 40km to Riobamba and I had nothing more to give. A combination of nausea, diarrhoea, altitude, and a complete lack of energy had floored me. As Edita continued up the hill, I twice walked over to my bike and prepared to resume the ride. Each time, I staggered to the verge and had to close my eyes as a wave of dizziness suddenly gripped me; each time, it seemed pointless and I walked back to lie down again. Then I heard Edita's voice from higher up the hill, encouraging me to continue. For a third time I got up and tried to get back on the bike, but again my head span and my stomach churned.

I was flat on my back when Pablo arrived. He seemed disappointed, even angry with me.

'It's a shame. There are only a couple of kilometres, and after that it gets easy.'

'I don't care any more. I'm not here to kill myself or break records. I'm just here for an enjoyable holiday.'

I knew this was true. I wasn't making excuses. I genuinely didn't care about anything at that moment except relieving myself.

We overtook Edita on another long, straight stretch. Three minutes later we reached the familiar stone archway of the Chimborazo park gate and drove underneath. The restaurant was shut – which was going to be a problem for Edita – but my only aim was the toilet. I hoped I wouldn't miss. When I climbed out of the jeep I could barely walk. At the toilet I discovered there was no paper, so I staggered back to the jeep to get some. I was badly dehydrated, and this little excursion dashed any hopes of continuing to Riobamba on the bike. I wasn't getting any better. In fact, I was getting worse. If I were to recover enough to continue with this adventure, then I needed rest.

The holiday would continue, but for me the sea-to-summit challenge was over – that little tick in the box to say that I'd done it and I'd played by the rules. But for Edita it was still on.

I don't know how long I spent on the toilet. I lost track of time. Glaciers melted; civilisations came and went; they had even invented trousers that told you when your flies were undone. When I returned to the vehicle, Edita was sitting in the back, drinking juice and feasting on snacks.

She offered me some nuts, but the thought of eating them made me want to retch. I raised the palm of my hand and turned my head away.

'Eat!' she said.

'I've tried. I've been trying since Guaranda. It's no use.'

'How can you hope to get to Riobamba on an empty stomach?'

'I've given up that hope. I'm going with Pablo.'

There was a brief moment of silence that seemed to go on much longer.

'I don't believe what I'm hearing,' Edita said eventually.

I turned away and hung my head.

'I'm sorry.'

There was another pause. I couldn't bear to look her way and see the anger on her face. When I did look up, she seemed to be holding back tears, but I couldn't be sure because they were hidden behind a look of defiance. I knew from our conversation in Scotland that if I abandoned the ride, she would continue alone. I had never doubted for a minute this was true.

'I can't believe you're going to abandon me to cycle down to Riobamba alone.'

'We won't abandon you. We'll stay behind you in the support vehicle, and make sure you're safe.'

I don't know whether she was listening when I said this, or if she wilfully misunderstood, but when Pablo returned to the vehicle, she gave him a different set of instructions.

'I'm going on,' she said. 'You take Mark to Riobamba then come back to support me.'

'No,' I said, 'I'll stay in the vehicle and we'll drive behind you.'

'You're abandoning me.'

My heart was melting. Of course I didn't want to abandon her, and in my mind I wasn't. I didn't want her to stick beside me as I limped home like an injured soldier. I had become an invalid, and heaven knew how long it would take me to reach Riobamba. By contrast, Edita was still strong and could probably get there in half the time without me. By no means would we abandon her; we would follow her every inch of the way.

But she wasn't seeing it this way, so what could I do?

I took a deep breath and closed my eyes. I opened them and gazed through the front windscreen at the bleak desert landscape that it seemed I would have to endure for a little longer. I didn't know how I would be able to do it, but I would just have to try one last time.

'OK. I'll come with you. But we still have 40km and I'm totally exhausted.'

Pablo had been silent, but now he decided to speak.

'Maybe it is better to rest,' he said.

He had seen me stagger to the toilet and back again, agony written across my face; it would have been obvious those 40km would take me a painfully long time.

'Tomorrow you will be better and you can continue the ride. But if you keep going today, then who knows how long it will take.'

I looked at Edita again and our eyes met. We held our gaze, neither of us willing to look away. Her manner was still defiant, but she appeared to be thinking.

Then, suddenly, she opened the door.

'OK, let's go then. It's getting late.'

When we left the park gate at 2.30, Edita was on fire. Perhaps she was still angry and channelling it into the ride.

Perhaps my presence that day had been holding her back. Whatever the reason she shot downhill like a bolt of lightning as we followed her in the vehicle. There were times when Pablo had to put his foot down to keep up with her.

We passed two more restaurants. Neither of them was open. Though Pablo seemed concerned, nothing could deter Edita.

'Let's keep going to Riobamba,' she said.

She hurtled onwards, down into the pine trees of the forest zone. The Scottish cyclist Graeme Obree famously claimed the world hour record (for cycling the furthest distance in one hour) using a home-made bike fashioned out of the parts of an old washing machine. I wondered if Edita hadn't secretly attached bits of an old lawnmower to her bike to provide a little extra oomph. On the downhill sections, she cycled so quickly that we could follow behind without feeling like we were driving slowly. We reached a flatter section, overtook her and continued for what felt like a few kilometres.

'I think we should stop and wait for her,' I said when we reached a village.

'Wait for her? It's OK, she is right behind us. I can see her in my wing mirror,' Pablo replied.

'She's right behind us?'

'Yes, she is very quick. She is going almost as quickly as we are.'

A second later, she sped past without even stopping to wave. Pablo started the engine and continued. Edita never stopped as we passed through farmland and villages. The road appeared to flatten, but this didn't slow her relentless pace – she was a machine, swallowing up the distance in a way we had never done before. It was as though I had been a burden to her, as if she had been towing me up the hill like a horse with a cart. Now the burden was lifted and she was free to gallop away.

I lost track of time, but I continued to measure the distance by the roadside markers. After 31km we passed Edita at the top of a steep hill that joined the Pan-American Highway at its foot. She was steaming onwards like a bat out of hell. The hill continued for many kilometres and we stopped at the bottom, expecting a long wait. But had we put the song 'Bat Out of Hell' on the stereo, then the intro would still be playing, Meat Loaf's dulcet tones yet to be heard, when Edita pulled up alongside us.

'There are just ten kilometres to Riobamba,' Pablo said. 'It's going to be difficult for us to stop again until we reach the city.'

'It's OK. I will keep going. See you at the hotel,' Edita said. And then she was gone.

We waited for five minutes at the junction, then turned onto the Pan-American Highway, expecting to catch her soon. But we didn't see her for a long time, and I started to get worried.

'We should have seen her by now,' I said.

'It's OK. She is quick, very quick,' Pablo said.

We finally caught her on the outskirts of Riobamba – I had no idea how she managed to get there so quickly. Determination must have been welling inside her like a furnace. As we passed through the city, Pablo crawled behind her like a support driver in the Tour de France. Edita led us through a maze of streets using Google Maps on her phone, which was mounted on a handlebar, and soon we were passing through many traffic lights on a tree-lined dual carriageway. I was expecting a small town, but Riobamba sprawled for miles. Exhaust fumes mingled with the steam coming out of Edita's ears.

We reached the Hotel Monte Carlo at 4.30. Our room was spacious, with a curtained window overlooking a small central courtyard. By now, Edita had forgiven me for abandoning her, but I still felt nauseous and no better than I had 24 hours earlier. The hard physical labour of the morning had given my body no chance to recover; I hoped my rest in the afternoon would help.

As if to underline my decrepitude, I logged in to the hotel Wi-Fi and learned that Mark Beaumont (who was, you may remember, the lunatic who cycled the North Coast 500 in 38 hours) had just become the first person to cycle round the world in 80 days, at a rate of approximately 400km a day. That was further than we were cycling on this entire trip – every day, for two and a half months. The only thing we had in common was the name 'Mark'. Even his second name was more evocative than mine.

Had he finished here, in this very hotel, then I would probably have crouched down on both knees, rammed my head between the spokes of his front wheel and screamed at the top of my tired voice.

'Cycle away, Marky Boy, you son of a gun – I'm not going anywhere.'

It was some consolation that, thanks to Edita's superhuman effort, the sea-to-summit challenge was still going strong.

An hour later we had showered and changed. We walked past the old colonial railway station to find somewhere to eat. During dinner, Pablo talked about what it takes to complete a challenge like ours.

'It is ten per cent physical and ninety per cent mental. The mental part comes with experience. If you look at the people who complete crazy endurance challenges, they are usually in their thirties and forties. People in their twenties may be fitter and stronger, but they haven't yet developed the mental part.'

How that accounted for me with my ageing joints, I

didn't know. I was in my forties too, and only a little older than Edita, but her mental capacity for this challenge was far in excess of mine. Pablo was right: I hadn't been in the right mental state up there on the plateau. Endurance athletes have the ability to push to their limits and then go beyond – sometimes a long way beyond. What takes them to such extremes is a mental quality: determination. They don't give themselves the option of giving up.

When I descended from the summit of Everest in 2012, I was easily as tired as I had been today and more besides. But I managed to fight on until I reached our high camp because I had no choice. Had I not done so, I would have died up there.

Today I did have a choice and I took a different path. I was able to get in a support vehicle and continue our adventure the following day. Some people might call this soft, but I don't care. Give me some feathers and I will wallow in them. I have no more craving to be an endurance athlete than I have to win a TV cake-baking contest. I don't even want to be a cyclist.

There wasn't far to go. I would be overjoyed to get off the bike and back on my feet. Our final day of cycling was a short one: only 30km and 850m of ascent straight up the Pan-American Highway to Urbina on the east side of Chimborazo.

I was feeling better after a good night's rest. My stomach was still giving me discomfort, but I no longer felt as nauseous, and my appetite had improved. On the downside, Edita was now feeling tired and had suffered broken sleep.

I was liberal with the butt cream now that the end was in sight (of the cycle ride, that is). I smeared great handfuls into my cycling pants like there was no tomorrow (which there wasn't as far as the butt cream was concerned). We left at 8.30 and cycled for several kilometres up a long dual carriageway, enjoying the beautiful morning. Chimborazo rose above the haze as we biked through the traffic of Riobamba. From the south the mountain exhibits its most distinctive shape, with three summits – the Whymper (6,310m), Politécnica (5,878m) and Nicolás Martinez (5,702m) – each diminishing in size as we looked from left to right. Its snowy top looked like it was floating in the air.

The city gradually petered out, but it was many kilometres before we left it behind. The road climbed gradually for most of the way. It would have been an easy ride, but we made slow progress in our jaded state, and I was dismayed to find that this part of the Pan-American Highway had no cycle lane, like it did near Quito. This put us more on edge. Only when the road shrank to a single lane were we granted the luxury of a metre width to cycle in.

Chimborazo rises above the Pan-American Highway

The exhaust fumes presented a bigger problem and my nausea returned. We passed a road sign to a place called Guano, which more or less reflected my condition at that moment. Pablo met us at a toll station 10km out of town, and once again I struggled to eat, queasiness welling with every bite. My water bottles were laced with fruit-flavoured hydration salts to replace some of the nutrients that I'd lost over the last few days. But my body was becoming sick of these and craved the refreshing taste of plain water.

We struggled on, mile after tedious mile up the main road. Relief washed over me when we reached the turn-off to Urbina. By then, we had climbed from 2,800m to 3,600m and cycled around to the east side of Chimborazo. We were looking at the mountain end on, and it now appeared as a single snow-capped dome. To the north, Carihuairazo had now come into view. It was much smaller, but its three jagged teeth held plenty of snow, and it looked a tricky proposition.

A lovely peaceful road led for 1km to the handsome train station at Urbina. The white walls of the station building were immaculately clean, and a series of gable ends patterned its walls like festival tents. They were crowned with a rust-red roof that complemented the blue sky overhead and the emerald green of its well-tended lawns.

Immediately opposite the station was our lodge, the Posada la Estacion. We rolled our bikes across the road and came to a halt.

'My god, this is such a relief. I'm so glad to get off this sodding bike,' I said to Edita as I dismounted. I swung my leg over the crossbar, but clipped it with the end of my toe. I let go of the bike as I lurched sideways, staggered, then fell face-first into the verge.

Edita roared with laughter. I started chuckling along as I wheezed in time to my breathing. I lay prostrate for longer than I needed to as the relief pattered over me like rain. I meant it, like nothing I had ever meant before.

13 CARIHUAIRAZO

Opposite the train station at Urbina stood a colourful two-storey building painted with green and blue stripes. A wooden balcony overlooked the entrance, and its sloping roof was decorated with ancient terracotta tiles.

This was our lodge, the Posada la Estacion, and Edita remembered it well. It was here, on the evening of 16 April 2016, that she experienced her second 7.8-magnitude earthquake. Most people are lucky to get one.

A man stood in the doorway with a silver-grey beard and a colourful bandana over his head. He was compact and wiry, rather like a pirate. It's probably what the Italian cyclist Marco Pantani would have looked like had he survived into his sixties. His eyes shone with a keen intelligence; this was a man who had remained humble despite having seen a lot in those 60 years. I was a little jealous. If I look as cool as that in 20 years, I thought to myself, then I'll be a happy man.

There was an amused expression on his face, and I wondered why; but then I realised that a minute or two earlier he had probably watched some idiot park a bike in front of his hotel then dive head first into a bush.

Edita wheeled her bike forward and greeted him.

'Hey, Rodrigo, it's me, Edita. Do you remember last year,

the *terremoto?'*

He smiled. 'Yes, I remember, with your friend Margaret. I don't forget an evening like that.'

I had heard a lot about Rodrigo Donoso, the owner of Posada la Estacion. He had been a trekking guide for over 30 years, and worked closely with members of the indigenous communities on the fringes of Amazonia. He used to own the station building and ran it as a hotel before it was taken back by the government and he moved across the road. There was also a rumour that he had many sons and daughters by different wives. I don't know if this held any truth, or whether it was just part of the legend that he didn't feel he needed to correct. I was looking forward to meeting him. Javier had hired him as our guide for the circuit of Chimborazo, partly because he knew him to be an interesting character who would enhance our trip.

The lodge had a lot of character too. Ancient wooden ice axes adorned the walls. The rooms were named after volcanoes, and ours – Antisana – had framed prints of Edward Whymper's engravings, including my favourite. When Whymper stayed in Cayambe village a few days before making the first ascent of Cayambe, he watched a lady emerge onto a balcony and empty a bucket of slops over a minstrel who was serenading her with a guitar. The incident left such a deep impression on him that he made a line drawing of the incident and published it in his book. And there, hanging over our bed was the very same picture of the feisty damsel in mid-toss, while the minstrel strums on, oblivious to the unconventional gift he's about to receive.

After lunch we said our goodbyes to Pablo. We were sorry to see him go – he had been an integral part of our team effort. He was a great fixer, and his knowledge of bikes and cycling was invaluable.

Before he left, we discussed our sea-to-summit challenge.

We still believed it was the first time it had been done in Ecuador, but we couldn't be sure. We were taking such a roundabout route by doing a full circuit of Chimborazo that it's unlikely anyone will ever follow in our footsteps. But were sea-to-summit challenges to become a thing in Ecuador, what would a sea to summit of Chimborazo involve? There were many well-qualified athletes in Ecuador, such as Karl Egloff and Santiago Quintero, who could make a far better job of it than us. They wouldn't ponce around doing a circuit of Chimborazo. They would go straight up and down while I still had my head over a toilet bowl in Guaranda.

Straight from Guayaquil up to the Carrel Hut would be the obvious way if you were acclimatised, but purists might even argue with our starting point in Guayaquil. Although we started at sea level, strictly speaking Guayaquil is not on the coast but on the Guayas River, a few kilometres upstream from its mouth in the Gulf of Guayaquil. A stricter version of the Chimborazo sea to summit would start on the beach at Playas on the Pacific Ocean, a day's cycle ride from Guayaquil.

'Is there anything else you would do differently?' Pablo asked.

'I wouldn't have that shitty bike,' Edita replied. 'A mountain bike with lots of gears is the right kind, but mine was missing some. Mark's bike was OK.'

This was a feed line I couldn't let pass.

'I think if I did it again,' I said, 'I would use one of those bikes with an electric motor.'

We laughed.

As he stood to shake our hands, Pablo was wearing the same grin I remembered from when he walked into Javier's house. There was a thoughtful expression on his face. I wondered if he would remember this cycle ride as deeply as we would, or whether it was just a job to him, with a pair of potty gringos just like any other.

'It's been wonderful,' he said. 'When I first met you, I didn't know whether you would be able to do it, but now I have no doubt. You will succeed.'

'Yes, we should be able to finish it now,' I replied. 'We've done the hard bit. We've climbed Chimborazo once already; we can do it again.'

'Thanks to you, Pablo,' Edita said. 'We couldn't have done it without your support. We're a team.'

'I just drove the car. It's easy. You guys did all the hard work. Good luck with the rest of your adventure, and I hope we meet again sometime.'

But as we watched him climb into the Land Cruiser and drive away with a wave, I knew that he couldn't possibly believe that. His support had been psychological as much as physical. He had given us confidence and company. We would miss him a lot.

We had 24 hours to rest in Urbina before continuing with our trek around the northern side of Chimborazo. It was now three days since I ate that poisoned pizza in Guaranda, and I still had a delicate stomach. I needed to replace a lot of calories, but I could only pick at my food. Rodrigo recommended that I drink some of his 'special tea'. I agreed eagerly, ready to spend the afternoon sitting under the table singing Bob Marley numbers and giggling uncontrollably, but I was disappointed to find that his special tea was just normal tea laced with oregano.

He asked me to sign his 'Everest book'. This was a photographic edition of Jon Krakauer's *Into Thin Air*. A few blank pages at the back had been signed by Everest summiteers who had stayed at the Posada la Estacion. The two most recent signatures belonged to Edita and Margaret, and the other two belonged to the Ecuadorian climbers

Rafael 'Chapico' Cáceres and Esteban 'Topo' Mena. I wondered if it was compulsory to have a nickname, and I thought about scribbling one of my own – Mark 'Still Has the Shits' Horrell, for example – but it didn't seem right.

Not for the first time on this trip I felt uncomfortably out of place. No disrespect to my fellow signatories, but the autograph of the one really important guest was missing. Rodrigo told us that the great Italian alpinist Reinhold Messner had stayed here when he came to interview the 'Ice Man'. Messner was famous for being the first man to climb all the 8,000m peaks. He ascended many of them solo, carrying minimal equipment, and often survived overnight bivouacs somewhere up in the death zone. He had somehow survived into old age, and was in the process of opening a series of museums in the Alps, celebrating mountaineers and other people who made a living from the mountains. The Ice Man, Balthazar Ushka, would certainly have been of interest to him. He was a 73-year-old local man who made a living climbing up to 4,800m to chop blocks of ice off one of Chimborazo's glaciers and carry them down to sell at the market in Riobamba.

Crazy man, I thought to myself. There had to be easier ways to earn a living. But that's enough about Messner – he probably thought the Ice Man's way was tough as well.

The next morning Rodrigo showed us around the garden. There were two huts at the back built in the indigenous style with adobe walls and thatched roofs. The first was a single room with a fire in the corner (which he retained as a museum piece). The second hut was his home, which had a mezzanine level and living quarters. Other interesting features included a porcelain plant pot made from a gentlemen's urinal nailed to a tree, and – most intriguing of all – a 3m-deep guinea pig pit. On a bed of straw at the bottom, half a dozen furry rodents were looking up at us with wistful faces. Rodrigo told us that guinea pigs are easier to keep than rabbits because they don't jump and they don't burrow. They were not pets but meals.

'People ask me if they have names, but they are for eating, so I tell them Monday, Tuesday, Wednesday, Thursday...'

It came as a surprise to learn later that Rodrigo was a vegetarian.

Even more surprisingly, he told us that although he is now 61, he still holds the record for running around Chimborazo, in a time of 14 hours.

'Like that crazy guy who ran up Cotopaxi in only one hour,' I said casually, to keep the conversation flowing.

'Ah, you mean Karl Egloff. Actually, he is my cousin.'

But before I had time to apologise, Rodrigo was continuing. He was unstoppable.

'Karl said if he knew he would be such a good runner, he would never have become a cyclist.'

I sensed an opening and leapt into it, like a corpulent bather plunging into a paddling pool.

'Do you know if he's ever climbed Chimborazo from sea to summit, like Edita is doing?'

'And you,' she said.

Rodrigo shook his head. 'No, not yet.'

I looked at Edita. 'I cheated, but you can still be the first.'

Javier arrived for lunch with another guide. Marco Castillo had just completed his UIAGM certification, becoming the latest mountain guide in Ecuador to obtain the Rolls-Royce of mountain guiding qualifications (no connection with the Rolls-Royce of butt cream, though we still had some left over). He turned out to be the same Marco who had led

Pablo and his friend Steve up Cotopaxi when they completed their Cotopaxi sea-to-summit adventure. Javier had a hunch that the Chimborazo circuit with an ascent of Carihuairazo could be a good commercial trip, so he'd brought Marco with him to learn the route off Rodrigo so that he could lead it.

You may think that three guides would be overkill to escort two of us around the mountain, but we were happy to have the company, and it meant that we shouldn't have to do any map reading ourselves. In any case, Javier would be supporting us in the vehicle, driving from camp to camp while we walked.

We left the lodge in Urbina at 2.30. I was alarmed when Rodrigo immediately mounted the railway embankment and started walking along the track.

'We'll walk along here for about a kilometre, as it's quieter,' he said.

'Er… you've checked the timetable?' I asked.

'There are about two trains a week.'

I walked with Marco to begin with. He was quietly spoken but inquisitive. Later he produced a notepad and pen, and took notes and GPS coordinates for the hike as he followed behind Rodrigo.

The railway line ran parallel with a smooth, metalled road that passed through farmland on its journey across the foothills of Chimborazo. The track was slightly higher than the road, and we were able to look into the distance across this verdant pasture – such a contrast to the barren desert of the Gran Arenal on Chimborazo's west side. The road was quiet, with very little traffic. It looked peaceful, and I couldn't help wishing that we'd followed it from Riobamba, instead of suffering the choking fumes of the Pan-American Highway.

To my relief, after 2km Rodrigo left the railway line and

turned up a dirt track. We followed it for several kilometres as we ascended through farmland into increasingly idyllic scenery. The afternoon sun was lowering directly over the summit of Chimborazo, and the mountain was masked by a bright band of fluffy cloud that hid its features like a shawl.

This handed the stage to Carihuairazo over to our right. Its trio of jagged summits appeared to be laden with glaciers, but Rodrigo assured us that most of this was snow. The summit on the left was more snow capped.

'That is Maxim,' Rodrigo said. 'Five thousand and twenty metres. It is the highest summit of Carihuairazo.'

It looked lower than the other summits from our position because it lay at the end of a summit ridge that we were looking along. The summit on the right was a black pyramid carrying only a few patches of snow. It rose up on the near end of the ridge.

'That is Mocha,' Rodrigo said. 'That is the summit I take my clients to when we trek from Urbina.'

'Maxim and Mocha sound like types of coffee,' Edita said. 'What's the middle one called, Macchiato?'

'Central,' Rodrigo replied.

Edita looked disappointed.

A broad snowy couloir separated Central from Mocha. All of the summits looked accessible, and the mountain stood proudly over the páramo landscape.

Our destination for the evening, Urkuhuasi Hut, was Rodrigo's second home – a thatched cottage that he had built on top of a grassy hillock, looking across the broad valley of the Rio Mocha to Carihuairazo. To reach it we walked across a plain of tufted paja grass, shining with mirror-like dew ponds. Clumps of golden ragwort, with their yellow flowers and silver leaves, added splashes of colour. We had climbed to 4,100m and found ourselves in a lush wonderland. It was the same altitude as the place where I'd collapsed on

Chimborazo's west side. There I could find only rocks and sand to lie on. Had I collapsed here, on the east side, I would have had a comfortable bed of fresh grass. I could have had a nice snooze and carried on.

By the time we reached the hut, the clouds had cleared off Chimborazo's flank to our west, exposing its three summits once again. This time they increased in size from left to right, with the broad dome of the main Whymper summit last of all. To the east the land fell away to the Amazon far beneath us. Beyond our grassy plateau was a sea of cloud, with the tall summits of Tungurahua and El Altar just peeping above the horizon.

Carihuairazo from Urkuhuasi

Shortly after our arrival the sun dropped behind Chimborazo and the temperature dropped with it. Inside the hut there was a single small room with a table and a wood stove. Upstairs was a wooden platform with three beds. Both Marco and Javier have their serious sides, and we ended up having a deep conversation about religion, rather like a church service. It went on for two hours, which – coincidentally, was the same length of time it took my obstinate stomach to eat a plate of rice. Had I eaten it grain by grain with a pair of tweezers I couldn't have been any slower.

Over breakfast, Rodrigo told us about the plane crash on Chimborazo in 1976, and his part in its discovery. On 15 August, Saeta Airlines flight LU-232 set off from Quito for the short 45-minute flight to Cuenca, carrying 4 crew members and 55 passengers. It disappeared 20 minutes later somewhere over Ambato. Its fate remained a mystery for 26 years, but in October 2002 two climbers who were exploring a new route up the Garcia Moreno Glacier stumbled upon the wreckage.

They didn't report the discovery immediately, believing that the plane they found was already known about. Four months later, Rodrigo was contacted by a television channel, Teleamazonas. They told him that a retired army major now working in the Directorate of Civil Aviation had approached them, offering an exclusive story about the plane's discovery for $10,000. The major had learned about it from the two climbers, who eventually became curious and approached him for documents about the 1976 crash. Teleamazonas refused to pay the major, but they wanted the story, so they asked Rodrigo to go and look for the plane.[35]

It took Rodrigo and his team only three days to locate the wreckage at 5,310m. He was interviewed on live television. Although the plane was badly damaged, frozen into the ice, and much of the debris had disappeared under the glacier, they were able to uncover human remains with identification cards of known passengers, and even some newspapers from the day the plane disappeared. These confirmed beyond all doubt that the wreckage belonged to flight LU-232. One 26-year-old mystery was solved, but another emerged: Rodrigo said that the plane had been looted of all valuables when they rediscovered it. He believes that someone else must have found it much earlier – maybe even before 2002 – and also kept quiet about it. There was a story about a lady from Cuenca who found her husband's wedding ring being sold at a market in Riobamba. She believed he had been wearing the ring on the day the plane vanished.

Eventually Rodrigo paused for breath, and we were able to leave Urkuhuasi at nine o'clock. For the next six hours we enjoyed the nicest trekking I had experienced in Ecuador, across thick, treeless grasslands, under a clear cerulean sky with views as wide as an ocean. The jagged ridge of Carihuairazo remained a constant shape on the horizon to our right, while Chimborazo's changing outline formed a wall to our left as we walked around it. Clouds obscured parts of both mountains from time to time.

I walked slowly, happy to be trekking once more and using my legs in the way they were designed, but I still didn't feel 100 per cent. My stomach was empty and I was surviving on snacks.

Almost as soon as we began walking, Rodrigo resumed the conversation.

'Do you know Alexander von Humboldt?' I heard him say to Edita.

'The guy who climbed Chimborazo?' she replied.

'No, he did not climb it. I have a book with his story back in Urbina. He exaggerated many things about his climb. He only reached about 5,200m and said he was bleeding from the ears because of the altitude. Imagine that – and he was a scientist!'

I listened only partially. Rodrigo was one of those people who can talk endlessly about any subject. And he did. As

Edita indulged him enthusiastically, I ambled slowly behind and heard snatches of conversation about the indigenous tribes of Ecuador, plants of the páramo, animal behaviour... At one point I swear I even heard them having a discussion about the faeces of the vicuña.

'They dig pits in the earth and huddle together to sleep,' Rodrigo said. 'You can tell it's a vicuña pit. There will always be a pile of dung nearby, with little green rosettes growing on the top. The dung is shaped like little beads, like you find on a necklace.'

'Really? That's amazing,' Edita said.

Was it? I was tempted to dispute this; there's nothing so amazing about very small stools. But I didn't want to get drawn in, so I slowed my pace again. Like me, Marco was lingering at the back, taking notes, admiring the landscape and enjoying the experience of being in the mountains.

He looked up and smiled.

'They're talking about turds, Marco,' I said.

'It's OK, it's better back here.'

As we slowed, Rodrigo's voice gradually faded into the wind, and peace and solitude washed over us. We crossed over a brow of hillside and saw them waiting for us. It was about the 57th time it had happened that morning. They were still talking animatedly. I looked at my watch. Exactly 2 hours and 47 minutes had passed by since we started walking.

They paused in their conversation and looked at us.

'Are you OK?' Edita said.

'Is my pace too quick?' Rodrigo said.

'Your pace is just right,' I replied. 'Marco and I are walking fifty metres behind in the "no talking" group. If we can hear what you're saying then we're too close.'

They looked quizzical. I scratched my chin and feigned curiosity.

'Rodrigo, in Ecuador, what is the record for the longest amount of time someone can talk without stopping?'

'I don't know.'

'It's two hours and forty-seven minutes. I've been timing you.'

He roared with laughter.

'My girlfriend is always telling me that no one can talk as much as me,' he said.

'She's right.'

Yet in spite of the talking I felt perfectly relaxed. We stopped two or three times by pools in the grass, where we rested in the sun and ate sandwiches. Edita spent a lot of time studying the glaciers to the north, trying to work out the route she had taken the previous year. It had been wet and grey then and she had seen little of the surrounding landscape.

Chimborazo gradually changed shape as we traversed around it. At one point we could see as many as four summits – the Nicolás Martinez, Politécnica, North, and Veintimilla summits. By the time we had circled to the north side we could see only the Whymper and Veintimilla. We walked across a grassy plain to a gentle pass where a herd of llamas grazed, then descended a dirt track for half an hour. Vicuñas grazed in the moorland to our left. They squeaked like birds when we stopped to film them. We learned later that vicuñas are reared in this area, known as Mechahuasca, and released into the wild as part of a reintroduction programme.

We reached Refugio Mechahuasca, at an altitude of 4,200m, at 3.30. There were two huts, each with bare concrete walls, three small rooms with double bunks, and a small adjoining kitchen. It was the most basic refuge I had stayed at in Ecuador. The local community owned it, but nobody took much interest in its upkeep apart from a warden who (according to Javier) didn't feel empowered to do anything to improve it without their agreement. But it did the job for us as a staging post to climb Carihuairazo.

I was still struggling to eat while we had a robust discussion about our start time for the climb. Edita and I wanted to leave as late as possible. But the guides, led most vocally by Marco, wanted to leave at stupid o'clock – which, as you will know by now, is the standard departure time for most climbs in Ecuador.

I explained my views on early starts.

'We miss the enjoyment of the climb when we complete the ascent in the dark,' I said. 'I know it's safer to climb at night, but surely the risks are manageable?'

'Excuse me,' Marco said, 'but these mountains are tropical. The snow melts quickly here. If we leave too late then there will be rockfall.'

His use of the word *tropical* made me think of pineapples.

'I know it's tropical in the lowlands, where the bananas and rice fields grow,' I said, 'but surely up here in the mountains, conditions are alpine?'

There was silence as I looked around the table. Rodrigo was smiling, but Marco and Javier glared. I even discerned a scowl on Marco's lower lip. I sensed that my remark had been considered unhelpful.

'We wake up at two o'clock and leave at three,' Marco said.

I tried my best not to smile, but it wasn't easy.

'Marco is UIAGM-certified,' Javier said.

This was too much, and I started laughing. The tension had been broken, but not everyone in the room understood why.

'What's so funny?' Javier said.

'I know the UIAGM issue you with an alarm clock that only works before midnight,' I said.

I don't know how deep a brow can furrow, but wide trenches were appearing above Javier's eyebrows and I was worried that he might injure himself.

'OK, we will get up at two,' I said, 'but I should warn you that I will be grumpy at that time in the morning.'

Nobody knows if Whymper made the first ascent of Carihuairazo in 1880, and nor was Whymper very sure himself. He made *an* ascent of *a* summit – whether it was the main one is open to debate. In June he camped south of what he described as its two principal summits, believing the eastern one to be higher. It was cloudy when he set off for the top, and remained so for the entire ascent.

He left his camp by lantern light, accompanied by the Carrels, his interpreter Francisco Campaña, the 'pleasant-tempered' David Beltran from Machachi, and a dog called Pedro that had attached itself to the party. They followed a ridge they had noted when the sky was clear. When daylight came they could rarely see more than 50m in the thick cloud, and the last man on the rope couldn't see the first. After less than two hours they reached a glacier and cut steps up it. The snow steepened until Pedro started whining and refused to go any further. They took it in turns to carry him the rest of the way; his achievement in being the first canine to climb Carihuairazo was therefore tempered by the fact that this was clearly cheating.

They reached the summit at 11am, 'a snow cone too small to stand upon'.[36] Whymper believed at the time that it wasn't the highest point, and he confirmed this on the way down when the clouds cleared. They looked back and could see they had climbed 'the western of the two principal peaks, which is distinctly, though slightly lower than the eastern one'.[37]

In fact, it wasn't even one of the two principal peaks. It's likely from a sketch in Whymper's book that they climbed the central one; which, as we know, had the evocative name Central. In 1951, Arturo Eichler, Horacio Lopez Uribe and Jean Morawiecki made the first undisputed ascent of the Maxim summit.

I was dreaming of being followed by dogs when my alarm woke me at 2am. I never enjoy getting up while I'm still half asleep, but I'd been through this process for night-time ascents many times before. You just get up, get dressed, and get on with it.

'How are you feeling?' Javier asked me at breakfast.

'Tired and grumpy. But don't worry, that's normal,' I replied.

Despite trying hard to look miserable in the forlorn hope of making our guides feel guilty about the early start, I was actually feeling much better. I rarely feel hungry in the middle of the night, but the fact that I didn't have any trouble getting down some granola and coffee suggested that my appetite was returning at last. Had I finally recovered? I hoped so. It was more than five days since I'd eaten that pizza in Guaranda, which made it a good four days longer than food poisoning should reasonably last.

We put our packs and climbing equipment in the back of Javier's Land Cruiser. To reach the foot of Carihuairazo, we had to return up the dusty road we'd walked down the previous afternoon. Javier and Marco decided to take the jeep up the first section – but, unlike me, Edita hadn't been in a vehicle since we left Guayaquil (apart from a reluctant lift to the restaurant in Balsapamba). She wanted to walk all the way from the hut so that no one could accuse her of cheating. I didn't give a toss about that, having cheated once already, but I agreed to accompany her, and so did Rodrigo.

We set off at 3am and walked briskly for 45 minutes until we reached the place where Javier and Marco had parked the vehicle. To the right the land dropped away in the direction we had come from yesterday, while to the left it sloped gently upwards towards Carihuairazo. At least that's what it did when we'd passed that way the day before. This morning we could see nothing.

It took us 10 minutes to sort out our climbing gear and put on our mountaineering boots, and at 4am Marco led us into the páramo. Quite why he was leading was unclear. We could see nothing in the darkness, and Marco was there to learn the route from Rodrigo (who was the one who knew it best). I wondered how he was managing to keep to the trail. Ours was not to question but to follow, so I said nothing, trusting that our guides knew best.

But as we passed through beds of tufted grass and loricaria, following no clear trail, Edita was not so sure. She had her phone out and was checking the GPS. After a few minutes she called a halt.

'Hey Marco, do you know about the Maps.me app?'

He turned around. 'What is that?'

Marco, Javier and Rodrigo crowded around as she gave a demonstration of the free mapping software she had downloaded in Quito. Although the map was basic we knew from experience that the trails were accurate. I decided to stay out of this conversation, and stood silently a few metres away. I was already in their bad books due to our argument about the early start, and I knew that questioning a guide about their navigation could lead to bruised egos.

'Can you really trust this app for navigation?' Javier said.

'For sure. We used it on Sincholagua, and the trail took us all the way to the summit,' Edita replied.

The app showed that we were walking between two trails that eventually met. The one on the left was closest.

After a short discussion it was decided that Marco would angle towards it. We all agreed that as long as we stayed in the middle, we couldn't go wrong, and would eventually meet one or other of the trails.

This was a schoolboy error. Only later did we discover that the two trails on Edita's app were skirting round each side of a mountain – a mountain that we had no need to climb. Staying in the middle meant that we were going straight up it. For the next hour Marco led onwards, stopping from time to time to consult Edita's app. At five o'clock we started climbing more steeply until we found ourselves traversing difficult terrain along the side of a very steep ridge. My head torch was too dim to see clearly where I was putting my feet. The trail must have been somewhere far below us, and I couldn't help thinking that we were lost. We stopped; while the rest of us waited, Marco scrambled along the ridge to see if he could find a way down.

'It will be easier when the sun comes up,' I said to Javier to help pass the time.

He snorted.

A few minutes later Marco returned. 'It's too steep – let's go down here,' he said.

The sun was rising as we scrambled down the bank to our left. After 20m we reached an obvious trail: the one we should have been taking all along.

'Aha, I know where we are,' Rodrigo said.

We had probably lost only half an hour at most. Our guides may have had some red cheeks, but luckily it was still too dark for any of us to see them. As we continued on our way, I amused myself by composing mountain guide jokes; the only problem was that I had no one to share them with.

'And then, at first light, just as we had lost all hope, our three guides found the true path with the help of Edita's

Maps.me app.'

The sun rose quickly as we continued to a col. It was broad daylight by the time we walked across a barren, rocky plateau. The face of Carihuairazo rose forbiddingly into mist above us, black rock laced with snow. Javier noticed some iron stakes sticking out of the snow. He explained that they were put there 15 years ago to measure the retreat of the glacier. It had shrunk by hundreds of metres. It wasn't so much a retreat as a rout, and it looked like the ice couldn't race up the mountain quickly enough. The warden at Mechahuasca later told us that the glacier is now just $300m^2$, which is only slightly bigger than a tennis court. It seemed probable that Roger Federer would still be playing when the last ice cube melted.

We reached the snow line and began climbing. It gradually became steeper, and when we reached a patch of rocky moraine Marco decided it was time to rope together and put on crampons. Edita and I joined his rope, while Javier and Rodrigo climbed behind us on a second one.

Now that we were on snow and actually climbing, Marco came into his own as the guide. This was what he was good at. We were a little quicker than Javier and Rodrigo, and rapidly zigzagged up a steep snow slope. I seemed to have completely recovered from my illness – either that or I found climbing much easier than riding a bike.

Marco headed up a gully with a rock tower to our right. It was much steeper. We had to turn in to the slope and use the front points of our crampons for 20-30m, digging our ice axes into the slope above us for balance. This was proper climbing, and I was just starting to enjoy it. We turned to the right and traversed above the rock tower until we reached the projecting spur of a ridge. I looked to the left and there appeared to be nothing above a high point 50m to our left.

'Is that the summit?'

Marco nodded. I couldn't believe it. It was eight o'clock and it seemed to have taken us next to no time to get there. Compared to the cycling, the climbing had been a piece of piss.

But there was a catch. Weird cauliflower-like ice formations laced the summit – which we soon realised hid a 5m rock tower as we walked along a rocky ridge. There was a small cleft in the very tip. Whymper would no doubt have thought it looked like a giant snow phallus. The same funny cauliflowers filled a gap in the ridge at the tower's base. The ice was soft and delicate, and fell away easily to the touch.

We climbed up onto the fore-summit, and the summit itself was in pancake-tossing distance just above us. Marco climbed down into the gap to see if there was a way across. It was possible if we were careful, but the last metres onto the summit would be very hazardous. He estimated that it would take time – perhaps as long as an hour – for him to clean it by knocking away the soft ice formations. We didn't have time. The sun was rising and soon the ice would start melting. Despite my jokes about the start time, it had been a good call to leave early because we had climbed a face rather than a ridge. When the ice melted there would be a risk of rockfall. We would have to leave those last 5m for another time.

We took our photos on the fore-summit, then stepped down onto a small snow basin just below to eat snacks. At that moment a tiny gap appeared in the cloud.

Edita gasped. 'Look at that,' she cried.

There, right in the gap, were four of the summits of Chimborazo rising 1,000m above us and framed in grey. It looked like a work of art. Few people get to see this completely unexpected view. We took photos, the clouds closed, and soon we could see bugger all again. I couldn't help reflecting that if we hadn't got lost earlier in the day we'd have been on our way down by now. Marco had brought us here at just the right moment. I silently thanked the UIAGM that they place a greater emphasis on climbing skills than navigation.

We descended quickly. Marco set up a sling and belay to protect us as we climbed down the steep gully one by one. I attached the rope to my harness, faced in to the slope and carefully watched where I was placing my feet as I inched my way backwards. At the bottom I untied and watched the others come down behind me. Last of all was Marco, who had to bring the rope with him, and therefore had no protection. He skipped down like a mountain goat.

Back on the páramo, the day took a bizarre turn as we tried to locate our vehicle. What seemed like straightforward terrain from a distance was in fact a series of gentle hillsides teeming with all the plants of the páramo – thick paja grass, *cojines* cushion plants, chuquiragua, and the juniper-like loricaria, known as the palm of the páramo. Our vehicle nestled somewhere among those gentle folds of green, but we hadn't taken a waypoint to mark it, and we couldn't get high enough to see where it was.

We zigzagged from left to right, up and over hillsides, but still we couldn't see it. It was as if the car were parked in the centre of a vortex, and we were being tossed in spirals around it without getting any closer. I kept expecting to crest a rise and stumble upon the Tardis.

We split up, and when I eventually found the car Rodrigo and Marco were already there and lying on the grass. Edita and Javier weren't far behind me.

Edita and I changed into comfortable trekking shoes, and we walked back to Mechahuasca with Rodrigo. It wasn't a pleasant walk. A gale blew from behind and tossed the dust around in waves. This was a different type of vortex, one where you had to keep your mouth closed to avoid swallowing a sand salad.

Some distance along the trail we looked back and saw the ridge that we had blundered up first thing in the morning. Standing in front of the main peak of Carihuairazo there was a whole mini peak, Loma Piedra Negra – or Pointless Peak, as I decided it ought to be named. We had tried to climb it in the dark when we could have just skirted round the edge. Still, it had been a useful reconnaissance trip for Javier, and I was feeling a lot better.

We could now turn our thoughts to Chimborazo and the climax of our adventure.

14 CHIMBORAZO ONCE MORE

'We should try to leave at six o'clock tomorrow. Maybe we can get up at five,' Javier said.

'Very funny,' I replied between mouthfuls. 'We could stay up all night, get pissed and leave in the middle of the night in just our boxer shorts.'

I was happy to find that my appetite had returned, but I was looking forward to a lie-in after this morning's early start. I assumed that Javier and Marco were trying to wind me up. But it turned out they were serious. We had another seven-hour trek ahead of us, and then they had to drive back to Quito. They were keen to get the walk over as early as possible.

It wasn't just Javier and Marco who were going to make the final day of our trek a bit harder. Although he didn't know much about it, Reinhold Messner was to play a part too. Over dinner Rodrigo mentioned that while he was staying at Posada la Estacion conducting research into the Ice Man, Balthazar Ushka, Messner – who was famous for having hair as thick as paja grass – walked from Mechahuasca Hut to Carrel Hut in only four and a half hours. Rodrigo believed this to be a record.

Javier and Marco had their way (again), and we started walking at 6.30, contouring around the foothills of

Chimborazo on a grassy four-wheel-drive track. We knew it would be a long day for the others, so Edita and I started briskly. We saw a profusion of the vicuña dung pits that I'd overheard Rodrigo talking to Edita about a couple of days earlier. At some point during the morning – I don't know when – it became clear that Rodrigo was having a crack at Messner's record. He turned up a narrow trail to the left and took over the lead up a dusty hillside through thickets of paja grass. Then he pulled away as we crossed ridge after ridge. The wind was howling, but after the first couple of ridges the land became more sheltered. We followed Rodrigo's footprints in the sand, gradually ascending. He glided up the slopes like a vicuña. Nobody could keep up with him. He paused only briefly at the top of each ridge until we saw him, then he glided on.

Where did he get the energy? He was supposed to be 61 years old, but was he? Maybe he wasn't even Rodrigo. Perhaps when – or if – we eventually caught him up, he would remove his grey beard, peel his skin off like they do with the villain at the end of Scooby Doo, and underneath would be Karl Egloff.

'And I would have broken the record if it hadn't been for you meddling kids.'

It was the only explanation.

The land became increasingly barren. The paja grass thinned out, but the desert sands remained fertile. Waist-high loricaria bushes extended their tentacles into the air. Eventually the land became completely dry, just desert and rocks, and the occasional chuquiragua bush with its flame-orange flowers.

I started to drop behind Edita too, and struggled to see either her or Rodrigo as I crossed each ridge. But I was beginning to recognise the topography of the mountain from our ascent the previous year, so I wasn't concerned about getting lost. I was keen to follow the quickest route, though. Only Rodrigo knew this – and as the end drew closer he showed no intention of stopping to wait.

I recognised the ridge that we had come down after our previous ascent, with the rock formation of El Castillo on its shoulder. I knew that beyond the ridge it was only a short walk across a plain to Carrel Hut. I had no wish to hurry, and plodded along at my own slow pace. They were all in an ungodly rush to reach the hut and beat Messner's record, but I had a different agenda. It was a rest day for me – I didn't want to overexert myself. Above all, I wanted to enjoy the experience of being in the mountains.

I hadn't a hope of keeping up with them, so I stopped trying. I took off my pack and sat down on a rock as I watched all three of them turn a corner and disappear behind a ridge. It was a lovely spot, and I decided to have my lunch. Time seemed to stand still. All of life's troubles were forgotten. By the time I had finished eating and cleared my head, 45 minutes had passed.

I walked slowly up a gully and across a couple of stony platforms. The route was easy to follow, and I was in a buoyant mood. Soon I saw Marco coming the other way. He had been sent back to find me, but he didn't see me, so I walked towards him. I wondered how close I could get before he noticed. Could I walk up behind him, tap him on the shoulder and shout 'boo', then follow it with an evil laugh? But he looked up, and as soon as he saw me, a smile of relief (or was it amusement?) crossed his face. He immediately pulled out his radio and spoke to Javier.

'We have been worried about you,' he said to me as he put his radio away. 'I am the rescue party.'

'What were you going to rescue me from – stampeding vicuña?'

'We thought you had fallen.'

I looked around me and the rocky hillside. 'And tripped over a rock? Sliced my hand open on a branch of chuquiragua?'

But I was being unfair. They had probably told Marco off for abandoning me, when in reality I had chosen to take my time. The normally taciturn Marco gabbled incessantly, like a relieved childminder who had mislaid his charges in the fairground and scampered around like an excited chicken, only to find them happily playing hook-a-duck.

Edita and Rodrigo waited in the main car park with Javier – and they also looked excited. I found them dressed in gym kit. For the last couple of days they had discussed running down from Carrel Hut to the park gate so that Edita could complete the circle with a cycle ride, walk, climb, and finally a run. I had shrugged this off as boys' banter (yes, I know Edita's not a boy, but that's not the point). Now I could see they were serious, and would have set off an hour ago had they not been waiting for Marco to recover my corpse from the aftermath of a vicuña rampage. Edita didn't look very happy with me, so I silently thanked Rodrigo and hoped the run would help to work off some aggression.

For me, running down a dusty 4WD track at 4,800m after a full circuit of the mountain seemed as appealing as turning around and walking back again. I waved them off, then sat down to eat my last sandwich. I discussed summit routes with Javier. He said the mountain was much drier than it had been two weeks ago, and the Whymper Route, which we were hoping to climb, was going to be harder. But I wasn't concerned. We had given ourselves a five-day window to wait for the best conditions.

We drove down to the gate on the winding road that dropped 500m. Edita and Rodrigo were already there when we arrived. It had taken them only 15 minutes to run down. Javier took us the short distance down the road to *Estrella del*

Chimborazo ('Star of Chimborazo'), the lodge on its flanks that he said would be the perfect place for us to rest before our climb.

Now, you're probably wondering what we were doing taking a vehicle again when we were supposed to be cycling or walking. But by our rules, as long as we started again from exactly the same place, Carrel Hut, then it wasn't cheating to make use of a motor. We needed to rest before our climb, and the Estrella del Chimborazo was a better place for it than the hut. The lodge comprised a series of timber chalets in a grassy valley beneath the south-west face of Chimborazo.

Javier, Marco and Rodrigo were still in a rush. We hurriedly said our goodbyes and let them leave. Still in tortoise mode, I settled comfortably into the dining room at the lodge. I could see why Javier had chosen this place for our rest day – it was like a museum. It was owned by Marco Cruz, a legendary figure in Ecuador's tourism industry, who had completed many significant ascents as a climber, and was one of the country's first instructors of mountain guides. He is considered by many people to be the grandfather of all Ecuadorian mountain guides (metaphorically speaking, that is, not literally – that would have been exhausting).

The dining area consisted of a single room made of wood, with long tree trunks as beams. Marco's old climbing equipment adorned the walls. There were ancient crampons, ropes and carabiners; old mountaineering boots were being used as flowerpots (which was more pleasant to look at than the gentlemen's urinal we'd seen at Rodrigo's place in Urbina). There were also photos of the various plants of the páramo, black-and-white photos of Chimborazo from various angles, Whymper engravings, and historical photos of climbers. It was clear that Marco Cruz was an important man, because there was a photo of him with Reinhold

Messner, and Messner was sporting a rare smile.

We spent a day and a half resting. The staff kept a wood stove burning as we sat and read our books, occasionally looking up to see a hummingbird dancing under the eaves. Chimborazo appeared briefly in the morning, but for most of the day it remained hidden behind cloud.

The next morning Romel arrived to take us back to the Carrel Hut. He was to be our guide on Chimborazo for a second time. I don't know what was going through his mind, but I expect he was keeping his fingers crossed that I was in better shape than I had been during our epic fifteen-and-a-half-hour ascent the previous year.

He suggested a little acclimatisation hike up the Whymper Route that afternoon to examine conditions. He had climbed the route a few weeks earlier, when there had been plenty of snow. We knew that conditions were drier now and there was more rock. If not the Whymper Route, then there were two alternatives. We could take the El Castillo Route up the west ridge, beneath the fortress of rock called El Castillo. This was the route we had taken the previous year; we knew we could do it that way, but it was long and we fancied a change. The second alternative was the Normal Route, straight up between the other two routes from the Whymper Hut, 200m above the Carrel Hut in the basin between both ridges. This route was shorter, but it was known to carry a significant rockfall risk.

We drove up to the Carrel Hut and grabbed bunks in the dormitory. My appetite had returned in full, and I had no problem wolfing down a large pork chop. After lunch, we set off to walk up to the Whymper Hut. It was cloudy, but we hoped the clouds would clear to let us have a look at the route.

As we were passing the hut we saw a figure high above at the Whymper Pinnacles. These shark fins of rock were easily recognisable from Whymper's engraving 'Chimborazo, from a little above the third camp'. In the engraving, taken from lower on the south-west ridge, two figures skirt the pinnacles on their left, while another stands on a snow slope with his ice axe just behind him. It looks as if he's bending down to tie his bootlace. Our figure was higher, and we continued up a scree slope above the hut to meet him. We reached the pinnacles after an hour and a half of walking. We were now at 5,200m, and had climbed 400m.

Suddenly, just as we were resting with a snack, a rock the size of a beach ball crashed down the ridge above us out of nowhere, falling right across the trail.

'Shit, did you see that – where the hell did that come from?' I said.

'Let's put our helmets on,' Romel said. 'There's someone up there.'

'Good idea. But that boulder was enormous. It looks like we'll also be needing cricket pads.'

We continued cautiously. A short distance above, we met a lone climber coming back down. He looked youthful and a little unsure of himself.

'Are you going up?' he asked Romel.

'We are going for a look at the route.'

The stranger had no climbing gear. Romel asked if he intended to climb Chimborazo.

'Yes, I hope so. I've not done anything like this before. My guide arrives tomorrow. I've been coming up here every day to walk up and down the ridge several times. I hope it will help me to acclimatise.'

He told us he was Canadian and that he'd been staying at the hut for several days. If he's been going up and down here every day, I thought to myself, knocking rocks that size down behind him, then I was surprised there was any ridge left. He was in a state of despair that hardly anyone seemed to be reaching the summit. Many climbers were turning back with altitude sickness.

'It's a long day. You have to be fit and you have to be acclimatised,' I said with all the assurance of a master mountaineer. I didn't tell him that last time it had taken me fifteen and a half hours, and that by the end I had the energy potential of a lettuce leaf.

We bade him goodbye and walked up to where the snow started at 5,400m. The clouds remained firmly in place and we could see nothing beyond. It was 4.30. The walk had been good acclimatisation but we were no nearer deciding which route to take for our summit attempt. Back at the hut, six or eight new people had arrived and were trying to get some sleep. Downstairs in the kitchen, the Canadian showed us photos of the Whymper Route that he had taken the previous day when the sky was clear. Romel thought the route might still be possible.

We had a seven o'clock dinner that evening, and the staff went to sleep soon afterwards. There was a strange atmosphere in the hut. We were the only people awake; everyone else would be getting up from nine o'clock onwards to start their overnight summit attempts.

Romel told us about the scouting trip he did on the Whymper Route three weeks earlier.

'Javier contacted me and said "Edita and Mark want to climb the Whymper Route. Can you find out the condition?" So I went up with my girlfriend, who had been up Chimborazo three times, but never reached the—'

'Wait, you have a girlfriend?' Edita said.

Romel blushed. 'Didn't I tell you? She is from Colombia. She is a professional boxer.'

Now it was my turn to interrupt the flow as I started choking on my soup.

'Are you OK?' Romel said.

'Are *you* OK, Romel?' I said after I'd recovered my dignity. 'It sounds like you will be needing additional protection.'

'It's OK. We use condoms.'

'Not that sort of protection. I mean... she's a boxer.'

Romel blushed again. 'It's no problem. Being in a relationship with a boxer isn't as dangerous as it sounds. I'm a mountain guide.'

This last fact was indisputable, and we returned to the subject of the Whymper Route. Romel had found it in good condition, with plenty of snow. In the course of reaching the summit, they broke a trail between the Veintimilla and Whymper summits. I remembered the maze of penitentes last year, with no trail in between.

'I guess your girlfriend was handy at knocking down the penitentes?' I said.

'There are no penitentes this time,' Romel said. 'The route is much easier.'

This was good news. Wrestling a way through the penitentes had been extremely tiring. I knew these weird ice pinnacles were temporary features, and we would be much quicker without them.

'This is great. Perhaps I will only take fifteen hours this time, Romel,' I said.

He laughed nervously.

We sneaked back up to the dormitory and climbed into our sleeping bags. That night I was often woken by people returning from their summit attempts. They all came back too soon to have reached the summit. In the morning we learned that nobody had been successful that night, but it seemed that in all cases they had altitude sickness or were too tired. The Canadian had been discouraged by this, but we found it reassuring that nobody was being thwarted by conditions.

It was a clear morning, and this gave us a chance to study the traverse from the Whymper Route to the Normal Route. We saw a lot of black ice. Romel didn't think it looked promising, but he decided to go for a scouting trip to examine the traverse from a different angle. He returned at noon after walking all the way up to the same point we'd reached the previous day. He said it looked much better from up there, and he now thought there was a 60-70 per cent chance of us getting through. Edita was excited about the prospect of climbing Chimborazo by a different route – we agreed to give it a try. If it weren't possible, we still had enough time to come back down and try one of the other routes the following day.

Back in the dining room, Romel introduced us to another guide, a cheerful character with big glasses. As we shook hands it occurred to me that he looked familiar.

'Haven't we climbed together before?' I said.

He didn't hesitate.

'Of course, Antisana 2009. I remember your video. It's the only video on YouTube of the whole Antisana climb.'

It was Ramiro the poet, who dragged an exhausted Tony to the top of Ecuador's fourth-highest peak all those years ago. His presence at the hut underlined how my connection with this country was deepening.

Romel suggested that we leave from the Carrel Hut at 10.30 that night. This time I didn't argue about the early start. We both knew how long this mountain took me to climb last time, and I didn't want to give him the satisfaction of reminding me. We got up at nine o'clock. The hut was much quieter than it had been the previous night. We three, the Canadian and his guide appeared to be the only people heading for the summit. We made sandwiches in the dining room and had coffee, bread and jam. It was tropical in the hut, but I knew it would get steadily colder for the next seven hours, so I wrapped up in three layers of fleece, PrimaLoft and Gore-Tex.

We left at ten o'clock and trudged slowly up to the Whymper Hut under a bright half moon. We reached the hut at 10.45 and continued up to the Whymper Pinnacles, reaching them shortly before midnight. It felt like a mild night, but it started to get colder when we reached the start of the snow at 5,400m and put on our crampons for the climb. I zipped up, put up my hood, and wore extra gloves. By one o'clock we were on our way again. As the snow angled to the left across the west face, we climbed steadily, and I lost track of time. There was one steep section where the ice was hard and we had to use our front points, but we were soon over it.

After about an hour we stopped climbing and traversed to the left. The angle was about 45°, but the ice was firm, and my right arm started to ache. I'd been training my arms for this moment by lifting pints of beer to my lips at sea level, but I clearly hadn't done enough; I asked Romel to stop so that I could give my arm a rest. In the back of my mind was the black ice section that we had seen from the car park and I knew we still had to cross. This would be the crux of the climb; if we could get across it, there should be nothing to stop us reaching the summit.

We reached the end of the snow and began crossing the section that had looked like a sheer cliff of red rock from below. But slopes can be deceptive when you look at them head on. It wasn't a cliff, but a slope of around 45° hiding a layer of ice beneath a surface of red pebbles. Only when this layer became thin and the ice poked through did the way become hazardous.

Then, just when I thought that it was going to be easy, the moment I had been dreading came.

Out of the darkness loomed a ramp of ice pitched like a

church spire. Although only a few metres across, the ice was as hard as a diamond and smooth as glass. Romel crossed it easily, facing into the slope and stepping sideways, kicking the front spikes of his crampons into the surface. I could see that the spikes didn't penetrate far, but Romel was an expert and crossed with such speed that we hardly registered the difficulty.

Then it was Edita's turn and my heart was in my mouth. She edged her way sideways, trying to kick her spikes into the ice, but could only manage a few millimetres of depth – nor could she get any purchase with her axe when she swung it overhead. With each strike, fragments of ice came away, but the axe wouldn't stick. Imagine climbing a ladder by balancing on each rung with your toenails alone, using only the tips of your fingers to steady yourself against the side rails. Beneath the ladder yawns a chasm, hundreds of metres deep.

The Whymper Hut lurked somewhere far below us in the darkness, and we were one tiny slip from plummeting towards its roof. I didn't dare breathe. Edita climbed upwards a couple of steps, but by her strained posture I could tell the ice was just as hard. I wondered how long my nerves could stand it.

'I'm stuck, I think, Romel.'

'Come back down.'

Safety was a few metres below her to the left.

I braced myself, expecting Edita to fall at any moment. My stance wasn't much more stable than hers. I belted my axe into the ice, but it bounced off like a hammer on rock; I jammed it in again, wiggled it around to gain what little purchase I could, then leaned into it. It was like attaching a roof tile with a smear of Pritt Stick. I was in no position to hold her if she lost her footing, and I didn't know if Romel's stance was any more solid on the other side. If either of us fell, he would need to hold both of us. In all likelihood, we'd all be ripped off the face and hurled into the darkness below.

I could hardly watch as Edita edged across inch by inch. They could hear my heart beating down in Carrel Hut; I knew that one slip and it could be beating its last. I closed my eyes, then opened them immediately. I needed to keep alert.

Minutes went by. They seemed to last a lifetime. Then suddenly she was across onto a safer area of flat stones and I heard Romel congratulate her.

My turn. I eased my way across two steps, a few millimetres of ice holding my crampons in a precarious grip. I needed to whack hard with my axe to get any security for my arms, but I couldn't whack too hard or I would lose my balance. It was going to take an age to get across that way; I decided to try another tactic. I would make a leap across to the safe area. It was only about two metres away – it seemed so close – but jumping isn't so easy when you only have two millimetres of toe to push with.

I took a deep breath, then leapt, forcing a pirouette. It was a move that would have scored zero for style on *Strictly Come Dancing*. Even Ed Balls would have been ashamed of me, but at least I wasn't wearing a sequinned leotard. My pulse thudded in the heart-stopping moment before I landed on the rocks. I looked up, and Edita was smiling. We were all across.

After this, the traverse of the Whymper Route held no more difficulties. Romel expertly picked a route that stayed on rock. Within half an hour of leaving the glacier on the Whymper Route, we rejoined the ice on the Normal Route. We had made it across the gap between, and although a few more hours of climbing remained, I felt confident now.

Romel climbed a little further onto the glacier, then cut a platform to give us a chance to sit down. It was nearly four o'clock and our first rest for several hours. As I took off my pack to take a swig of water, I suddenly realised how cold it was. Both of my water bottles were frozen. I could barely unscrew the tops, and when I did, a thick layer of ice filled the neck. I knew that they wouldn't unfreeze until later that morning when we were heading back down again. I might just as well have been carrying 2kg of Keith Harris and Orville CDs for all the use they were now. At least I could have used the CDs as toilet paper in the event of an urgent need (mountaineers have improvised with stranger items).

We put on our down jackets then continued steeply up the cone of the volcano to join the Normal Route. Now we were back on familiar ground from our ascent the previous year. Edita checked her altimeter. We were at 5,900m. There was more snow than there had been last time, and it felt much safer.

Two monotonous hours lay ahead of us as we climbed steeply on the featureless snow cone, waiting for the sun to rise. Crunch, crunch, crunch went my feet as they trudged up the frozen snow. There wasn't much to engage my mind in the darkness and unchanging terrain, and my thoughts began to wander. I looked up and saw what I thought was a torch high above us: the Canadian and his guide, perhaps, on their way to the summit? But the torch remained stationary for many minutes and I decided it couldn't be human.

Was it a will-o'-the-wisp, the mythical light that lures weary travellers into a peat bog? If so, then what was it doing here? Perhaps it was a mountain version that lured climbers into crevasses. But as I imagined will-o'-the-wisps, I couldn't stop thinking about an old BBC children's programme of the same name. I pictured a giant, cartoon version of Kenneth Williams in the sky above us, smiling down with his pointy nose and hands spread apart.

'Tonight the creatures of Doyley Wood are going to climb a volcano. Arthur the Caterpillar is leading the way, followed by Mavis the fairy with her magic wand.'

I plodded along behind them, and Kenneth looked away, turning his nose up to the sky.

'And at the back comes the Moog, the stupidest creature in the forest.'

I willed him out of existence and cleared my head. Eventually I decided the light must be a star.

Dawn on the Veintimilla summit

Gradually, as the sky lightened, the ground became less steep. We stepped onto the Veintimilla summit at six o'clock. Although Romel had told me what to expect, I still couldn't quite believe it. Last year a field of penitentes had blocked the approach to the lower of the two summits, but now the penitent monks were no longer here. I looked across to the dark curve of the Whymper summit, rising a few hundred metres away. All that stood between us was a crust of firm snow. The penitentes that had caused us so much trouble last time were nowhere to be seen. These ghosts of the snow had melted away.

We could see two black figures approaching the top of the Whymper summit. It was still extremely cold, so we didn't linger. We took our packs off and left them on the lower summit. Then we unroped – the trail was easy and there were no crevasses – before dropping slowly down to the saddle and back up again. The sun was rising directly behind the Whymper summit and it lit our way as we completed the final section. It was just a walk on firm snow, like a procession, and I let the sweet taste of achievement wash over me.

The Canadian and his guide returned past us as we approached the top. I slapped him on the back, but he seemed too tired to respond.

'Don't believe the statistics,' I said. 'It's a hundred per cent success rate from Carrel Hut tonight.'

This was true. Only five of us had left the hut, and we were all here.

Cold but elated, we reached what was now the huge snow plateau of the Whymper summit at 6.30. I hugged Edita and started jumping up and down.

'Sea to summit, sea to summit,' I cried.

The others got caught up in it, and soon all three of us were jumping up and down and squealing like a trio of clubbers on a dance floor. It was something I remember doing once or twice on a Saturday night when I was in my twenties, and only now, doing it again on the furthest point from the centre of the earth, did I realise what a prize tit I must have looked.

For the second time in as many years, we had a clear view of all the volcanoes in Ecuador rising above a sea of cloud: Cotopaxi, Cayambe and Antisana in a line to the north, and the seldom-climbed big three of the south, Tungurahua, El Altar and Sangay. We were blessed to have the place to ourselves.

I took some still photographs, but my camera batteries had gone the way of my water bottles and were too cold to let me take any video. Happily Edita's GoPro was still working. She wanted some summit video footage, and she pointed the camera at me to make a speech.

I rose to the challenge, but I hadn't expected to be heckled by the camera operator.

'I'm going to try and say something without swearing. It's 6.30, the 27th of September, 2017, it's jolly cold and I'm jolly tired, but we're here on the Whymper summit of Chimborazo. And I'm going to turn the camera around, because Edita here has just completed the sea to summit.'

'And Mark too.'

'I cheated, I cheated.'

At this point, the recording ended abruptly.

'Stop saying that.'

'What?'

'That you cheated. Why do you keep saying that?'

'Because I cheated.'

'No, you didn't.'

'Yes, I did. I got in the vehicle.'

'So did I,' she insisted.

'No, you didn't.'

'Yes, I did. To go to the Marco Cruz Lodge.'

'Ah, but that's different. You returned to the same point that you left.'

'Why is that different?'

'It's the rules.'

'Whose rules? They're not my rules. Why do you care that you cheated?'

I smirked. 'Ah, so you're agreeing that I cheated?'

At this rate, it looked like we were going to need an eruption on Cotopaxi to end our argument. If it didn't, then we were in danger of taking even longer than fifteen and a half hours this time.

But in one respect, Edita was right. It didn't matter to me that I'd cheated – only that it had happened, and I wasn't going to pretend that it hadn't. Only one of us had completed the sea-to-summit challenge in its entirety – and it wasn't me. But I'd had a nice holiday, and that was what mattered. It was great to be up here on the summit again.

After 15 minutes on top, we turned and left. I had never expected to be there again, and perhaps this really would be the last time, but I was in good company. At the very end of his seven months in Ecuador, Whymper also made a second ascent of Chimborazo with the Carrels to satisfy the handful of locals who doubted their first ascent. To appease these people, Whymper took David Beltran and Francisco Campaña with him, the two Ecuadorian staff who had climbed Carihuairazo with them.

The ascent was something of a rush before they caught their boat back home. They chose the north-west ridge along what is now known as the Pogyos Route because they were already on that side of the mountain after their ascent of Carihuairazo.

It was an ascent like no other. They left at 5.15, just as the sun was beginning to offer enough light to recognise features in the gloom. The air was still, and they could see that it was going to be a crystal-clear morning.

Or was it?

Whymper lingered behind the others because his hands were cold and he wanted to beat them into warmth before he departed. Just at that moment he chanced to glance across at Cotopaxi and…

Duh, duh, duuuuuh…

There was a drum roll and the clash of a cymbal (at least, there might be in *Whymper: The Movie*, if such a film ever gets made).

At that precise moment, Cotopaxi erupted. Within seconds, Whymper estimated that a column of ash rose 6,000m into the air and started drifting towards them. There was no hope of outrunning the ash cloud. It chased them up the ridge and drifted across the sun a few hours later. When this happened, Whymper swore that the sun went through a cascade of colour changes, from green to blood red, tarnished copper to shining brass. By midday the cloud of ash was directly overhead.

Like it had for us, their route eventually joined what is now the Normal Route up the Thielmann Glacier. At one o'clock, they sighted the 10ft flag pole they had left on the summit after their first ascent. Beltran and Campaña thus became their witnesses. They reached the top at 1.20, and 10 minutes later the dust from Cotopaxi started falling on the summit. It filled their eyes and nostrils, and made eating and drinking impossible. By two o'clock the dust was so deep that the summit resembled a ploughed field; by this point they were breathing through handkerchiefs. The ash cloud obscured all view of the surrounding countryside and Whymper drolly observed that 'our last ascent in Ecuador, like all the rest, rendered no view from the summit'.

The temperature had dropped. By 2.30 it had become so dark that they decided to halt their scientific observations and head back down to camp. Before they left, Whymper took one last summit photograph of a place where, unlike us, he knew for sure he would never return. It wasn't exactly how he liked it to be.

The sky was dark with the clouds of ash, the people shivered under a temperature of 15°F, the wind fluttered everything

that could move, the snow gave a poor foundation for the
stand, and the gloom made focusing uncertain. All the
conditions were favourable for the production of a bad
photograph, and the result was just what might be
expected.[38]

Still, at least his camera was working, unlike my more
modern contraption.

We had more luck with the weather. It was warmer by
the time we regained the Veintimilla summit. Here we
stopped to have a sandwich. Both Edita and I felt ourselves
nodding off to sleep, so we perked up and left the lower
summit at 7.30.

I hadn't forgotten my epic, multi-hour descent on a
super-dry glacier the previous year. This time it was much
easier; there was more snow. But it was still unbearably
tedious. The summit is worth the effort, but Chimborazo
could never be described as an engaging climb. We decided
to descend by the Normal Route rather than returning by the
Whymper. I remembered the ice traverse, when I'd needed
to pirouette like a cavorting celebrity shorn of dignity, and I
didn't want to go through that again. But this decision
proved to be a mistake. It was such a boring old plod down
a steep and monotonous glacier. Had we returned by the
Whymper Route, we would at least have been able to
practise our dance moves.

Once back on rock, we remained roped up with our
crampons on. The mountain was crumbling, and it had
crumbled considerably since our last ascent. I reacquainted
myself with the red cliff the consistency of cheesecake. A few
bites had been taken out of it since our last visit, but I didn't
like it any better.

'This mountain's shit,' I said to no one in particular. 'Why
did we come here again?'

But I knew why, and in my heart I also knew it had been worth it.

We traversed beneath El Castillo, the rocky outcrop on the west ridge. The terrain was unrecognisable from the previous year, and the trail had crumbled to nothing. Parts of it were sliding down the slope. There was a lot of ice too. Chimborazo was trying my patience. It had been a straightforward walk on rock, but now we remained roped together, taking great care where we put our feet.

When we reached the safety of the firmer ridge, the Carrel Hut was still far below us, but this time I was in much better shape. We descended quickly. The terrain remained awkward, peppered with loose rocks, but we didn't stop. We reached the hut at 10.30, after twelve and a half hours of climbing – a good three hours quicker than last time.

I strode into the hut with my head held high. There was no sign of the lumbering wreck I'd been a year earlier. I felt triumphant as I plonked myself down in a chair in the dining room.

'Yay, we've done it,' Edita said, falling into the chair beside me. 'We need medals.'

'We need beer. That's what we need. Lots of it.'

It had been much easier the second time around, as mountains often are. Conditions were better; I was in better shape. We had been doing a lot more exercise, and we were well rested. But most importantly, we had climbed the mountain before and we knew we could do it again. So much of mountaineering (and anything in life) is in the mind.

I hadn't found the whole sea-to-summit adventure quite so easy. The bike ride had taken me to the limits of my endurance. I had been found wanting, and had to take the support vehicle for a short distance.

But, for Edita, it had been a complete success. She had

cycled from sea level at Guayaquil, done a complete circuit of Chimborazo, then climbed to the summit. She had even done a short run from Carrel Hut down to the park gate. We didn't know for sure, but it's likely this was the first time the feat had ever been accomplished. She was truly a superstar.

In any case, whatever the achievement, we'd had a great adventure, and would be returning home with many happy memories of a fabulous country.

Outside Carrel Hut, some cyclists were preparing to cycle down the hill. They had been driven up in a bus, and their bikes were being unloaded from the roof. It seemed to be a popular activity for tour companies to bring their clients here in order to zoom down the dirt track to the park gate. A tour leader was handing out knee pads and elbow pads. I don't know whether any of them were serious cyclists, or simple, everyday tourists on activity holidays.

It's wrong, I know, but I felt a gentle waft of superiority.

EPILOGUE

Just before we embarked on the North Coast 500, Edita and I spent a week back in London getting some last-minute logistics arranged for our two cycle rides. My father emailed me to say that he was going to be in London later that week, and to see if we would be able to meet up. This reminded me to do something I had been meaning to do for a while.

'You mentioned some time ago that you might be able to help me out with a ring. Is that offer still available?' I wrote back to him.

My mother had died suddenly in 2003, before any of the events described in this book took place, and long before I met Edita. My father had kept her wedding ring, thinking I might be able to use it one day. He offered it to me in the early stages of our relationship, but I laughed it off. Edita had been married once already.

'I doubt she'll want to make that mistake again,' I quipped.

Time went by. We continued to spend much of our time living and working in different countries. Then, one day, after a failed attempt to make a home for ourselves in Italy, Edita decided to leave her job to move to London and start a new life. It was a time of Brexit chaos. Despite all the uncertainty for EU citizens living in the UK, Edita was undeterred. We had to find a way of living together somehow.

This showed a lot of trust. I owed her something in return.

Supposing I proposed to Edita on the summit of Chimborazo? Of course, proposing on the summit of a mountain is a bit cheesy these days. Edita might even be half expecting me to do it there. What if we reached the summit and I didn't do it? She might be mad at me for the rest of the trip when we should be celebrating.

We were doing a few interesting things before we got to Chimborazo. There were other places where I could pop the question that would be more original than a mountain summit. If I could get hold of a ring and carry it around with me, I could just ask on the spur of a moment, while we were doing something that I could never have imagined us doing until it actually happened. Watching a dolphin leap out of the water playfully as it followed our boat… Slumped on my back in a grass verge having a camera shoved in my face… Watching Edita wrestle with a langoustine that dangled between us on a portable gallows. These are all examples that never entered my mind.

Dad confirmed that the ring was mine to give to Edita if I wanted. He also confessed – unnecessarily I thought – that, to be honest, he'd given up hope of me ever needing it.

But later in the week he emailed back with bad news. You will have to forgive his strange, old-fashioned use of the English language, but he used to be a university lecturer.

I fear that I've so far failed to find that circular object you requested. I've ransacked the corner of the roof space where I thought it was without success (but managed to use the 3-4 hrs I was up there to clear out some redundant papers). You may have to improvise in the short term. Your brother

hacked a ring out of a chunk of wood with his pocket knife
for the initial purpose. Very sorry, but I'll get there.[39]

Hacked one out of a chunk of wood? Bloody typical, I thought to myself. I'm sure it didn't feel like that to Perran as he carefully carved the ring out of the branch of a walnut tree in his garden.

But I shouldn't have been surprised. When we were growing up, Dad never parked his car in the garage because it was too full of other crap. Later, when he moved house and had a new garage built, he deliberately made sure it was a double garage so that he could store crap alongside his car. As you can probably guess, he now has a double garage full of crap, and still has to park outside.

I imagined holding a roughly hewn bit of wood out to Edita as the hill mist drifted over a damp bog and midges crawled down our necks. Perhaps Scotland wasn't such a romantic place to propose after all. If I got down on one knee to do it then I'd probably end up sinking into the peat. Other adjectives spring to mind. Farcical maybe, but not romantic.

The Andes, on the other hand – there's a land that conjures up romance. There would be lots of places where I could pick up quite a simple handmade ring that Edita could wear until Dad had moved enough of his old papers around to find my mother's wedding ring hiding underneath.

My first opportunity to buy a ring arose at Rodrigo's guest house in Urbina, at the end of our bike ride. He had a craft shop where he and his partner made various items out of polished stone. The shop was usually locked, but the staff would open it on request. Edita asked Rodrigo's cook if we could go in for a look around. Among the postcards, mugs and clothing there was some simple jewellery, including a few undecorated rings. While Edita was busy collecting a few items that she wanted to buy, I sneaked upstairs to fetch my wallet. I would offer to buy everything for her, and slip a ring in too.

Alas, by the time I returned, she had finished her shopping and the cook had locked up the shop and gone away.

Many days later, after we had climbed Chimborazo for a second time and completed our challenge, we decided to go for a few days' rest and relaxation at a jungle resort on the banks of the Napo River, one of the major tributaries of the Amazon. On the way there, we were driving on a good road down a forested gorge east of Riobamba when our bus pulled up unexpectedly in a car park.

It was hot and humid, and I understood that we were expected to walk down a muddy footpath into the gorge to look at some waterfall. So much for rest and relaxation.

'This place is amazing,' Edita said. 'I came here last year after the earthquake.'

'You know about this? I'm not really into waterfalls, you know. I mean, they're OK. But at the end of the day they're just big bits of water gushing over a ledge.'

At the top of the gorge were some souvenir stalls, and I started to formulate a cunning plan. A path dropped 100m or so through forest to the riverbed. There were lots of other tourists, and I couldn't help noticing that the ones coming the other way were dripping in sweat.

'I hope this is going to be worth it,' I said to Edita, trying to sound as grumpy as I could.

Before we reached the bottom of the gorge, the path climbed back up another 50m to a viewing platform above a rock pool. The sheer walls of the gorge hemmed the pool in on three sides. A waterfall crashed down into the pool from a crack in the rock high above. It wasn't bad, if I'm honest, though the waterfall spilling down into Smoo Cave on the north coast of Britain probably pushed it into second place.

The path continued through a cave formed by an overhang in the cliff face. The roof was very low, and there were places where we had to crawl on our hands and knees. I followed behind Edita, ducking my head as I scraped my back along the ceiling above me. We reached the second viewing platform, and I could see that the path beyond continued underneath the waterfall and across a bridge high above the gorge. If I wanted a cold bucket wash then clearly this was the place to come.

I sensed an opportunity.

'Is that path a dead end?' I asked Romel. 'Do we have to come back the same way.'

'Yes.'

'You and Edita have fun then. It looks like a good laugh, but it's not my thing. I'm allergic to cold water.'

Without further ado, and without saying goodbye, I turned around and crawled back through the cave, down the path and back up the other side. My T-shirt clung to me like a rash and I sweated like a pig in the humid air, but I was driven onward by the thought of those souvenir stalls. As long as one of them sold jewellery everything was good. Our luxury safari lodge in the jungle, or in a canoe floating down the Amazon – these would be romantic places to propose. I just needed a ring.

Towards the top of the climb I chanced to glance around.

'Why are you walking so quickly?' Edita said, who was just a few steps behind me.

Oh shit.

'You've caught me up. Why didn't you stay to look at the waterfall?' I replied. 'I thought you wanted to see it.'

'I came here last year. And why are you being so grumpy?'

Our trip to the jungle wasn't as romantic as I expected. Our lodge was on the fringes of the rainforest, and I'm told you have to go deep into its heart to see the unusual wildlife that the Amazon is famous for. Our wildlife spotting was mainly confined to frogs, giant crickets and spiders, including one big hairy tarantula crawling across a computer workstation. It wasn't the right moment, and I still didn't have a ring.

We did visit an indigenous village with another souvenir shop, but alas there were no rings. In any case, on this visit Edita discovered a hitherto unknown talent for using a 6ft Amazonian blowpipe with poison darts. We had several shots at a carved wooden owl across a grassy field. By the end of the session Edita was hitting the owl squarely in the forehead with almost every blow. This was scary, and the symbolism might have deterred me, even if I had a ring in my possession.

I was beginning to think my chance would never come while we remained in Ecuador. My final hope was Quito, and the Mercado Artesanal, a covered market in the Mariscal Sucre area, a few doors down from the hotel where we stayed for our last night in Ecuador. Twenty corridors of tiny stalls, crammed from floor to ceiling with arts and crafts, were crowded into a single block. Alpaca blankets, chocolates, paintings, woven bracelets, mugs, leather bags, key rings, and of course jewellery were just a few of the things on offer.

As we walked through the aisles, I hovered behind, ready to slip away and do some shopping of my own as soon as Edita was distracted by something. But every time she hinted at stopping for long enough to haggle with a stall keeper, and I dropped back away from the action, she turned around and followed me. It was infuriating. Aisle after aisle we explored. It wasn't until the 15th aisle – by which time I'd pretty much given up hope and was yearning for a bar where I could stop and have a beer – that some embroidered table mats suddenly drew her eye.

'What do you think of these? Perfect for our coffee table.'

If I'm honest, I didn't give a toss.

'They look amazing, but don't let the lady rip you off. Make sure you haggle with her for ages until you get a good price. I think I'm just going to look for some T-shirts.'

I rushed off to the furthest jewellery stall I could find, where I bought a simple dark brown band carved from coconut. It only cost a dollar. Many people might consider this a drawback, but choosing rings wasn't my biggest strength. I was worried that, if I spent a fortune on one without asking her, Edita might think me a prize-winning idiot – especially if she thought the ring was shit. Anyway, it was better than a chunk of wood hacked with a pocket knife. Most of all, though, it was just a bloody relief that I'd managed to get hold of the damn thing before we went home.

I had one more important task to perform.

Quito's position in a valley surrounded by mountains gives it one huge advantage on the restaurant front. On its fringes, houses sprawl up the hillsides, presenting plenty of opportunity for long views across the city. Later that night we were sitting on a candlelit balcony with a glass of wine, looking out over the lights of Quito far below. Perhaps this was more romantic than the summit of a mountain, or a Scottish bog, or a jungle lodge surrounded by creepy-crawlies. It wasn't as original, but there's a reason why the old tried-and-tested ways are the best.

For all the difficulty I'd had trying to furtively get hold of a ring, I'd not actually considered how to deliver the question. I thought that would be the easy bit. I expect a few of you have some tips, but it's too late now.

'Oh, I've got something for you,' I said towards the end of the meal, nonchalantly producing the ring from my pocket and holding it up. 'I was wondering if you wanted to get married when we move back to London.'

Maybe this wasn't the best way of asking. In fact, it clearly wasn't.

'Very funny,' Edita said.

'But I'm serious. If you don't like the ring we can go back to the market and get another one,' I said. 'It only cost a dollar.'

This didn't have the effect I'd intended either. Edita roared with laughter.

Anyway, I don't want to bore you with the details, but a few minutes later, after I'd managed to convince her that I really wasn't joking, she said yes.

'What was your favourite part of the whole trip?' Edita asked me as we held a celebratory glass of *pisco sour* and gazed across the lights of Quito.

This is what's known as a trick question. Luckily I spotted it.

'How am I supposed to answer that?'

'Just be honest.'

'But if I say the summit of Chimborazo, you're going to be really offended, aren't you?'

Of course, the answer to that question depends on the criteria you use to judge it. If your criterion is the view, then 1,000 points of light in the city below us didn't remotely surpass the summit of Chimborazo, where a golden sun lit up a blanket of cloud that stretched to the four horizons, and all the major volcanoes in Ecuador broke the surface. If your criterion is sheer terror then, believe me, discovering that your wife-to-be is a champion shot with a 6ft blowpipe is pretty scary.

It had become abundantly clear that neither of us really gave the squeal of a guinea pig whether our Chimborazo sea-to-summit achievement had been a world first or not, but the idea had been a good one. We'd had a great adventure on the back of it, and both Chimborazo and Quito would always command a special place in our hearts. These were more profound rewards than claiming some obscure record.

I could put Chimborazo, its crumbling glacier, unrepentant penitentes and walls made from cheesecake from my mind. I wouldn't be climbing them a third time – no way, Javier. With my two ascents and two exhausting bike rides out of the way, it was time to turn my attention to life's next great adventure.

Sea to summit completed, 27 September 2017

ACKNOWLEDGEMENTS

This wouldn't be the book it is without the help of a number of people.

I would like to thank my editor Alex Roddie, who doubles as one of Britain's top outdoor writers and commentators, for his help throughout.

I was very lucky to have the mentoring support of another indie author, Roz Morris, energetic novelist, travel writer, editor and writing coach, who provided many suggestions to improve the book.

My brother Perran and father Ian have been particularly helpful, annotating the manuscript with many improvements.

I am extremely grateful to my other beta readers Dia Carstens, Andy Lintern and Grant Rawlinson, who read early versions of the manuscript and provided much constructive feedback.

I would like to thank Andrew Brown of Design for Writers, for producing a cover to rival that of my first book *Seven Steps from Snowdon to Everest*.

My thanks to all my friends on Facebook and readers of my blog who provided enthusiastic feedback about the cover. I have frequently trialled content for this book in blog posts, and I would like to thank the many readers of my blog who have provided feedback in comments.

I would like to thank the many people I have met and travelled with over the years, who have made all my adventures special. Some made it into the finished book, some into earlier drafts, while others didn't make it at all. This in no way reflects their importance to my journey. In particular I would like to thank our friends in Ecuador who made an important contribution to this story: Pablo, Romel, Marco, Rodrigo, Felipe, Ramiro and Domenica.

This journey wouldn't have been possible without the logistical expertise of 'El Jefe', Javier Herrera, the owner of Andeanface, for whom, it seems, nothing in Ecuador is impossible. I am also extremely grateful to his wife Helma and family for being such welcoming hosts.

Of course, I would not have carried out this journey at all had it not been for the star of this book, my amazing wife Edita. I will never be able to thank her enough.

I am very grateful to all the readers of my blog and travel diaries. I enjoy the writing nearly as much as the travelling, and you are the people who make it worthwhile.

Last, but by no means least, I would like to thank *you* for reading this book (especially if you have got all the way to the last sentence of the acknowledgements). I hope you have enjoyed it, and I look forward to welcoming you back sometime.

PHOTOGRAPHS

If you're wishing this book contained many more photos from my journey, thanks to the miracles of the internet you can view all my photos from every expedition via the photo-sharing website *Flickr*.

Each trip has its own album, and I have grouped them by the relevant section of the book. You can access them all at: www.flickr.com/markhorrell.

Part 1 – The Avenue of the Volcanoes

Avenue of the Volcanoes, Part 1. Ecuador, *December 2009 to January 2010*:
    www.markhorrell.com/AvenueOfTheVolcanoes1
Avenue of the Volcanoes, Part 2. Ecuador, *December 2015 to January 2016*:
    www.markhorrell.com/AvenueOfTheVolcanoes2

Part 2 – The North Coast 500

North Coast 500. Scotland, August *2017*:
    www.markhorrell.com/NorthCoast500

Part 3 – The Sea-to-Summit Adventure

Chimborazo Sea to Summit. Ecuador, *September to October 2017*:
    www.markhorrell.com/ChimborazoSeaToSummit

NOTES

1. Ferreiro, *Measure of the Earth*, p.185.
2. Whymper, *Travels amongst the Great Andes of the Equator*, p.133.
3. Ibid., p. 298.
4. Hall, *Excursions in the Neighbourhood of Quito, and Towards the Summit of Chimborazo*, p.28.
5. Whymper, *Travels amongst the Great Andes of the Equator*, p.195.
6. Ferreiro, *Measure of the Earth*, p.215.
7. Hall, *Excursions in the Neighbourhood of Quito, and Towards the Summit of Chimborazo*, p.54.
8. Humboldt, *Views of the Cordilleras and Monuments of the Indigenous Peoples of the Americas*, p.64.
9. Ibid., p.65.
10. Whymper, *Travels amongst the Great Andes of the Equator*, p.147.
11. Ibid., p.154.
12. Math Encounters Blog, *The Farthest Mountaintops from the Center of the Earth*, http://mathscinotes.com/2015/01/the-farthest-mountaintops-from-the-center-of-the-earth/.
13. Volcano Discovery, *Cotopaxi eruption August 2015 – news & updates*, https://www.volcanodiscovery.com/cotopaxi/activity/aug2015-eruption.html.

14. Wulf, *The Invention of Nature*, p.83.
15. Humboldt, *About an attempt to climb to the top of Chimborazo*, p.198.
16. Whymper, *Travels amongst the Great Andes of the Equator*, p.27.
17. Ibid., p.77.
18. Boussingault, *Ascent of Chimborazo*, p.53.
19. Whymper, *Travels amongst the Great Andes of the Equator*, p.49.
20. Ibid., p.52.
21. Ibid., p.58.
22. Ibid., p.66.
23. Ibid., p.69.
24. North Coast 500, *An Alternative Guide to the NC500 for Cyclists - Part One: Inverness to Garve*, http://www.northcoast500.com/blog/blog/october-2016-(1)/route-descriptions-and-recommended-nc500-alternati.aspx.
25. North Coast 500, *Level Crossing Dangers and Cycling Safely on Single Track Roads*, http://www.northcoast500.com/blog/blog/june-2016-(1)/nc500-cycling-blog-june-2016.aspx.
26. Robertson, *Mountain Memories*, p.86.
27. Munro, *Bens Laoghal, Hope, and Clibrig*, p.186.
28. Naylor, *From John O'Groats to Land's End or 1372 Miles on Foot*, p.31.
29. Brown, *Hamish's Mountain Walk*, p.276.
30. Pennant, *A Tour in Scotland and Voyage to the Hebrides*, p.379.
31. King, *An Teallach: Ross-shire*, p.10.
32. Whymper, *Travels amongst the Great Andes of the Equator*, p.260.
33. Ibid., p.160.
34. Ibid., p.19.

35. El Universo, *Se confirma que hallazgo de avión fue el año pasado*, https://www.eluniverso.com/2003/02/21/0001/12/DDAB5EEFC28C4E5AB6E5ED8E122C46A5.html.
36. Whymper, *Travels amongst the Great Andes of the Equator*, p.315.
37. Ibid., p.317.
38. Ibid., p.326.
39. My father found my mother's wedding ring two years later, while clearing his possessions to move house, and kept his promise to give it to Edita.

BIBLIOGRAPHY

All of the following books and journal articles served as reference while writing the historical sections of this book.

Bennet, Donald, ed. *The Munros: Scottish Mountaineering Club Hillwalkers Guide, Volume One.* 2nd ed., Edinburgh: Scottish Mountaineering Trust, 1991.

Biggar, John. *The Andes: A Guide for Climbers.* 3rd ed., Castle Douglas: Andes, 2005.

Bonington, Chris. *The Next Horizon: From the Eiger to the South Face of Annapurna.* Sheffield: Vertebrate Digital, 2016.

Bouguer, Pierre. *An Abridged Relation of a Voyage to Peru* in Pinkerton, John. *A General Collection of the Best and Most Interesting Voyages and Travels in All Parts of the World.* Vol. 14, London: Longman, Hurst, Rees, Orme, Brown, Cadell and Davies, 1813.

Boussingault, Jean-Baptiste. *Ascent of Chimborazo* in Thomson, Robert D. *Records of General Science.* Vol. II, London: John Taylor, 1835.

Brain, Yossi. *Ecuador: A Climbing Guide.* Seattle: The Mountaineers Books, 2000.

Brown, Hamish. *Hamish's Mountain Walk: The first non-stop round of all the 3000ft Scottish Munros .* Dingwall: Sandstone Press, 2010.

Cadell, Henry M. *The Mountain Scenery of the North-West Highlands.* The Scottish Mountaineering Club Journal, Vol. 1, 76-82, 1891.

Cieza de Léon, Pedro de. *The Discovery and Conquest of Peru.* Durham: Duke University Press, 1999.

Dickinson, Greg, and Amanda Tomlin. *The Rough Guide to the North Coast 500.* London: Rough Guides, 2017.

Eichler, Arturo. *Ecuador: Nieve y Selva, Snow Peaks and Jungles.* Quito: Edicion del Autor, 1970.

Ferreiro, Larrie D. *Measure of the Earth: The Enlightenment Expedition That Reshaped Our World.* New York: Basic Books, 2011.

Garcia, Marcela, and Bernard Francou. *The Heart of the Andes.* Quito: Ediciones Libri Mundi / Enrique Grosse-Luemern, 2002.

Hall, Colonel. *Excursions in the Neighbourhood of Quito, and Towards the Summit of Chimborazo* in Hooker, William Jackson. *Companion to the Botanical Magazine.* Vol. I, London: Edward Couchman, 1835.

Hart, Matt (2015, March 5). *Where in the World Did Karl Egloff Come From?* Retrieved from https://www.outsideonline.com

Henry, Emil. *Triumph and Tragedy: The Life of Edward Whymper.* Leicester: Matador, 2011.

Humboldt, Alexander von. Translated by Vera M. Kutzinski. *About an attempt to climb to the top of Chimborazo.* Atlantic Studies: Global Currents, Vol. 7:2, 191-211, 2010.

Humboldt, Alexander von, and Aimé Bonpland. *Personal Narrative of Travels to the Equinoctial Regions of America, During the Year 1799-1804.* London: George Bell, 1885.

Humboldt, Alexander von. *Views of the Cordilleras and Monuments of the Indigenous Peoples of the Americas.* Chicago: University of Chicago Press, 2013.

Humphreys, Sara and Stephan Küffner. *The Rough Guide*

to Ecuador & the Galápagos Islands. London: Rough Guides, 2016.

King W.W., and H.T. Munro. *An Teallach: Ross-shire*. The Scottish Mountaineering Club Journal, Vol. 3, 10-18, 1895.

La Condamine, Charles-Marie de. *Journal du voyage fait par ordre du Roi, L'Equateur*. Paris: Imprimerie Royale, 1751.

Macfarlane, Robert. *Landmarks*. London: Penguin, 2015.

MacInnes, Hamish. *Beyond the Ranges: Five Years in the Life of Hamish MacInnes*. London: Victor Gollancz, 1984.

McCosh, F.W.J. *Boussingault: Chemist and Agriculturist*. Dordrecht: D. Reidel Publishing Company, 1984.

McNeish, Cameron. *The Munros: Scotland's Highest Mountains*. Edinburgh: Lomond Books, 1998.

Montillier, Philippe. *Chasseurs de Glace en Équateur (Ice Hunters / Hieleros)*. Vétraz-Monthoux: Editions La Boussole, 1999.

Moore, Robert T. *Chimborazo, Bolívar's "Watch Tower of the Universe"*. American Alpine Journal, Vol. 1, No. 2, 93-105, 1930.

Munro, H.T. *Bens Laoghal, Hope, and Clibrig*. The Scottish Mountaineering Club Journal, Vol. 5, 182-187, 1899.

Murray, W.H. *Undiscovered Scotland: The second of W.H. Murray's great classics of mountain literature*. Sheffield: Vertebrate Digital, 2015.

Naylor, Robert, and John Naylor. *From John O'Groats to Land's End or 1372 Miles on Foot*. London: Caxton Publishing, 1916.

Neate, Jill. *Mountaineering in the Andes*. 2nd ed., London: Royal Geographical Society, 1994.

Patey, Tom. *One Man's Mountains: Essays and Verses*. Edinburgh: Victor Gollancz, 1971.

Pennant, Thomas. *A Tour in Scotland and Voyage to the Hebrides, 1772, Volume 1*. 2nd ed., London: Benjamin White, 1776.

Pfaffl, Fritz A., and Wolf-Christian Dullo. *The first ascent to the volcano Cotopaxi in Ecuador by Wilhelm Reiss (1838-1908)*. Vol. 103, 1175-1179, 2014.

Prebble, John. *The Highland Clearances*. London: Penguin, 1963.

Prescott, William H. *The History of the Conquest of Peru*. London: J.M. Dent & Sons, 1847.

Rachowiecki, Rob, Mark Thurber and Betsy Wagenhauser. *Climbing & Hiking in Ecuador*. 4th ed., Chalfont St Peter: Bradt, 1997.

Roberts, Alasdair. *Midges*. Edinburgh: Birlinn, 2005.

Robertson, A.E. *Mountain Memories*. The Scottish Mountaineering Club Journal, Vol. 24, 81-86, 1952.

Robertson, A.E. *The "Munros" of Scotland*. The Scottish Mountaineering Club Journal, Vol. 7, 10-14, 1903.

Robinson, Andy. *The End to End Trail: Land's End to John O'Groats on Foot*. Milnthorpe, Cicerone Press, 2007.

Salkeld, Audrey, ed. *World Mountaineering: The world's great mountains by the world's great mountaineers*. London: Mitchell Beazley, 1998.

Shulman, Neville. *Climbing the Equator: Adventures in the Jungles and Mountains of Ecuador*. Chichester: Summersdale Publishers, 2005.

Smith, Anthony. *Explorers of the Amazon*. Chicago: University of Chicago Press, 1994.

Snailham, Richard. *Sangay Survived: The story of the Ecuador volcano disaster*. London: Hutchinson, 1978.

Sobel, Dava. *Longitude: The True Story of a Lone Genius Who Solved the Greatest Scientific Problem of His Time*. London: Fourth Estate, 1996.

St Louis, Regis, et al. *Ecuador & the Galápagos Islands*. Victoria: Lonely Planet, 2009.

Townsend, Chris. *Scotland*. Milnthorpe: Cicerone Press, 2011.

Ulloa, Antonio de. *A voyage to South America: describing at large the Spanish cities, towns, provinces, &c. on that extensive continent*. 4th ed., London: John Stockdale, R Faulder, Longman, Lackington and J Harding, 1806.

Ulloa, Antonio de, and Jorge Juan y Santacilia. *Noticias Secretas de América*. Madrid, Editorial-América, 1918.

Webster, Paul and Helen. *The Munros: A Walkhighlands Guide*. Moffat: Pocket Mountains, 2012.

Whymper, Edward. *Scrambles amongst the Alps*. London: John Murray, 1871.

Whymper, Edward. *Travels amongst the Great Andes of the Equator*. London: John Murray, 1892.

Wulf, Andrea. *The Invention of Nature: The Adventures of Alexander von Humboldt, the Lost Hero of Science*. London: John Murray, 2015.

ABOUT THE AUTHOR

For nearly ten years Mark Horrell has written what has been described as one of the most credible Everest opinion blogs out there. He writes about trekking and mountaineering from the often silent perspective of the commercial client.

For more than fifteen years he has been exploring the world's greater mountain ranges and keeping a diary of his travels. As a writer he strives to do for mountain history what Bill Bryson did for long-distance hiking.

Several of his expedition diaries are available as quick reads from the major online bookstores. His first full-length book, *Seven Steps from Snowdon to Everest*, about his ten-year journey from hill walker to Everest climber, was published in November 2015.

His favourite mountaineering book is *The Ascent of Rum Doodle* by W.E. Bowman.

Seven Steps from Snowdon to Everest

As he teetered on a narrow rock ledge a yak's bellow short of the stratosphere, with a rubber mask strapped to his face, a pair of mittens the size of a sealion's flippers, and a drop of two kilometres below him, it's fair to say Mark Horrell wasn't entirely happy with the situation he found himself in.

He was an ordinary hiker who had only read books about mountaineering, and little did he know when he signed up for an organised trek in Nepal with a group of elderly ladies that ten years later he would be attempting to climb the world's highest mountain.

But as he travelled across the Himalayas, Andes, Alps and East Africa, following in the footsteps of the pioneers, he dreamed up a seven-point plan to gain the skills and experience which could turn a wild idea into reality.

Funny, incisive and heartfelt, his journey provides a refreshingly honest portrait of the joys and torments of a modern-day Everest climber.

First published in 2015. A list of bookstores can be found on Mark's website:

www.markhorrell.com/SnowdonToEverest

CONNECT

You can join Mark's **mailing list** to keep updated:
www.markhorrell.com/mailinglist

Website and blog: www.markhorrell.com
Twitter: @markhorrell
Facebook: www.facebook.com/footstepsonthemountain
Flickr: www.flickr.com/markhorrell
YouTube: www.youtube.com/markhorrell

DID YOU ENJOY THIS BOOK?

Thank you for buying and reading this book. Word-of-mouth is crucial for any author to be successful. If you enjoyed it then please consider leaving a review. Even if it's only a couple of sentences, it would be a great help and will be appreciated enormously.

Links to this book on the main online book stores can be found on Mark's website:

www.markhorrell.com/FeetAndWheelsToChimborazo

Printed in Poland
by Amazon Fulfillment
Poland Sp. z o.o., Wrocław

56131907R00223